FARRAR
STRAUS
GIROUX

Enchantress

Enchantress

MARTHE BIBESCO
AND HER WORLD

Christine Sutherland

Farrar, Straus & Giroux

NEW YORK

Published simultaneously in Canada by HarperCollins*CanadaLtd*
Printed in the United States of America

Designed by Abby Kagan

First edition, 1996

Library of Congress Cataloging-in-Publication Data
Sutherland, Christine.
    The enchantress : Marthe Bibesco and her world / Christine
Sutherland.
        p.   cm.
    Includes bibliographical references and index.
    ISBN 0-374-14814-7 (hardcover: alk. paper)
    1. Bibescu, Martha, ca. 1887–1973.   2. Princesses—Romania—
Biography.   3. Authors, Romanian—20th century—Biography.
I. Title.
DR262.B5S87   1996
949.8'02'092—dc20
    [B]   96-15654
                                                                              CIP

Contents

Illustrations

Frontispiece: Marthe in her twenties, from a portrait by Boldini. *Courtesy of Jane Lady Abdy*

Illustrations following page 174:

Princess Marthe Bibesco, by Boldini. *Courtesy of Weidenfeld & Nicolson Archives*
Marthe as a child in Bucharest, age five. *From the archives of the Ghika family*
Posada, Marthe's house in the Carpathians, reconstructed after the 1916 fire. *From the archives of the Ghika family*
Mogosoëa. *From the archives of the Ghika family*
Prince Charles-Louis de Beauvau-Craon, Marthe's great love. *Courtesy of his granddaughter, Princess de Beauvau-Craon*
Princess Bibesco in her drawing room at Mogosoëa as painted by Vuillard. *Courtesy of São Paulo Museum*
Marthe in her thirties. *From the archives of the Ghika family*
Prince Emmanuel Bibesco, Marthe's handsome and mysterious cousin; friend of Marcel Proust. *From the archives of the Ghika family*
Prince Antoine Bibesco, Emmanuel's younger brother; friend of Marcel Proust; married to Elizabeth Asquith, daughter of Henry Asquith, Prime Minister of Great Britain. *From the archives of the Ghika family*
Anna, Countess de Noailles, poet, Marthe's hostile cousin. *From the archives of the Ghika family*

Author's Note

I first met Marthe Bibesco years ago, when as a young girl in Paris I came across her book *Catherine Paris*. I recall walking around the Ile de la Cité holding the book in my hands and imagining Catherine gazing out on the river from the windows of the Hotel Lambert. I know of no other book that conveys so vividly and in such magical prose the beauty of that particular part of Paris.

Years later I encountered Marthe again in the pages of Proust's correspondence and in the memoirs of the various literary and political figures of the interwar period. I resolved to explore the life of this brilliant, talented and beautiful Romanian woman, the Egeria of statesmen and prominent politicians, who long before the days of Monnet and the Common Market devoted herself to the vision of European unity. Her home was a Byzantine-Venetian palace a few miles away from Bucharest, in which she entertained the European elite. When the Communists took over Romania, she was forced to escape with a few personal possessions and her diaries. She eventually reached Paris, her spiritual home, where she lived until her death in November 1973.

My quest for Marthe Bibesco led me to Bucharest and to that city's Central National Archives, where I found packing cases confiscated from her house, unopened since 1945. There were letters, photographs, house accounts, a multitude of personal notes, but few diaries. Back in London I was introduced to Marthe's grandson Brigadier Prince John Ghika, who with great kindness and trust handed over to me sixty-five volumes of Marthe's diaries, brilliantly transcribed and assembled by Mademoiselle Claudia Verhesen. They cover a period of sixty-five years of her life from 1908, when she was twenty-two, to 1973, the year she died. I was also allowed to research a collection of her voluminous correspondence and personal mementos, the property of the family. The residue of Marthe Bibesco's papers, including manuscripts for her books, can be found at the Bibliothèque Nationale in Paris, Department of Manuscripts (Don. 29738), and in the Department of Humanities of the University of Austin, Texas.

In spite of the tragic events in the days of Ceausescu, Romania is still one of the lesser-known countries in Europe. In the nineteenth century it was called "the kingdom at the edge of the Western World." Born from the ashes of the Ottoman Empire, breathtakingly beautiful, wrapped in mystery and age-old legends, it is a land of towering mountains and rich pastures, powerful rivers and fertile plains that merge into the eastern steppes. It was said to have been the habitat of mythical-sounding princes—Michael the Brave, Mircea the Old, Vlad the Impaler, Brancovan the Good, whose names now belong to the pantheon of local folklore.

Vienna wits used to say that "the Renaissance arrived in the Balkans panting in the nineteenth century," and Romanians easily admit that they lack the poise and balance that an undiluted Western civilization provided its northern neighbors. Their history and tradition, like their climate, are full of contradictions and age-old struggles. Lying at the crossroads between two very different civilizations and cultures, Romania has been fought over by successive invaders: first the Romans, then the Goths, Huns, Bulgars, Moguls, Tartars and, finally—after the collapse of Byzantium— the Turks. With its frequently shifting frontiers Romania's geographical position remained awkward, situated as it was between Austria and Hungary in the west and the steppes of southern Russia in the east, gateway to Tartar invasions in years past. The only natural frontiers are the great arc of the Carpathian Mountains in the north and the delta of the Danube, which flows into the Black Sea at Constantsa. From the fourteenth to the end of the nineteenth century danger always came from the east, be it Mogul, Tartar, Turkish or Russian foe. In earlier days the conquerors came from Rome.

The Roman colonization lasted for two centuries, and its influence went so deep that all the subsequent invasions, even those of the Dark Ages, were unable to uproot it. To this day the average Romanian takes enormous pride in what he considers his Roman heritage and Latin-based language.

Christianity came to them from Byzantium and with it relative peace, interrupted by sporadic forays by the Turks. Then, after the fall of Constantinople, all Danubian provinces became part of the Ottoman Empire. But the Turks did not interfere with their Christian religion (to this day there are no mosques in Romania) or tribal structure. The country was ruled by native princes, called hospodars, who in return for their rank and privileges paid tribute to the Sublime Porte. The first great hospodar, the hero of local legends and ballads, was Mircea the Great of Wallachia, who allied himself with the Serbs and the Poles to fight the Turks at Kosovo in 1389, a date remembered in the Balkans to this day. Mircea lost the battle and was forced to pay tribute to the Sultan, but returned a few years later and through crafty dealings at the Sultan's court, managed to preserve not only his dynasty but also the territorial integrity of the country and its Christian religion. After Mircea the most infamous and dreaded hospodar was Vlad the Impaler of fifteenth-century Dracula fame, who enjoyed impaling his enemies while alive and dining outdoors, surrounded by screaming victims dangling and twisting on their stakes. Vlad's ferocity frightened even the Turks, whom he defied for years until he was deposed by another chieftain, Radu the Fair. Perhaps the most legendary hospodar was Michael the Brave of Wallachia, who succeeded in uniting Wallachia, Moldavia and Transylvania, the three provinces corresponding to present-day Romania. Though Michael's reign did not last very long—he was murdered in 1607—his accomplishments inspired generations of his countrymen, including Queen Marie of Romania, who at the 1918 Congress of Versailles insisted that the three territories remain joined together under the Romanian crown.

In the eighteenth century the Turkish sultans tightened their grip on the country and Romanian nationals were no longer permitted to hold the title of hospodar. The privilege of exercising provincial authority fell to the Phanariots, the Sultan's Greek bankers. The Phanariots, who derived their name from the Phanar, the Greek Quarter of Constantinople, were a cohesive and extraordinarily able lot. They controlled the Sultan's finances and most of the highest offices of the Ottoman state, which they used to enrich themselves. When it came their turn, they applied the same principle to administering Romania. The Phanariot rule is remembered for its ruthless exploitation of the native Romanian population.

Phanariot princes had as little security in their tenure as did the hospodars. For in distant Constantinople, at the court of the all-powerful Sultan, raged a continuous maelstrom of egocentricity and intrigue and it was easy to fall victim to the machinations of other would-be princes. According to eighteenth-century chronicles, they liked to keep their possessions in ornate traveling coffers "so as to be able to leave at any moment." Contemporary paintings preserved in museums and monasteries show them dressed in long velvet mantles, trimmed with fur, fastened with jeweled clasps, wearing turbans with diamond aigrettes or high fur bonnets. In spite of the insecurity of their tenure they lived in great opulence and enjoyed ostentation. It is remembered that one of the Phanariot princes made his official entry into Bucharest riding in a sledge drawn by a pair of stags with gilded antlers.

The tide of Ottoman dominion, however, was ebbing fast. After the Crimean War (1853–56), Wallachia and Moldavia were placed under the guarantee of six nations (Austria, Britain, France, Russia, Turkey and Sardinia), and the Congress of Paris decided that elections should be held to determine their future government. In 1861 Alexander Cuza, a local chieftain, was elected head of the country. He turned out to be corrupt and dissolute, and five years later was forced to abdicate. Parliament then asked Ion Bratiano, Romania's first statesman, to journey to Western Europe to look for a foreign prince willing to take charge of the newly born country and help it to climb out of the slough of inertia and corruption, the legacy of years of Turkish rule. It was hoped he would be a member of a dynasty powerful enough to impress local clan leaders and of sufficient wealth to pay for his own court expenses.

It was not an easy assignment. For European royalty the Balkans were not an appealing destination, and to many Bucharest seemed even farther away than St. Petersburg. The position of Prince of Romania was first offered to the younger brother of the King of Belgium. He turned it down. The Parliament's next choice went to Prince Karl von Hohenzollern-Sigmaringen, second son of the ancient Hohenzollern family of Bavaria.* Small of stature, with piercing blue eyes, little charm and no sense of humor, the future King Carol had nevertheless an inborn strength and great natural dignity. From his strict Catholic ancestors he had inherited promptness, willpower and moral rectitude. No greater contrast to the easygoing Romanians could be imagined. Yet Prince Karl was eager to accept; there was a residue of ambition in his makeup and the prospect of power, even in a faraway country, was tempting. On April 20 1866—Good Friday—Ion Bratiano arrived at the massive, turreted feudal *Schloss*, seat and home of the Hohenzollern dynasty since the thirteenth century, to offer Romania to the twenty-eight-year-old Prince. Bratiano was told that, as an officer in the Prussian Army stationed in Berlin, Karl had to consult his

---

* There were two branches of the Hohenzollern family, both dating back to the thirteenth century: the Hohenzollern-Sigmaringen in Bavaria and the Hohenzollern-Brandenburg, who ruled Prussia.

kinsman King Wilhelm I of Prussia. He also wanted to explore the views of Emperor Napoleon III, as the support of France would be vital to him in the future. After an encouraging visit to Paris, where he was prompted by the Empress Eugénie to accept, Prince Karl went on to Berlin. The King of Prussia was doubtful. "All the people of Eastern Europe put together are not worth the bones of one Prussian officer," he told his cousin. But Bismarck, the redoubtable Chancellor, who five years later brought about Germany's unification, advised Karl to proceed. "Try it out," he said. "If you fail it will at least give you something to remember from your dull youth." He told him simply to ask for leave to travel abroad. "The King will guess your intention, but it will remove the need for him to make a decision."

The young Hohenzollern thus embarked on a journey that was to become half comedy, half adventure. As the Emperor of Austria was opposed to the scheme, he refused to grant him right of passage. Karl had to travel incognito. Undaunted, he borrowed the clothes of his valet and secretly made his way through Austria, traveling in a second-class compartment on a slow train with a crude basket for his clothes and a sack of provisions. After a miserable passage down the Danube and a two-day ride in a bumpy carriage, he arrived in Bucharest, where he was welcomed by Bratiano and a small crowd of supporters, more curious than enthusiastic. "Where is the palace?" he asked. With some embarrassment the minister pointed to a square, undistinguished wooden structure, surrounded by muddy fields, in front of which a group of pigs wallowed in the mud.

Undeterred by the primitive conditions around him, the twenty-eight-year-old Prince, with immense courage, set about governing and organizing his adopted country. The task ahead was gigantic. He could not rely on the Army, which was ill equipped and badly disciplined; the peasant masses were illiterate, half starved and very angry; and the aristocracy and the newly emerging middle classes—greedy and bent on pleasure—seemed unconcerned with the fate of their country. Turkish rule with its age-old tradition of baksheesh had corrupted the law enforcement agencies and the police. The treasury was empty, and road and rail communications nonexistent. Prince Karl stood alone among people whose language he did not speak, whose religion was alien to him, facing rebellious and mocking local satraps, whose riches were an insult to his poverty and who regarded him as a usurper —worse, a German usurper. Few rulers faced such an uphill task.

Displaying considerable diplomatic cunning, he first secured recognition from the neighboring powers Austria and Turkey. Next, so that he could govern effectively, a new constitution was enacted. Providing for an upper and a lower house, it gave the Prince an absolute and unconditional veto on all legislation and settled the throne on Prince Karl and his heirs. Then an immediate and successful attempt was made to reorganize the Army and build a network of railways. In a comparatively short time trade and commerce expanded; the country was beginning to function.

Prince Karl was by now thirty. It was time for him to find a wife and found a dynasty. Encouraged by Frederick, the Crown Prince of Prussia, and his English wife, Vicky, a daughter of Queen Victoria, Karl proposed to Elizabeth de Wied, a German princess from the Rhineland. Known in history as Carmen Sylva, Elizabeth turned out to be eccentric and neurotic. It was a stormy marriage; when she failed to produce the expected heir, she was temporarily banished from the country by her husband. A nephew, Prince Ferdinand, son of Karl's younger brother, was adopted as heir to the princely title and future throne.

Prince Karl's efforts to rebuild the Romanian Army bore fruit when, in 1877, at the time of the last of the Russo-Turkish wars, he seized the opportunity to wrest Romania's independence from the disintegrating Ottoman Empire and win the title of King for himself. His coronation, approved by the Congress of Berlin, took place on May 22, 1881. It was a moment of supreme triumph for the man who fifteen years previously had arrived in the country penniless, wearing the clothes of his valet. Henceforth he was to be known as Carol I of Romania.

In the last decade of the nineteenth century Bucharest was a rapidly expanding city, still primitive, but picturesque and intensely alive. It was a compound of French, Russian, Viennese, Turkish and Greek influences, and startling contrasts. Its wide tree-lined avenues, fashionably dressed people, the multitude of outdoor restaurants and the luxuriant social life mirrored late-nineteenth-century Paris. But just behind the two elegant thoroughfares lay ill-paved winding streets, with rows of small wooden houses, most of them hovels. Couples dressed at the height of Parisian fashion mixed unconcernedly with crowds of beggars and half-naked gypsies. In the poorer quarters, the so-called Devil's slums on the banks of the Dambovitsa, the small river that runs through the city, street vendors still carried the traditional wooden yokes supporting baskets of seasonal fruit, hampers of live, squawking fowl, loads of pistachios, sweet pastries and containers of the popular honey drink, *braga*. There were open markets, varied and noisy like Asiatic souks, and flower girls, gypsies with flashing white teeth, crouched over their wicker baskets of fragrant blooms.

With a population of half a million inhabitants, Bucharest was unusually widespread, covering more than twenty square miles. Part of its charm was its distinctly rural character. Even today most of the larger houses stand apart surrounded by gardens. In Marthe's day it was not unusual to find a cow grazing within the walled confines of a boyar's family mansion. Out of the city center the houses were set sideways, their entrances opening not on the curb but on narrow strips of garden and backyards usually full of chickens. Bucharest has very hot summers, followed by exceedingly cold winters with deep snow. Throughout the summer and the long, lovely autumn, no business was ever conducted between midday and late afternoon. People dined late, and all over the city, from the multitude of small cafés, even in the poorest of districts, rose the strains of gypsy violins, blending with the haunting tunes of age-old national songs. Tradition connects Bucharest with the word *bucurie*, Romanian for "pleasure." Founded in the fourteenth century by Prince Mircea of Wallachia, occupied and destroyed by successive Tartar, Turkish and Russian invasions, the city rose again and again, loud and lively, dedicated to commerce and earthly pleasures. "They live at the crossroads of Europe and are the most resilient race on this earth," Queen Marie used to say of her subjects.

Enchantress

Introduction

$\mathcal{T}$uesday, October 24, 1901. Bucharest, the elegant capital of the newly created kingdom of Romania, is *en fête*. Crowds line the sidewalks, bands play, gypsies dance in the streets, the air vibrates with gaiety. In the open-air restaurants that line the principal avenues, men with Roman profiles and lively dark-eyed women raise glasses to celebrate "the betrothal." It is autumn, the most beautiful season in the Balkans, and today Bucharest, with its wide tree-lined avenues, is golden. A procession of carriages winds its way to the ancient Orthodox church of Domnita Balasa, where the ceremony is to take place. There, in the full panoply of the church, amidst the glow of hundreds of candles, the golden vestments and incense, the profusion of orchids and lilies, the glitter of jewels, Bucharest society has assembled to celebrate the engagement of George Valentine Bibesco, scion of the most illustrious family in the land, descendant of the legendary hospodars of Wallachia, to Marthe Lahovary, daughter of the Foreign Minister of Romania, friend and confidant of the monarch, who, like

his brothers, has long been distinguished in public service. George
Valentine is twenty-two, handsome, willful and exceedingly rich;
Marthe is only fifteen, already a dazzling beauty. Dressed in a gold
brocade tunic, her red-blond hair streaming unadorned down to
her knees, she appears in the flickering light of the candles, a
vision descended from the Byzantine frescoes on the wall. "Pure
like the Virgin," whispers the old prince, the groom's father, an
old roué, whose own marriage to a divorced Frenchwoman with
two children had once caused a huge scandal in the Central European beau monde. "The boy *is* lucky."

The Patriarch pronounces benediction on the young couple;
they are betrothed; the music surges. Because of Marthe's extreme
youth, the wedding is to be delayed for a year; she is to go home
to her parents, while George serves his commission in the Army.
But tonight there will be a huge family banquet, a torchlight parade at the Bibesco estate in the country; wine will flow all over
Bucharest, and the ancient ritual of the hora, the national dance,
will be performed by gypsies.

The Lahovarys

*M*arthe Lahovary, the future Princess Bibesco, was born in Bucharest on a late snowy afternoon on January 28, 1886, as gas lamps flickered in houses and horse-drawn sleighs dashed across the wide expanse of the semi-Oriental city, driven by coachmen in red or blue caftans fastened with silver buttons and cinched with Circassian belts. Her family, the Lahovarys, belonged to a particular elite in Romania: the new bourgeoisie, a class that appeared on the national scene as the Phanariot princes were departing and the Ottoman Empire drifted into impotence. Hardworking and endowed with remarkable civic sense, this class filled the gap between the boyars and the peasants. Many were rich, for they had learned in Constantinople how to make money, and with the arrival of Karl von Hohenzollern, they rose in importance to become the backbone of the country. Leaving the countryside to the boyars, they built themselves impressive town houses, married into the great families of the land and gradually took over the running of the government. The majority were of Greek or Asia

Minor origin; as with the Phanariots in years past, France was their model.

The Lahovarys came originally from Antioch in Asia Minor and settled in the latter part of the eighteenth century in Constantinople, where they held a number of important posts in the service of the Ottoman Empire. Contemporary accounts mention a Petraki (Peter) Lahovary as one of the directors of the Ottoman Central Bank and Inspector General of Orthodox Monasteries, both influential and undoubtedly lucrative positions. His son, Manolaki (Emmanuel), held a number of equally prestigious posts until one day, due to the intrigues of the Grand Vizier, he fell out of favor with the Sultan and narrowly avoided decapitation. Manolaki's fortunes were restored a few years later, when a cousin of his, a Prince Soutzo, was appointed Hospodar of Wallachia and Manolaki became his Minister of Finance. From then on the family lived in Romania and prospered. Married to daughters of prominent boyars, who brought fat dowries and innumerable children, most of them male, the Lahovarys soon became one of the most influential families of Bucharest. They were presidents of banks, judges of the peace, directors of mines, owners of national newspapers and key members of government. "Out of ten chairs around a table at a meeting, eleven will be Lahovarys," remarked a contemporary wit.

Marthe's father, Jean Lahovary, was sent to Paris at the age of eleven to study at the celebrated Lycée Louis-le-Grand. A brilliant student, he was determined to succeed in spite of his contemporaries, who made fun of his name and called him "the Turk." Having won first prize at the Concours Général—a nationwide university graduates' competition—he was asked to remain in France and was offered some excellent jobs. But he turned them all down, returning to Romania to take part in the 1877 war against Turkey. Decorated for heroism at the Battle of Plevna, Jean Lahovary next decided to enter government service. The recently created kingdom of Romania needed all the able men it could muster and the Lahovary clan served it well. At the time of his daughter Marthe's birth, he had just entered Parliament and was soon to be named Minister of Agriculture. Meanwhile his brother Jacques, the General, whose statue adorns one of Bucharest's principal squares, was already Minister of Defense, and his other brother, Alexander, was about to take up the post of Deputy Foreign Minister. The three brothers, the "great Lahovarys," as they were called, were much admired for their erudition and professional integrity—a rare virtue in Romanian government circles of the day.

Jean Lahovary married Emma Mavrocordato, member of an illustrious family of the Phanar, reputed to descend from Othello.

Othello was chieftain on the Greek island of Levkas (white) and bore the title of *mavros* (black), which was also the name of the highest mountain on Levkas. After the island was conquered by the Venetians, he was sent to Cyprus, as their vassal, to command a garrison. There he married a local girl, Miss Cordato, whom he strangled in a jealous rage. The two family names were joined. In Cypriot dialect the girl was known as "Desdemoni," the unfortunate one. The story was picked up by Shakespeare. Another ancestor was Alexander Mavrocordato, Hospodar of Moldavia, who unsuccessfully tried to abolish slavery in Romania. A younger Alexander Mavrocordato, leader of the Greek War for Independence, a soldier and a poet, became famous as a friend of Byron and Shelley; it was said that Byron had died in his arms at Missolonghi.

Unlike the Lahovarys, the Mavrocordatos were a family of eccentrics. Marthe's maternal grandfather, Alexander Mavrocordato, nicknamed "l'Ours"—the Bear—was a leading member of the local Conservative Party and prone to outbursts of sudden, terrific temper. Having quarreled with the King's ministers, he retired to his country estates, where he led a "voluptuous and savage existence" and fathered a large illegitimate progeny.

His wife, exasperated by his rages, tired of living in what she called "a wilderness, surrounded by packs of dogs and illiterate servants," and resentful of his attempts to make her constantly pregnant, decided that she would be far better off bringing up the children on her own. One day in early spring she called for her carriage, and, gathering her two sons and a daughter, she drove into Bucharest, bought a ticket for Paris and embarked on a new destiny. They settled in a modest apartment in the Latin Quarter of Paris, where they led a quiet bourgeois existence among local French people. Contacts with other Romanians were avoided. The children did well at school, life was peaceful; they all enjoyed themselves. But once a year chaos erupted. Leaving his dogs and mistresses behind, the Bear arrived in Paris to visit his legitimate offspring. Luckily he never stayed very long, for he usually found much to criticize in the household, venting his fury in loud out-bursts, which frightened the passersby and the pigeons on the quays.

The moment the boys passed their final exams they were summoned back to Romania by their redoubtable father "to take up positions suitable to their talents and their rank." Young Emma, knowing that her father was not interested in daughters, had every reason to hope that she would escape her brothers' fate. She wanted to remain in Paris at all costs, for she had fallen in love with a young Monsieur de la Marinière, a friend of one of her brothers. They became engaged with the enthusiastic approval of her mother, who liked the idea of her daughter living in France. But they had not thought of the Bear. Having got wind of the situation, he set off for Paris forthwith and, impervious to his daughter's objections and the tears of the assembled household, he "repatriated" Emma to Jassy, the second town in Romania, but deeply provincial after Paris. Emma hoped to die of boredom and a broken heart, but survived thanks to the company of another victim of love, a young Olga Sturdzo, who had been forced to give up Milan I, King of Serbia. Then one day her father informed her: "A gentleman has arrived from Bucharest—your future husband. You will be meeting him shortly." "But I don't know him," said poor Emma. "I know him," he responded, "that's enough."

Emma was married to Jean Lahovary, Marthe's father, in the Orthodox cathedral of Jassy on January 20, 1880, at midnight, as was the Orthodox custom. In spite of the memory of her youthful love, which took a long time to recede, the arranged marriage turned out to be reasonably happy. A poem, preserved in the Bibesco archives, written by Jean Lahovary on the seventeenth anniversary of their wedding, talks of their "serene life together" and thanks her for "unfailing support" in bad times.

At the time Marthe was born, her parents had just returned from Paris, where Jean Lahovary was serving as Minister of Romania to France. Madame Lahovary, remembering her happy childhood in the Latin Quarter, had hoped that they would remain there forever; France was her country of adoption, as it later became her daughter's. Throughout her life Marthe attributed her love of France and everything French to the fact that she had been conceived in Paris; with the passage of years she even convinced herself that she had been born there as well. Marthe was the Lahovarys' third child; a daughter, Jeanne, had been born in 1882 and a son, George, two years later. The arrival of a second daughter was a disappointment for the parents; they had hoped for another boy to safeguard the family line, just in case anything should happen to George.

On the day of the new baby's arrival Jean Lahovary was elected deputy to the National Assembly. It was an impressive victory for the Conservative Party, and in spite of the acute cold, cheering crowds surrounded the Casa Cantacuzène, the elegant family mansion on Calea Victoriei. While her husband stood on the balcony responding to the cheers, Madame Lahovary retired to her bedroom in tears, disappointed at being deprived of a hoped-for son and of Paris.

Marthe's childhood was difficult. To realize at an early age that one's birth has been a bitter disappointment to one's mother would be a devastating blow for any child. "I suffered too much when I was very young to be able to ever forget it," she confided to her journal some years later. "Because I was the youngest of three I was always being left behind. The rest of the family went off to Paris or Cabourg [a French watering place] while I was sent to the country with my nurse." The country in this case was Bratachanka, an estate near Bucharest, belonging to her great-uncle George Lahovary, president of the Romanian Court of Appeals. Not wanting to pay the cost of two extra sleepers on the Orient Express for Marthe and the nurse, Madame Lahovary decided to leave them behind in Romania for the summer, claiming that Marthe was too young to undertake such a long journey. Sixty years later, when revising her early memoirs, Marthe still remembered the episode with undiminished bitterness. She could not have been more than five years old at the time.

But there were also compensations, and life in the sprawling family house was on the whole very pleasant. The Casa Cantacuzène, in spite of its rather grandiose-sounding name, was like most of the boyar houses of the period: a simple square wooden structure, whitewashed with wooden floors painted in a variety of colors. Its distinguishing feature was a large stone balcony, overlooking a garden, which looked onto the main street. It was furnished in a version of the post-Second Empire style with plush sofas and heavy velvet wall hangings. According to the customs of the time an entire bevy of servants hovered around the Lahovary household. Marthe's early upbringing was left almost exclusively in the hands of two nannies: Anika, a jolly young peasant girl from Balotesti, and Maria, an old woman of Czech origin, who had lived in Romania for years. Anika was eighteen; she had dark brown eyes, red cheeks and long, glistening black hair, which she wore in two braids, thick as her arm, coiled on top of her head like a turban. It was a style much favored by girls in the villages, for the hair served as a pillow on which to carry heavy baskets or pitchers of water. When Anika loosened her hair it fell down over her shoulders like a mantle, reaching all the way to her knees. In the evenings, before going to bed, little Marthe liked to be stood on a dresser in her room, take the pins out of Anika's hair, unwind the braids, cover her face and play hide-and-seek with the silky curtain. Anika's hair, she recalled, smelled of almonds and frankincense. Bath followed in a round wooden tub and, amidst much laughter and hugging, Marthe was finally put to bed.

Marie—the old nurse—had a more lasting influence, for she introduced Marthe to the world of fantasy and folklore. Though illiterate, she possessed a rare gift for spinning colorful, endless yarns in which Grimm's fairy tales, popular at the time, intermingled with legends from the Romanian past. She particularly liked to tell sinister and scary stories. "I was quite often frightened," Marthe told her friend the Abbé Mugnier in later years, "but I savored the frisson of fear and found comfort in getting hold of Marie's hand."

A sensitive and precocious child, Marthe went through what she later described as "an acute religious and patriotic phase." When seven she rebelled against "the terrible injustice of the passion of Christ"; a year later she shed tears for Joan of Arc. "I used to sob for hours in my bed recalling how the poor girl was burned at the stake, and passionately wanted to be like her . . . save my country, lead my people . . . hear the voices." At one point between the ages of seven and ten she even contemplated entering a convent.

In the summer of 1892, when Marthe was six and a half, her brother George contracted typhoid and died. It was a blow from which the family never recovered. George was an enchanting child: affectionate, clever, good-looking; he was adored by his parents and his two sisters. He and Marthe were particularly close. "You are so beautiful, like an angel," he used to tell her, playing with her long golden hair. Their closeness annoyed Madame Lahovary, who wanted her son's affection undivided; she once even admitted to her husband that she was "strangely jealous of Marthe." George fell ill suddenly after a weekend at Balotesti, the Lahovary country house about a forty-minute drive by carriage from Bucharest. Surrounded by fields and meadows, in the middle of a rather dull, flat countryside, Balotesti was a typical boyar residence of the time— an unpretentious, comfortable wooden family house, at the edge of a village dominated by the golden dome of the Orthodox church. (It is still there, now part of a suburban development on the way to the Otopeni Airport.) The cause of the little boy's illness remained a mystery; most likely, it was due to his drinking water from one of the antiquated wells on the place. All day he had been enjoying himself, but suddenly on the way home to Bucharest he was seized by a violent fever, which persisted in spite of frantic efforts by the best doctors in the capital. As typhoid was suspected, Marthe and her sister were moved to the house of an aunt, and stringent hygiene provisions put in place to minimize the risk of contagion to the household. All drinking and cooking water were now boiled, but little Marthe, in defiant solidarity with her brother, got hold of a glass of murky water from the river and drained it. "I want to catch the same illness as my brother," she declared. During the spring George got progressively worse; he lay on his bed, eyes fixed on the pretty painted ceiling in his room, while his mother read him stories from books by the Countess de Ségur, a popular children's author. He knew that the doctors were powerless to save him. "Why do I have to die?" he repeated, as he felt the end approaching.

One morning in early May, Marthe's father arrived at her aunt's house red-eyed, absentminded and wearing, unusual for him, rumpled clothes. "You must pray for your brother," he said, "he is not with us anymore." The next day Marthe and her sister Jeanne were taken to the Petit Parisien, a children's shop in Bucharest, to be measured for mourning clothes—black pleated skirts, black blouses, white marine collars and cuffs. When they were finally allowed to return to the family house they found the atmosphere funereal. Madame Lahovary made no effort to control her grief, punctuated by outbursts of hysterical sobbing. The house became a shrine to the departed son; a lock of his hair was permanently kept under glass in a jeweled frame, his first tooth mounted in gold lay on her bedside table, photographs were covered in black crepe. No affection was shown to the girls. On the contrary, they were made to feel vaguely guilty for being so triumphantly alive and healthy. Marthe was a particular source of irritation to her mother, for not even the hideous mourning outfits could diminish the growing beauty of the child. One day as she was waiting for her mother to alight from the carriage, a passerby turned to Madame Lahovary and exclaimed, "Your daughter, madame, is exquisite, like a painting." Marthe's mother turned to the unknown admirer and whispered, "If only you had seen her brother, you would realize she is nothing." Marthe, of course, overheard the remark and remembered. Years later, in one of her most successful books, *Le Perroquet Vert* (*The Green Parrot*), she described this unhappy period of her life and talked about the "*gloire funèbre*," the "glorious satisfaction" some people derive from incessantly dwelling on a tragic death.

Faced with her mother's neurotic hostility, life for Marthe would indeed have been grim had it not been for the intervention of the Lahovary men. Both her father and her uncle Jacques, the

General, as well as her grandfather Mavrocordato, took over the duties usually performed by the mother. Jean Lahovary, Minister of Agriculture at the time, soon to become Foreign Minister, was, in spite of his busy life, the most attentive of fathers. It was he who sat by her bed in the evenings, endlessly answering questions which sprang from the child's fertile imagination. It was he and not her mother who nursed her through a series of childhood illnesses and watched over Marthe's and her sister's physical welfare. And it was Jean Lahovary, the busy statesman, who in consultation with his brother the General engaged the carefully selected, outstanding teachers for his daughters. It was a happy coincidence for this gifted, sensitive child, who longed to be educated and whose facility for absorbing knowledge was astounding, that the Lahovarys were then at the zenith of their power. From a very early age Marthe had been conscious of her family's importance in the country, and now that she was growing up, she found it even more pleasing. "Like the sunflowers in our cornfields, which invariably turn to the sun, my instinct always leaned toward power," she recalled when describing her unconventional upbringing. That "instinct" was to remain with her all her life.

In her book of family reminiscences, *La Nymphe Europe*, which she never completed, Marthe pays a glowing tribute to her grandfather Alexander Mavrocordato for teaching her "how to think," how to take in new ideas, "but not before examining them carefully with complete confidence in my judgment." "You are well capable of it," he would tell her. The redoubtable Prince Alexander Mavrocordato, who had been so feared and detested by his own children in their youth, had turned into a doting grandfather. Little Marthe, with her inquisitive mind and love of history, was his favorite. Like her father, he supervised her education, saw to it that she was taught to read and write at an early age and liked to explain to her the complicated history of their country. But above all he introduced her to the "fairyland of French culture," as she was fond of saying in later years. Under the guidance of the eccentric old man, who had adored France in his youth, Marthe progressed from the world of Perrault's fairy tales to Ronsard and on to French classics, through Corneille and Racine to Chateaubriand, whose *Mémoires d'Outre-tombe* became her inseparable companion in later life.

Descendant of a great family of the Phanar, whose emblem was a soaring phoenix, Prince Alexander Mavrocordato gently led his little granddaughter through the "genealogical forest," reviving for her the half-forgotten exploits of her illustrious ancestors, bringing back images of the Ottoman court, the glories of the Phanariot princes. One day while Marthe delightedly perched on his knee, the old man, after reading through some family documents, produced a round box, dating back to the sixteenth century; it had a blue enameled lid studded with diamonds. On it, delicately drawn, its wings outspread, ready to take off into space, was the Mavrocordato phoenix. The so-called *montre armoiriée* (the crested watch), a precious family heirloom, was one of the earliest examples of watchmaking, sent from Nuremberg to Constantinople and presented to a Mavrocordato ancestor by the eighteenth-century sultan Ahmed III in recognition of his services. Marthe, as she later recalled, never forgot "the pride and excitement which surged through me at the sight of the miraculous bird, our family's emblem, decorating that precious family memento."

Marthe's education, as she was fond of recalling, was almost exclusively French, with daily lessons in English and German. (She became fluent in all three.) French was the language of the house; Romanian was used to communicate with the servants and the villagers of Balotesti. It was only when Marthe was eleven years old that, at the insistence of her father, a monk from a nearby monastery was engaged to teach her proper Romanian and a smattering of the national literature.

Each year Madame Lahovary, who had never liked Bucharest and hated the local society, arranged to spend at least four months in France with her daughters. Her husband, who by then had become Foreign Minister and a close adviser to the King, joined them whenever he could get away. After spending one rather unsatisfactory summer in a rented villa in Brittany, the Lahovary family decided to establish themselves in Biarritz. "Discovered" by the Empress Eugénie in the late 1850s, Biarritz was the fashionable meeting place for the international beau monde of the time:

French society figures, Spanish aristocrats, Russian grand dukes, rich Germans, Austrians and a smattering of South Americans. The English, led by the Prince of Wales, the future King Edward VII, came later. At the end of the nineteenth century Biarritz was an unspoiled, charming place; the ocean was pure and bracing, the scenery magnificent with the snowcapped Pyrenees in the background and the lush Basque countryside around it.

For Madame Lahovary the chief attraction of Biarritz at the time was the presence of Queen Natalie of Serbia, a distant cousin. Daughter of a Russian officer and the Romanian Princess Ghika, Natalie married Milan I, King of Serbia, but was divorced or rather "repudiated" by him in 1888. She was allowed, however, to keep her title of Queen and given a substantial financial settlement. Established in a large villa called the Sacchino Palace, Queen Natalie, who was about forty at the time, but looked much older, because "she never ceased to weep at the loss of her throne," was particularly fond of young people. Marthe was often asked to call on her "aunt" to accompany her on carriage rides through the town. "The Queen likes to have Marthe around, as if she were a little dog, because she is pretty," observed the ever caustic Madame Lahovary. She was about to forbid the visits, but her husband countermanded her orders. "I want Marthe to spend time with the Queen; she talks well and after all she is part of the history of our times," he told his wife.

The Lahovary ladies were in Biarritz when news came of the death of the old Prince Alexander Mavrocordato at the family seat in Jassy. Marthe, who adored her grandfather, was distressed and deeply shocked that her mother refused to return to Romania for the funeral. Madame Lahovary, since the death of her little son, considered all other deaths unimportant; she had never been close to her father and saw no reason why she should undertake a long, hot journey to Jassy in the middle of a Biarritz summer season. For Marthe her refusal was incomprehensible and contributed to the widening gulf between them. "I remember driving with my mother and my aunt Eugénie by the great cathedral of Bayonne the day after my grandfather had died," she wrote in *La Nymphe Europe*. "The doors were open; it would have been easy to go in and at least say a prayer. But no, my mother ordered the carriage to stop in front of the then fashionable tearoom The Arcades and we went in to consume cups of chocolate and be seen. I could neither drink the chocolate nor eat the pastries; I swallowed my tears nearly choking." Such was the child's indignation and sense of loss that sixty years later, as an aging woman, she still remembered "how she had hated her mother at that moment."

To fill the void caused by her grandfather's death and in need of a hero to admire, Marthe turned to her uncle General Jacques Lahovary, Minister of War and a much loved national figure. Two years younger than her father, Jacques Lahovary was a man of great intelligence, arresting physique and outstanding organizational talents. Put in charge of the Army by King Carol, he managed to weld together a disparate assortment of shepherds, peasants and city workers, drill them into effective military units and lead them to victory against the Turks at the Battle of Plevna, which resulted in independence for Romania. Tall and slender—he retained the figure of a young lieutenant all his life—the General seemed to be impervious to the elements and drove about lightly clad in his carriage even in the depths of the winter. Unlike Marthe's father and the rest of the Lahovary men whose eyes were blue or gray-green, the General's eyes were jet black, "piercing and unforgettable" under prominent black eyebrows. A long silky mustache, slightly droopy, which he liked to twirl and twist absentmindedly, reminded Marthe of the portraits of the Mogul emperors. Popular with his soldiers, the General was also very much admired by the young, who sensed that "under all that martial glitter" he possessed a real capacity for affection. From among the children in his family the little ten-year-old Marthe stood out because of her vivid intelligence and passionate desire for learning, while her beauty "went straight to his heart." He would often appear at the end of the day, when Marthe and her sister Jeanne had finished their lessons, and ask Mademoiselle Viaud, their excellent French governess, for permission to take the girls out for a drive. It was Marthe who always enthusiastically volunteered; Jeanne preferred to remain at home and practice her piano. Riding along the Chaussée Kisselev in his smart open carriage, driven by a team of black

horses, acknowledging greetings from the passersby, the General
and his niece discussed the serious issues of the day, the decline
of the Ottoman Empire, the ever recurring Balkan crises, the difficulties of governing Romania. "He talked to me seriously, as to
an adult, as if I were one of his political associates," Marthe recalled, "nor did he tire of answering my naïve questions, but tried
to explain everything. . . . Thanks to Uncle Jacques and my father
I learned that international politics is an endlessly fascinating
game; I vowed to remain close to it . . ." In the meantime, she
avidly continued to listen to the never ending flow of argument
and discussion in her own house, where politicians came and went,
foreign statesmen had to be entertained and messengers carrying
sheaves of paper for her father were constantly arriving at the door.
Jean Lahovary, who liked to breakfast with his daughters, was always hurried by his aides, "snatching a last cup of coffee between
the dining room and the street, while the horses whinnied outside." Yet in spite of all the daily pressures heaped upon him, Jean
Lahovary's rapport with his daughters and with Marthe in particular remained intimate throughout their entire adolescence. It was
a blessing but perhaps not full compensation for their mother's
neglect, and in the matriarchal tradition of the Balkans the situation was considered unusual. But then few women were as eccentric and neurotic as Marthe's mother.

Coming from a family of six brothers Madame Lahovary had
always wanted to be a boy. When she married, her dream was to
produce six sons; she failed at it and worse fate took away her only
son. As a result, she resented her daughters' existence and actively
disliked Marthe because of her rapidly unfolding beauty and feminine aura.

At the beginning of the twentieth century, the kingdom of Romania had been independent for twenty-two years. King Carol was
firmly established on the throne; his adopted successor Ferdinand
had married the beautiful English Princess Marie of Edinburgh,
granddaughter of Queen Victoria, known to history as Queen Marie of Romania. In the first two years of her marriage to Ferdinand,

"Missy," as she was known to her family, had already produced a son, the future Carol II, and a daughter, Elizabeth. Life in Bucharest was unbearably dull for the spirited young girl, who exchanged the glamour of an English court and later the freedom of her parents' countrified existence in the duchy of Coburg, for the somber atmosphere of a primitive, uncomfortable so-called palace, where she lived under the strict supervision of "der Onkel," the King, and his eccentric and often unkind artist wife, Queen Elizabeth (Carmen Sylva), recently returned from exile and anxious to resume the reins of power. "Poor Missy, what is going to happen to her in such an insecure country where society is so dreadful?" Queen Victoria wrote to her daughter Vicky, wife of the German Kaiser and Missy's aunt. A similar opinion was expressed by Emperor Franz Josef in Vienna, where the newlyweds Marie and Ferdinand stopped on their way to Bucharest after their honeymoon in Germany. At a dinner given in their honor the Emperor regarded the new Romanian crown princess with interest, tinged with pity. "You sent something far too beautiful to Romania" he told Lady Paget, wife of the British Ambassador, during the evening. "I don't understand how the Duchess of Edinburgh could make up her mind to do so." He later voiced reservations about King Carol's wife, Carmen Sylva. "She is stark mad," he declared. "How is this young girl going to cope with her?"

It has never been adequately explained why the Duchess of Edinburgh insisted on pushing her seventeen-year-old daughter into a loveless marriage to one of the dullest and most unprepossessing princes in Europe, when Marie's cousin George, the future King George V, was standing by, much in love, ready to offer his hand. They had known each other since childhood, and Prince George never made any secret of his desire to marry "darling Missy." It was also Queen Victoria's wish. The probable explanation is that Missy's mother, daughter of Tsar Alexander II of Russia, who had never liked English court life ("damp and dull") and did not get on with her mother-in-law, Queen Victoria, wanted Missy to remain "on the Continent." There might have been another reason: at the time of Missy's arranged engagement to the Crown Prince of Romania, George was only the second son of the future Edward VII; it was his older brother Albert Victor, Duke of Clarence, who was destined for the throne. Missy's mother, who herself was married to Queen Victoria's younger son, had been irked all her life by having to give precedence to Alexandra, the Princess of Wales. As the daughter of the Tsar of Russia (an "Imperial and not a Royal Highness"), she felt she deserved better treatment. She wanted her daughter to be Queen, no matter how shaky or distant the throne.

After the birth of her second child the Crown Princess Marie was finally able to get away from the strict regime imposed on her by King Carol and to begin building a life of her own. She now had an establishment: the palace of Cotroceni, a rambling, unshapely building set in a large garden on the outskirts of town, where she could entertain her friends and the Bucharesti "young set." Unlike many beautiful women, Princess Marie did not fear competition and took pains to surround herself with the prettiest women of her generation.

Marthe was only fourteen at the time, but already talked about as one of the great beauties in a city full of beautiful women. Her family had always been close to the throne; her father was still the King's most trusted adviser and had been so for the last twenty-five years. When Marthe was eleven years old Queen Elizabeth asked Madame Lahovary to allow Marthe to pose for her, as the Angel of Light, carrying the Cross of the Resurrection. Marthe obediently sat during the interminable sessions at the palace, though, as she later recalled, "I began to suspect that the Almighty had provided the Queen with more determination than talent."

For the young Crown Princess Marie, eleven years older than Marthe, it was "love at first sight." A remarkable friendship sprang up between the fourteen-year-old girl and the beautiful Crown Princess. On Marthe's part it was boundless admiration for a free, original spirit, an illustrious bloodline and exquisite physical perfection. For the Princess it was the pleasure of being adored without reservation by someone young, but infinitely mature for her age, who she hoped would fill the void left by the separation from her own sisters. Queen Marie's memoirs give an interesting picture of Marthe as an adolescent: "Marthe Bibesco," she writes, "carried the promise of great beauty and dreamt of grandeur. Brought up among famous men, she liked power, great achievers, talented artists, successful politicians, kings and princes . . . This young girl with huge green eyes and magnificent reddish hair had enormous vitality and thirst for knowledge, which I found stimulating; I was flattered by her admiration and amused by Marthe's almost encyclopedic knowledge of my ancestry. Not only was she unusually mature for her age, but she had a prodigious memory and powers of observation; nothing escaped her. I often had a feeling of being with someone older than myself. Most important—I knew I could trust her."

The two young women were alike in many ways: they shared the same romantic outlook on life; poetry—particularly love sonnets—moved them deeply, as did a fine sunset over the Danube delta. For the first time since she arrived in Bucharest the Crown Princess had someone she could laugh with when discussing the goings-on at court. Marthe, even at a very young age, had a wicked sense of humor and was an excellent mimic. Queen Carmen Sylva, an absurd figure outside her circle, was the frequent butt of their jokes. It helped the Princess to control her annoyance with "Auntie's" unwelcome forays into her household.

Marthe's beauty and her intelligence did not escape the notice of Crown Prince Ferdinand. Painfully timid, rather gauche, with an unprepossessing physique (his stuck-out ears made him look comic), obsessively prudish in a country of luxuriant permissiveness, Ferdinand developed a sentimental, Werther-like affection for Marthe, which remained with him until the end of his life. In a curious way the girl's presence, her charm and intuitive tact, helped to smooth the frequently strained relations between the young royal couple. They liked to have her around and she was often invited to cruise with them on the royal yacht on the Black Sea, a pastime she much enjoyed.

A young girl from a prominent family with a large dowry, great connections and sensational looks was a rare prize on the Bucharest marriage market. Even before she reached her fifteenth birthday pretenders began to line up for Marthe's hand. Her parents had already narrowed down a few choices: one of them was a Prince

Ghika-Comanesti, a fine figure of a man, bearer of a historic name, whose family had just come into the possession of a section of the Ploesti oil fields, which promised to make them millionaires. Marthe met him but was not particularly enthusiastic. "I addressed a fervent prayer to God: please make them think I am not worthy of him." Because of her extreme youth the project was temporarily shelved and young Ghika went off to Africa to shoot lions.* When he returned from his travels he found that Marthe was engaged to be married to Prince George Valentine Bibesco, grandson of the Hospodar of Wallachia.

* In a twist of fate Marthe's daughter, Valentine, later married Ghika's son.

2

❧❀❧

The
Virgin Bride

One day in late March 1901, Marthe and her sister Jeanne drove over to the Palais Stirbey on neighboring Calea Victoriei to pay a call on Aunt Valentine Bibesco, a distant relative of their mother. On entering the vast drawing room, furnished in the then fashionable mixture of Byzantine and Second Empire styles, Marthe saw leaning against a tall Byzantine chest a young man wearing the brown-and-black uniform of the 2nd Regiment of the King's Artillery. He was of medium height, dark and blue-eyed, and wore a slightly insolent expression. He struck her as the most handsome man she had ever seen. "I experienced a deep emotion," she confided to her diary that evening, "as if my heart had suddenly stopped." The object of this *coup de foudre* was George Valentine Bibesco, Tante Valentine and Prince George Bibesco's only son. Though well known to the Lahovary family, he and Marthe had never met until now. Seven years older than Marthe, George* was perpetually on the move: dashing between Bucharest

---

* George was the Bibesco family name by which all eldest sons had to be called.

and his country estates, completing his military service, courting women or establishing ever more ambitious sporting records.

On the surface, young Bibesco was everything that a parent might have wished for a daughter. Scion of a great family with immense wealth, possessed of splendid looks and an enviable reputation as a sportsman, George Bibesco shone in Bucharest society, as well as in the aristocratic circles of Paris and Vienna. His admirers were legion; men liked him and women found him irresistible. But hidden under this remarkable exterior was a self-willed and selfish man, a cynic, sensual but cruel by nature. Adored and outrageously spoiled by his mother, he brooked no interference with his whims, using charm to atone for his misdemeanors. Highly intelligent, he refused to study what bored him—books and literature were disregarded (it was said that he never read any of his wife's books). Mathematics and science interested him. But above all he loved machines: cars, speedboats, motorcycles and later planes. He was a sportsman without parallel. Only a few weeks before his introduction to Marthe, the papers had been filled with his most recent exploit—a record-breaking drive behind the wheel of his Mercedes 16/20cc between Geneva and Bucharest, accomplished in seventy-three hours and forty-five minutes in spite of adverse weather conditions.

To Marthe, imbued with romantic notions and longing to escape from her mother, George Bibesco appeared on that late winter afternoon as the longed-for Prince Charming who would lead her into a new and splendid world. George Bibesco was equally dazzled. He had never met anyone as beautiful as the Lahovary girl, whose future promised still greater beauty. Here she stood with huge, languorous green-brown eyes, a pink-and-white English complexion, so different from the swarthy Bucharest girls, and reddish-blond hair cascading onto her shoulders. He immediately noticed her elegant, long-limbed figure, her tiny waist and overall look of distinction. It did not take him long to realize that here was the most exceptional prize the marriage market had to offer, and because it was so exceptional, he, by right, should own it. It was the same reasoning he applied to horses, motorcars and speedboats. Not being in favor of marriage ties, he of course would have preferred to elope to Paris and take her as his mistress, but he knew this was out of the question.

Over lunch at the Jockey Club, Marthe's father told the impatient young man that his daughter was much too young to be married; he must wait—at least a year—perhaps longer. Lahovary explained that they could become officially engaged in the autumn, but the wedding would follow "sometime later." In the meantime they would be allowed to write to each other. There was no appeal from this verdict.

Restless and impatient by nature, unused to having his desires thwarted, young Bibesco decided to "kill time" and embarked on a series of travels. The couple saw comparatively little of each other, as George seldom alighted in Bucharest. His "letters"—bits of paper scrawled on in haste—have been lost, but Marthe's are still in existence. They are a touching mixture of childish affection and total commitment to their future life. She admonishes him "to be careful—not to drive recklessly," and chides him for being away from her for so long. She describes small events of her daily life in a fresh, original style, revealing a sophisticated sense of humor, unusual in a girl of fifteen. Did her fiancé read any of her letters? Probably not, as she often complained that he failed to answer the questions she put to him.

As the date of the official engagement drew near, George became more unpredictable and moody. In her innocence Marthe blamed herself and wrote sweet notes asking him "to forgive her if she had done anything to annoy him." It was not an auspicious beginning.

Old Prince Bibesco, George's father, well aware of his son's mercurial behavior, tried to smooth matters over. A connoisseur of feminine beauty, having spent a lifetime seducing women, he liked and admired his future daughter-in-law. He assured Marthe that his son would change dramatically as soon as they became man and wife. "Frustration is driving poor George to behave strangely; I can understand him." He smiled. "Don't worry, all will be well."

The Crown Princess sent her best wishes and a diamond pin in the shape of a star. "How amusing that you should be marrying the son of the Pretender," she wrote to Marthe. As Hospodars of Wallachia the Bibescos had indeed a quasi-royal status in Romania. The Liberal Party, most of whose members disliked the Hohenzollern dynasty, made sporadic attempts to rally around a *national* candidate for the throne. They even approached Prince Nicholas, George's uncle, but he refused to have anything to do with their "mad project." Married to Hélène d'Elchingen, the granddaughter of Marshal Ney, Prince Nicholas Bibesco was comfortably settled in Paris and determined to stay there. Father of two daughters, but no son, he had arranged for the "right of succession" to pass to his younger brother George, Marthe's future father-in-law, and his descendants. Though it was highly unlikely that the Bibescos would ever ascend to the throne of Romania, Marthe, passionately enamored of history, liked the prospect of marrying into a family with dynastic pretensions, famous in her own country as well as in France. "I stepped onto the European stage through the grand door," reads an entry in her memoirs on the day of her wedding.

After the official engagement in October, an occasion for protracted celebrations in Bucharest and on the Bibesco country estates, the fiancé accompanied his father on a mission to Constantinople, where they were to be received by the Sultan. Swept up in a welter of entertainment, dazzled by the exotic life on the Bosphorus, George forgot to write to his fiancée for several months. He was brought down to earth by Jean Lahovary, who suggested he return home forthwith if he wanted the marriage to take place. Leaving his father behind, the prospective bridegroom boarded a boat for Constantsa. He had not yet arrived when news came that on May 22, 1902, Prince Bibesco had died of a heart attack in his carriage while returning from an audience with the Sultan. (Rumor had it that he had been poisoned by the Grand Vizier, but there is no evidence to substantiate this.)

George was now heir to his father's riches and free to do whatever he wished. The family was in deep mourning and he seized on it as an excuse for dispensing with "the boring festivities" of a fashionable wedding in the autumn. He wanted to get married quietly in six weeks' time. There was some opposition from Marthe's family and acute disappointment in the social circles of

the capital, who had been looking forward to the festivities tradi-
tionally associated with such a grand wedding, but, as usual,
George had his way.

At the time of Marthe's marriage, the Lahovary family lived at
97, Calea Dorobantilor, an attractive two-story house built in late-
eighteenth-century style, with stone balconies and surrounded by
a large garden. It is now the American School in Bucharest; a stone
tablet at the entrance commemorates Marthe's childhood there
and her fame as a writer. The room where she spent her last night
as a Lahovary is now the kindergarten playroom, but the house
structure is unchanged. French doors open on the two balconies
in her room, the garden is slightly smaller than it was in her day,
but when I went there it was easy to imagine Marthe on the morning of her wedding day, exactly as she described in her memoirs.
"Dawn at last . . . I did not sleep all night from excitement. It is
the morning of my wedding . . . I jump out of bed and open the
doors to the balconies. One looks to the east, the other to the
south. . . . I let the sun stream into the room. It is a glorious
morning. Why am I sad? All went well yesterday; the civil marriage
passed without a hitch . . . We opened our presents . . . I am
overwhelmed by the splendor of George's gifts. My dear fiancé,
after weeks of moodiness and annoyance, caused by family quarrels, has regained his happy disposition. We laughed and joked
together like children and made fun of all the people who criticize
us for depriving them of the festivities they had so counted on."

They were married on June 29, 1902, in a quiet ceremony for
their immediate families. That same night they boarded the Orient
Express for Munich and Paris, accompanied by two chaperons:
George's mother and his old nurse Fraülein Hamm, who had
rushed over from Germany for Prince Bibesco's funeral. It was an
ill-starred beginning.

"The physical union of two people is like murder," Marthe
recalled with a shudder. "All at once one is obliterated; no identity
remains except pain." Years later, in her book *Où Tombe la Foudre*,
she proclaimed, "Giving a virgin to a man is like handing a Strad-
ivarius to a monkey."

What happened on the Orient Express? There is no doubt that

George, sensual and brutally selfish, treated his child bride the way he dealt with the women of the Bucharesti demimonde he frequented. He showed her no patience or tenderness—but simply raped her. The experience had a devastating effect on Marthe and colored her attitude toward sex for the rest of her life. "In spite of the best will in the world," she recalled, "I could not find any pleasure in yielding to my husband's demands." Gradually she formed the conviction that physical pleasures "are a slightly obscene and overrated pastime, unremarkable when compared with the sublime delights of intellectual pursuit."

After a few days in Munich, where Marthe visited the studio of the fashionable painter Franz von Lenbach, who was anxious to do her portrait, and accompanied her mother-in-law on a tour of the city's art galleries, the newlyweds continued on to Paris. There at last she could get away from the old Princess's supervision and revisit the places she had known as a child. As the family was in deep mourning, social calls were restricted to a minimum; only a handful of Tante Valentine's French relations turned up at the Liverpool Hotel, on the rue Castiglione, where they were staying. Their objective—as George acidly remarked—was to see how much his mother had aged since her divorce from Prince Bauffremont and her subsequent marriage to his father.

They returned to Romania in early August in time for George to take part in military maneuvers, scheduled that autumn. Marthe followed her mother-in-law to Posada, the Bibesco family country residence in the Carpathian foothills.

At this point, it is necessary to enlarge on the person of Aunt Valentine, Marthe's indomitable mother-in-law, one of the most colorful figures of the period, who was to play a crucial role in her life. Born Countess de Caraman-Chimay of distinguished French and Belgian lineage, granddaughter of Thérésa Tallien, a political hostess and a beauty at the time of the French Revolution, she married Prince Paul de Bauffremont, a professional soldier and later a general in the French Army, who led the ill-fated cavalry charge at the Battle of Sedan in 1870. Valentine hated garrison life and soon fell out of love with her husband, who turned out to be mean, selfish, quick-tempered and chronically unfaithful. According to her contemporaries and those who knew her at Napoleon III's Tuileries, Valentine had a strong character, immense energy, a sharp wit and a gift for manipulating people. Though not a renowned beauty, she had a lovely figure and there was a great air of distinction about her. Men found her attractive; she always seemed to be surrounded by a circle of *chevaliers servants* prepared to keep her company during her husband's frequent absences from home. Prominent among her admirers was a handsome Romanian officer serving in the French Army. His name was George Bibesco, heir to the Hospodar of Wallachia and father of Marthe's young husband.

Brought up entirely in France, where his father was living in voluntary and happy exile, the young captain was a graduate of the French Military Academy of St. Cyr, took part in the ill-fated Mexican campaign in which Napoleon III unsuccessfully supported Emperor Maximilian and was appointed an officer on the French General Staff. Valentine de Bauffremont, fragile, attractive and seemingly helpless, so obviously neglected by her husband, appealed to his romantic imagination; he decided she needed protecting; it was not long before they became lovers. But Bauffremont turned out to be an unexpectedly tough adversary. Not only did he continue to ill-treat his wife physically; he also tried to prevent her from seeing their two little daughters, whom he ordered to live in the country with his mother in the family château on the Loire. Matters reached such a pitch that Valentine sued for "a *séparation judiciaire.*" Divorce did not exist in France in those days and separation had to be granted in an ecclesiastical court. At first the Tribunal de la Seine granted her request, but a month later when Bauffremont appealed, the verdict was reversed. The 1870 Franco-German War, the fall of Napoleon III's Empire and the fact that both Bauffremont and Bibesco became prisoners of war in Germany delayed matters. Hostilities were resumed, however, when the two men returned home. Bauffremont and Bibesco fought a celebrated duel which resulted in the lover being sent to the Conciergerie prison for a time. Finally, two years later, Valentine managed to obtain the longed-for legal separation and custody of her two daughters. Determined to marry Bibesco, which she could not do in France, she transferred her residence to Saxe-Altenburg in Protestant Germany, where divorce was legally accepted.

In 1875 she and George Bibesco were married in a civil ceremony in Berlin, followed a few days later by an Orthodox wedding in Dresden. She thought she had outwitted her husband. But Bauffremont was not to be defeated. He promptly instituted a case for the arrest of his "bigamous wife" and petitioned the courts for the custody of his daughters. Valentine refused to give in, fighting the case passionately for two years until her money ran out. Menars, the Caraman-Chimay property, which she loved and which was to be passed on to her daughters, had to be sold to pay the lawyers. She finally emerged from the turmoil, having twice changed nationality and religion, duly married to her lover, her spirit intact and her joie de vivre undiminished. She settled with him in the old Bibesco family palace in Bucharest, where she produced three more children, including Marthe's husband, George.

For years the "affair Bauffremont" provided great copy for newspapers all over Europe. Every detail of the scandal was avidly scrutinized and enjoyed; poor Valentine was much condemned and turned into a social pariah. In Paris, in the staid Faubourg St. Germain, a citadel of propriety, all doors closed against her and, much to her distress, her name was dropped from the *Almanach de Gotha*, the bible of European nobility. The case became a classic in the annals of international jurisdiction, much relished by generations of law students, who for years used to choose it as a subject for their graduating theses.

It took Valentine a long time to adjust to life in Romania. She missed her family, her French friends, the excitement of Paris, and of course, for the "belle of the Tuileries," Bucharest and its court life remained provincial and dull. At one time in the 1880s, during one of the ever recurring Balkan crises, Prince Bibesco, supported by the French statesman Léon Gambetta, was considered a candidate for the throne of Bulgaria. Ever cautious, Valentine consulted her old friend the German Chancellor Otto von Bismarck; he wired her: "It would be most regrettable if a woman like you buried herself in Bulgaria." She promptly abandoned the project.

(The Chancellor, in fact, was pushing the candidature of Prince Ferdinand of Saxe-Coburg-Gotha, who in 1887 became Prince and later King of Bulgaria, known in history as Foxy Ferdie.)

With the passage of years the Dowager Princess, now firmly anchored in the haven of the Greek Orthodox Church and endowed with the respectability of old age, became reconciled to her fate. Having forgotten her own stormy past, she became a merciless critic of the vagaries of the young. Very well educated and a brilliant conversationalist, she insisted on maintaining the highest standards of speech and deportment, which she now proceeded to apply to her lovely newly acquired daughter-in-law. Marthe, she observed during the honeymoon trip, though badly mishandled by her husband, will survive, but in order to shine "in the real world," she would need coaching. In the severe solitude of Posada, enlivened only by social visits from a few neighbors and the intermittent appearances of her husband, the young girl was put to work harder than at any finishing school. She was made to read classical and modern authors, both French and German, practice her already fluent English, take notes, write digests, read prose and recite verses aloud; Valentine insisted on teaching her how to walk, enter a room and move gracefully around the echoing chambers of the vast, sprawling house. "It will all be useful to you one day," the old Princess assured Marthe, who believed her and accepted this harsh regime for nearly four and a half years.

"During the early years of my marriage," recalled Marthe, "I used to return to Posada with reluctance; I had been very lonely there, also bored . . . But as time passed, the house, the village and its people became part of me, my real home and a refuge. I called it 'my very own land of the willows.' "

In Romania the willow tree reigns supreme. Before starting to build a house for his family, a villager will first put a little willow shoot in the ground; in no time it becomes a weeping willow embellishing the entrance to his house. Willow trees surround water wells, providing shade around the water pump, the traditional village meeting place; they denote boundaries between individual peasant plots; they grow along the fast-flowing mountain streams and form closely knit clumps of greenery on the meadows. "As I

looked at my village from the windows of the approaching train,
all I could see were the willows, the houses were lost among
them," recalled Marthe. The willow is much praised in local song:
"We love you, O silvery waterside tree. You yield osier and timber
for our houses and you give us the flutes without which there
would be no music in our midst . . . you rustle and sing in the
wind to the glory of the rivers you protect."

An age-old tradition, going back to pagan times, ordains that a
village girl who becomes pregnant out of wedlock must undergo
a symbolic marriage to a willow tree. She is taken out of her house
by the village elders, conducted to the riverbank, tied to the trunk
of a willow (its branches cover her shame) and, after suitable in-
cantations, is pronounced duly wedded; henceforth she will be
allowed to walk with her head covered, like the rest of the married
women in the village, shame having been exorcised by the willow
tree.

When I visited Posada recently, the main house, in which
Marthe had lived with her husband and mother-in-law in the early
years of her marriage, was no more. It mysteriously burned down
in September 1915 after secret papers pertaining to the conduct
of the war had been deposited there for safekeeping. Marthe had
never liked the main house. "It reminds me of a villa in Deau-
ville," she used to say. She abandoned the burned-out ruin and
skillfully converted the servants' quarters and an adjoining barn
into a charming, comfortable, English-style country house with
modern facilities, where in later years she entertained a succession
of distinguished visitors and many friends.

Marthe's house is now a complex of government offices, unfortunately with some very ugly additions. What has remained unchanged, however, is the incomparable setting. Built with its back
to the road, the house—in Marthe's day—opened on a series of
ascending paved terraces planted with roses, laburnum, lilacs, jas-
mine and a multitude of scented shrubs, sheltered by giant chestnut and acacia trees. Behind the house, protecting it from the
elements, were the mountains, covered with dense oak and beech
forests, forever changing in color, alive with deer, stag, brown bear
and other wildlife. A paved path along a mountain torrent led up-

ward until it disappeared from view on the skyline. Along that path
Marthe used to walk on most afternoons at Posada. She walked
alone, dressed in her English sporting clothes, heavy boots and a
wide-brimmed hat, defying the local custom of the lady of the
house having to be accompanied at all times. Her mother-in-law
disapproved: "It is dangerous," said Valentine. "People expect us
to move around in a carriage . . . to keep our distance." Disre-
garding her remarks, Marthe set off to get to know the villagers,
learn about the local customs, bring help where it was needed and
establish channels of communication where none existed. The
half-pagan, half-medieval world in which the Romanian peasant
existed enthralled her, and as her writing capacity developed, she
began to take notes, filling a large blue exercise book with what
she called "my disparate scribblings." It helped to relieve the
loneliness of the young bride, left so soon to her own devices.

Where was George when Marthe walked alone in the mountains, or went through the dreary ritual of reading the newspapers
aloud to the Dowager Princess after dinner? Young Bibesco, having
acquired the most beautiful girl in Romania for his wife, saw no
reason why he should look after her to the detriment of his pleasures. Motor racing, gambling and an active Bucharest love life
consumed a great deal of his time; besides, he now had a business
to look after—a cement factory at Comarnic, the neighboring
town, which under the direction of a German manager was becoming extremely profitable. As a result, George seemed to be contin-
ually absent; even when his arrival was expected, he would turn
up hours late.

Marthe describes one of the many evenings at Posada waiting
for her husband to appear: "It is dinnertime; we sit by the fire all
dressed up . . . Zufall, the Swiss majordomo, comes in looking
anxious, obviously sent in by the cook. 'We shall wait for the
Prince,' says Valentine. As time passes, I become more and more
nervous; the roads are icy, George drives with reckless speed . . .
has there been an accident, or is he with a woman? . . . I try to
hide my tears; Valentine seems calm, but I know she is worried;
tension mounts . . . I go to the window and watch. Suddenly lights
become visible in the distance; seconds later the Mercedes, driven

at reckless speed, enters the courtyard; the dogs bark . . . doors are flung open. My husband enters the room, magnificent in his fur-lined cloak. He kisses his mother, pats me on the back and calls for dinner. Not a word of excuse or explanation."

Early in the New Year, Marthe realized she was pregnant. The Bucharest doctor they consulted warned George that her pregnancy would be difficult and the utmost care should be taken at the time of delivery. Chloroform had been available in Germany and in England for some time; it was used during the birth of Queen Victoria's seventh child and more recently when the Crown Princess Marie gave birth to the future King Carol II. In view of Marthe's extreme youth and delicate constitution, it is surprising that no preparations were made for what was obviously going to be a prolonged and painful birth. It was even more surprising that Marthe's mother, Madame Lahovary, refused to break her holiday in Normandy and travel back to Romania for the event. Only Valentine was left at her daughter-in-law's bedside. It was August; the heat on the plains was intense, though at Posada the nights were mercifully cool. The pains started on a Tuesday, and for the rest of the week Marthe underwent agony, hovering between life and death, assisted only by the local doctor and a midwife. Early on August 27, 1903, she finally gave birth to a daughter, whom they named Valentine in honor of the Dowager Princess. It took Marthe a long time to recover; there were moments in the first few weeks after the baby's arrival when she came close to dying. "She is too young," mused the midwife. "This is what happens when children are made to beget children—we must pray." The villagers prayed for her too. "Our poor little Princess," sighed the women, who gathered in the local churchyard; "they have ruined her . . . she may never be able to produce a son and heir for the Prince."

Marthe has been much criticized for what was reputedly a lack of affection for her daughter. It is true that during Valentine's childhood and early youth their relations were frequently strained. As Marthe describes in her memoirs: "I admit that at the very beginning I did not care for that little bundle which had caused me such enormous suffering. . . . She even disgusted me as a baby

. . . I had to force myself to hold and kiss her. I did not want her to come and truly resented her forcing herself upon me. As she grew up, I saw to it that she would be well looked after, but there was little closeness between us." It was only years later, when both mother and daughter underwent common suffering and separation, that their relationship altered, became close and affectionate on Valentine's side and lovingly protective on Marthe's.

For the moment, however, Marthe—in the opinion of her doctors—was too young to cope with motherhood. She was also too inexperienced to cope satisfactorily with her husband. As her correspondence reveals, she still loved him, was happy when he chose to come home, but feared and only reluctantly submitted to his lovemaking. She was much relieved when, six weeks after the baby's birth, a distinguished Bucharest gynecologist told George that it was essential they refrain from intercourse for at least two years—a harsh prescription for a man like Bibesco, who now felt justified to multiply his absences.

The next two years could have been years of crisis for Marthe. Isolated in the Carpathians with an aging mother-in-law and a daughter who did not interest her, conscious that her marriage was threatened by her husband's multiple liaisons, Marthe could have lapsed into a deep depression and rebelled. What happened to the glorious expectations she had cherished at the time of her engagement to George? In spite of her fragile health, she was more beautiful now than at the time of her marriage. Was she destined to remain hidden from the world, like a nun in a convent? George explained that because of the expanding cement business they must, for the time being, continue to base themselves in Posada, with only occasional stays in Bucharest. Her father, to whom she went for advice, uncharacteristically took her husband's side. So that was that. She had to resign herself to her fate. But in the course of her long solitary walks in the mountains, Marthe came to a remarkably wise conclusion for one so young: she would bide her time and "show them." In the meantime, she would concentrate on her education, taking full advantage of what Valentine had to offer, and devote all the available time to writing. Instinct told her that therein lay her salvation and her future.

From then on, her days acquired a definite structure. She woke up early, even in winter when it was still dark outside; her breakfast was brought to her at eight o'clock every morning, half of it going to the cat, for she had little appetite, much to the despair of the servants. After a short visit to her daughter and a look at the household accounts, she remained in her bedroom reading and writing until it was time to rejoin her mother-in-law for the midday meal. This was also the moment when the mail arrived—the highlight of the day. The newspapers were brought to the library by the solemn Swiss majordomo after lunch, and over coffee Marthe read aloud to Valentine excerpts from week-old French, German, or English papers with an occasional glance at an item in the current Romanian press. The Dowager then retired for a siesta and Marthe returned to her room to rest on her bed for a while. In the afternoons, regardless of weather conditions, she sallied forth for a walk. Undeterred by rain, heavy snow or the oppressive heat in the summer, she was bent on exploring her domain, getting acquainted with the villagers. She wanted to overcome their mistrust. "These people," she remarked in her diary, "have been so mistreated for centuries that they have no aspirations left . . . just survival." She describes one typical afternoon in the spring as follows: "Coming back from my walk, I slipped into the house through the servants' entrance to avoid running into my mother-in-law, who was in the music room. How could I explain to her that I really enjoyed walking in such terrible weather—she who always worries about my state of health. When I got back to my room I dismissed Virginie, my French maid. Her hands are too delicate to cope with the encrusted mud on my boots. It is Outza, the old Romanian peasant in my service, who takes away my wet coat, smelling of sheep; she kneels and pulls at the boots. The skin on Outza's hands is tough and gray, like the skin of the primeval tortoises which live in the swamps of Dobrudja."

Outza's presence in the house was the bridge that Marthe constructed between herself and the village. All the other servants were foreign, with the exception of the laundresses and stable boys. "Baba Outza," asks Marthe, "what are the women doing in the village at this hour?" Outza shrugs her shoulders, much

amused. "How do I know? Some are busy sewing or knitting, others sit around gossiping." "And the children?" "How do I know?
The naughty ones cry, the others play with the goats and jump
about."

To Outza, Marthe was a kind of divinity, a good but incomprehensible creature whose purpose she will never be able to
fathom. Why on earth does she insist on walking the hills in such
weather when she could stay home by the fire or ride around in a
carriage? Having taken Marthe's boots off, she rubs her mistress's
icy feet and softly wails, "*Vai, vai, vai . . .*"

In summer, when the weather was clement, Marthe was expected to partner her mother-in-law in a game of croquet on the
lawn. Valentine, who was adept at the game, loved winning to the
point that she often cheated. Dinner, for which they both changed
into formal clothes, was announced with the sound of a brass gong;
the ritual succession of courses took a long time; the conversation
lagged for lack of subjects. But sometimes, when in good humor,
Valentine took to reminiscing; Marthe listened with real interest
to descriptions of life in the Tuileries at the court of Napoleon III,
of the reigning personalities of the Faubourg, of the great contemporary scandals; she particularly liked to unravel the complex
genealogical links between Valentine's family the Chimays, the
Bibescos and the members of the old French aristocracy, who repudiated Valentine but who in a few years would open the doors
of their houses to Marthe with enthusiasm. Valentine retired early,
and by 11 p.m. Marthe returned to her room, wide awake; she
would spend the succeeding two hours writing.

It was not much of a life for a beautiful, talented girl of eighteen. She needed help; it would come unexpectedly from the
Bibesco side of the family.

Across the country in Bessarabia, near the Danube town of
Turnu-Severin, lay the domain of Corcova, the property of two
brothers, Emmanuel and Antoine Bibesco, George's cousins.
Noted in literary memoirs as friends of Marcel Proust, the two
brothers, who resided in Paris, were well known in France for
their intellectual qualities, splendid looks, great wealth and social
charm. Antoine, the younger of the two, belonged to a group of

young noblemen, who in Proust's *A la Recherche du Temps Perdu* merged into the unforgettable character of Saint-Loup. A handsome, virile man with chiseled features and the profile of a Roman emperor, Antoine combined natural vivacity with an arrogant, insolent manner and mordant wit. He fascinated women, whom he liked to seduce and discard. Proust adored him, though he complained of Antoine's multiple love affairs with beautiful women, "which took so much of his time." Antoine, though often exasperated by the writer's excessive susceptibility, admired Proust's genius and remained his loyal friend for the rest of his life. At the time of their first meeting in the Parisian salon of Antoine and Emmanuel's mother, Princess Hélène Bibesco, Antoine, who was then twenty-three, was studying for the Romanian diplomatic service. "The great thing about being a Romanian diplomat," he liked to say to his friends, "is that it will not be necessary to spend any time in Romania."

Emmanuel, two years older than Antoine, as aloof as Antoine was social, had an aura of mystery about him. Tall and lissome with Oriental dark eyes and fluid movements, he was nicknamed "l'Almée," the Dancing Girl, by his friends. Artistic and extremely knowledgeable, particularly in ecclesiastical architecture, he carried his passion for privacy to extremes. His only known hobby was visiting the cathedrals of France, which he liked to do on Sundays. Proust accompanied him on a few occasions, but the two never really got very close. Unlike Antoine, who adored women, Emmanuel was probably a homosexual, unable to reciprocate a woman's feelings, as Marthe was to discover a few years later. Proust, of course, guessed his friend's leanings and was frustrated. He called Prince Emmanuel "the enigma," liked and admired him, but, lacking encouragement, gave up the fruitless pursuit. As George Painter remarks in his biography: "Proust never even reached the point of calling Emmanuel 'tu.' "

In the summer of 1904, the two brothers, who were spending several weeks at Corcova, drove over to see cousin Marthe. It is not clear whether they had met before; as members of the family, they might have attended George and Marthe's wedding two years earlier; or they may have met in Paris during the Bibescos' short honeymoon. The encounter has not been recorded; at the time, Marthe would have seemed a mere child, while they would have had little in common with their philistine cousin George.

"They brought the air of Paris into our Carpathian retreat," Marthe recalled. They also brought understanding and compassion. Antoine instantly realized the extent of Marthe's loneliness, "abandoned by her husband in the depth of a forest, having to spend her days between an imperious and demanding mother-in-law and a child she does not particularly care for," he noted. He sensed her frustration and growing disillusionment with her marriage. A connoisseur of feminine beauty, he was bowled over by his young cousin's looks and agreeably surprised by her intelligence and budding literary talent. An immediate understanding based on mutual trust and amused observation of life grew between them. They were to meet frequently in the future; with the passage of years, Antoine would become Marthe's intimate friend and confidant (their correspondence now fills two volumes).

The relationship with Emmanuel evolved in a different direction; it was to cause Marthe much bewilderment and deep sadness, for he was not a man who brought happiness to those around him.

Before leaving Romania, Antoine introduced Marthe to his cousin and friend Elise Bratiano, wife of the distinguished statesman Ion Bratiano, head of the Liberal Party, and sister of Barbo Stirbey—"the power behind the throne of Romania." Marthe was in need of a woman friend, and no one could have filled the role better than Elise. A handsome, aristocratic woman in her late thirties, of a culture and intelligence rare among the Romanian women of her class, Elise and her brother Barbo were later successful in guiding Crown Princess Marie through the labyrinth of Romanian political life and remained her closest advisers for years to come. At Antoine's request, Elise agreed to visit her "abandoned young cousin," and in spite of their difference in age she was, as she wrote to Antoine, "most agreeably surprised. I have spent several hours in Posada and made some pleasant discoveries. Marthe is intelligent and talented. . . . I admire her powers of concentration—a rare thing; she is not a child anymore. We understand each other well . . . You were right to suggest that we meet; being with her gives me pleasure." Deprived of her mother's affection since birth, Marthe was grateful for Elise's friendship and her counsel so different from Valentine's nineteenth-century strictures. Elise, who had no children of her own, welcomed the admiration and the trust with which this charming and unusually gifted young cousin turned toward her. In her correspondence with Antoine, Elise always referred to Marthe as "the child."

Elise's occasional visits to Posada and the Bibesco brothers' infrequent appearances in the country were the only breaks in the grayness that enveloped Marthe's daily existence in her Carpathian eyrie. She spent more and more time observing the life and customs of her country people, made voluminous notes, wrote poetry and tried her hand at writing short stories. But "it is not living," she wrote to her sister Jeanne. "To retire into solitary writing at my age is to be sulking at life" (*bouder la vie*).

3

❧❀❧

Journey to Paradise

In the spring of 1905 came a break in the clouds—the voyage to Persia—an unforgettable episode that permanently changed Marthe's life. How it all unfolded is uncertain, but it is possible to detect the hand of Marthe's father, Jean Lahovary, who was then Foreign Minister of Romania. George Bibesco was told that the current state of affairs at Posada would result in the permanent alienation of his wife's affection. She needed a change from the country and some time to be with him. Conveniently, a mission to the Shah of Persia was arranged; George was named head of the delegation and his wife was to accompany him on the voyage. It was to be their second honeymoon.

George set about the preparations with gusto. Traversing Persia in an automobile would be quite a feat and would crown his career as sportsman. Never mind the delicate state of his wife's health; she would love the romance of the expedition, George told himself. Five others were co-opted for the delegation: Emmanuel Bibesco; Monsieur and Madame Phérékyde, George's cousins;

Martin Leonidas, a Greek friend; and Claude Anet, the Bucharest correspondent of the Paris *Le Temps*, who was to be the expedition's historiographer. They would drive in three cars: George's large 40cc Mercedes, a smaller 20cc Mercedes, belonging to the Phérékydes, and Martin Leonidas' Fiat 16cc. Two chauffeurs skilled in mechanics accompanied them. It did not occur to the men that spare parts might be needed on the primitive Persian roads; nor did they much bother about the increasingly threatening reports that emanated from the Crimea, to where the 1905 Russian revolution had apparently spread.

After sending the cars and the chauffeurs ahead, they embarked on April 11 on a Danube steamer to Galatz, the great commercial port at the mouth of the Danube delta. After crossing the Danube to Ismail, the travelers set off on a tedious two-day drive through Bessarabia, a flat, primitive former Romanian province that had been ceded to Russia. Weather conditions were appalling; torrential rain and mud ruined the cars' delicate engines, mud even drowned Claude Anet's watch, though he had carefully lodged it in his breast pocket, and there were no inns or hotels on the way. It was with great relief that they arrived in Odessa, the thriving Black Sea metropolis, and checked into the comfortable Hotel de Londres, where they rested for several days. Yalta in the Crimea was their next stop. To Marthe's somewhat naïve disappointment, the much talked-about revolution had not yet reached Yalta; the beautiful flower-strewn countryside instead lay peaceful in the April sunshine. She would have loved to explore it, but George insisted they keep to a schedule. Marthe did manage, however, to pay a visit to Maxim Gorky, exiled to the Crimea by the Tsarist government for his revolutionary views. The famous writer lived in a pretty Italian-style villa on the outskirts of Livadia, accompanied by his mistress. Claude Anet sent word that he would like to interview him, and Marthe prevailed upon George to let her come along in spite of the locals' objections that it would be unsuitable for "such a great lady to visit a couple living in sin."

Gorky was then thirty-six, a world celebrity, placed by Russian opinion at the side of Tolstoy. "He seemed prematurely old to me," Marthe reported. "His eyes were distant as if fixed on some inner vision." As neither Marthe nor Anet spoke Russian, it was left to the "companion," who spoke French, to interpret. According to Anet's recollection, most of the interview centered on a conversation about Tolstoy, of whom the "companion" disapproved. "How can a man with his aristocratic background pretend to speak in the name of the people," she kept saying. "Look at Alexey Maximovitch—he is their spokesman," she assured Marthe, pointing her finger at Gorky. Anet noted that the great man remained disappointingly silent most of the time, quietly puffing at his pipe. A year later Gorky left Russia to conduct his anti-tsarist campaign abroad.

When they arrived in Batum, Armenia, aboard a Russian vessel, the *Grand Duke Boris*, the city was in the throes of revolution. Chaos reigned, drunken bands roamed the streets and restaurants and hotels were boarded up. The manager of the International Hotel, whom George bribed, allowed them the use of a few rooms, but they had to provide their own food and drinking water. Contrary to what they had been told in the Crimea, Tiflis, the capital of Georgia, and Baku, in what is today's Azerbaijan, were also in the hands of revolutionary mobs. Wherever they went, the party had to be escorted by armed Cossack guards. It was thus with relief that they crossed the frontier into Persia at Lenkoran on May 8, three weeks after leaving Bucharest. Marthe was ecstatic. Not even the oppressive humid heat or the uninspiring landscape of the ill-smelling Lenkoran swamps could dampen her enthusiasm at having finally penetrated into Persia, "the land of the dreams of my childhood." She was thrilled at the sight of the local peasants in their native long tunics and turbans, "as if they had stepped down from a Tavernier print." Emmanuel declared that "it all looked exactly like Cochin China," from which he had recently returned.

Persia was in a state of considerable chaos. Shah Muzaffar-ed-Din, an irresponsible despot, had led the country down the road to bankruptcy by borrowing large sums of money from Russia, which he squandered on journeys to the fleshpots of Europe. As the fear of the Shah and his government disappeared, public order collapsed; bands of robbers roamed the countryside, attacking caravan routes. Undaunted, the voyagers got into their conspicuously expensive vehicles and drove over the dusty, rutted highway to Resht, where they thankfully accepted the hospitality of the Italian Consul. Comfortably installed at the consulate, Marthe at last had the leisure to explore the charming city of gardens and orange groves. It was the season of lilac and orange blossoms. "The air is humid and dense, filled with the undistilled scent of a thousand gardens on the sea. It is what I imagined the Orient would be like," she noted in her diary. "I keep telling myself that I am really in Asia, that it is true . . . Yesterday at sunset I watched the passing of a caravan—a majestic progression of camels, disciplined, dignified, tall like the arcades of the Sultan's Palace, balancing their mysterious loads on their backs. Summoned by the sound of their bells, a group of veiled women left the fountain and came forth to meet them. . . . I was back in biblical times."

The governor of Resht province, one of the many sons of Shah Muzaffar, was delighted by the arrival of distinguished foreigners and set out to entertain them. Marthe and Madame Phérékyde were invited to have tea with the wives in the Sultan's harem, a rare honor. "We sat in the inner sanctum, a Persian garden full of blue irises, around a fountain surrounded by blue mosaics, reflected in a basin of limpid water. Azodos Sultan is the third son of the Shah; he is twenty-two years old and already has seven wives; he rides a white horse with a red-painted tail; his power is absolute. . . . We waited. . . . Suddenly, coming toward us from a long blue-tiled alley, I see the son of the Shah followed by three of his princesses (we never saw the other four, apparently of a lower rank). He introduces them one by one. They are tiny, these little sultanas; they have girls' bodies and magnificent eyes, visible above their white Muslim veils; they proffer tiny white-gloved hands and bow deeply. They remind me of nuns in a convent. I would have liked to ask them so many things—like how do they manage to coexist, all seven of them, dependent on this one man, their master, who is young, spoiled, irritable, and strikes me as a slightly degenerate specimen of the human race. Does at least one of them love him? Has it ever occurred to them to unite and present a common front against the abuses and the infinite dreariness of their lives?

"As I was contemplating the abyss dividing us, in walked four incredible little boys, dressed in adult clothes, living miniatures of their father. They wore finely cut redingotes, dark striped trousers, red felt caps with black tassels. I was struck by the beauty of their eyes and their solemn, impenetrable expressions. The Prince took each one by the hand and presented to us: 'His Highness . . . son of Princess . . . ,' pointing at each of the mothers in turn. Then a eunuch appeared, carrying what seemed like a large green-clad doll, dressed in stiff, formal clothes. This was the baby son of the youngest and prettiest of the wives, aged one.

"We said goodbye. The Prince accompanied us to the doors of the harem. 'The happiest day of my life,' he said, bowing. Instructed in Oriental courtesy, we replied, 'It too was the happiest day of our lives.' We hurry . . . anxious to regain the fresh air and open spaces. One last look—the harem recedes in the shadow of the setting sun and with it the lives of its inmates."

Disappointment awaited them in Teheran with its preponderance of modern-style buildings, its imperial palaces filled with European furniture at its ugliest. "All plush and cheap imitations," Emmanuel scoffed with derision. In the absence of the Shah, who as usual was traveling in Europe, George and Emmanuel were received in audience by the Regent and handed over to him the Grand Cordon of the Order of Carol I.

Lodged in a small colonnaded palace, brand-new and surrounded by very fine gardens—one of flowers, another of fruit—Marthe enjoyed Teheran in spite of its ugly modern features. "I loved the altitude," she wrote. "It gave me a feeling of well-being . . . and the roses, huge, heavy bouquets of roses of all colors exuding the most heavenly scent; they are sold everywhere in the street and they fill the gardens that surround me. Spring here is like our summer in Romania—still and fragrant."

Because of the abysmal state of the roads and the difficulties of obtaining gasoline on the way, George decided that they would have to continue their journey to Isfahan, a distance of about 250 miles, in a horse-drawn carriage. "Had he known the discomfort that awaited us he would probably not have embarked on the journey," noted Marthe. And indeed the journey turned out to be a nightmare. The road was an ill-defined track in the desert, dusty and full of potholes; the springs of the ancient coach soon collapsed; the relays at which the horses were changed were primitive; the food covered with flies. Emmanuel, normally unperturbable, became so disgusted that he wanted to return to Teheran, but Marthe persuaded him to stay on. On the road to the holy city of Qum, their vehicle fell apart; George managed to find a replacement with more solid but much smaller springs, which increased the discomfort of the journey. Finally, after three more days of arduous travel, they arrived at the last relay before Isfahan. There waited a splendidly appointed carriage, driven by four frisky horses. A coachman in the livery of Prince Zil-el-Sultan, another son of the Shah, handed George Bibesco a letter welcoming them to his province and informing them that an entire palace had been put at their disposal. The offer of the palace had to be courteously refused, as George had already made arrangements to stay with the Russian Consul, Mr. Tchirkin. In great spirits, they drove into Isfahan, escorted by a detachment of Cossacks. "Between the desert and the city spread fields of opium poppies," Marthe remembered. "Some were white, the others scarlet; they went on for miles, like a gigantic carpet, as if to soften the transition between the hell of the desert and the paradise awaiting us."

The city of Isfahan, the former capital of the empire of Shah Abbas—the great sixteenth-century contemporary of Elizabeth I of England—of Suleiman the Magnificent of Turkey and of Akbar of the Moguls, is built on a plateau that dominates the countryside. At the time, one approached it by stately bridges, surrounded by luxurious gardens, which led to the immense Royal Square—the Maidan. Beyond it was the Hall of Forty Columns and the Hall of Audience, with its throne and endless rooms decorated with mural paintings. The famous Blue Mosque, its turquoise tiles shimmering in the sunshine, bathed the neighboring houses in soft blue light. "Isfahan is all blue, far bluer than I could have imagined," Marthe exclaimed in her diary. "It is like an enchanted city, well worth all the hardship to arrive in this paradise."

On the first morning of their stay the young Prince, governor

of Isfahan, sent baskets of white strawberries and white peaches
from his gardens; they were exquisitely arranged, interspersed with
the petals of red roses. Delighted to have such distinguished visitors to liven up the monotonous routine of his life, the young
Prince became their guide, ordering all doors and secret treasures
open to them. Whenever possible, Marthe escaped by herself to
wander in the bazaars, visit some hitherto hidden garden and explore the winding alleys, where medieval craftsmen still worked.
Often Emmanuel accompanied her. At night, back in the Tchir-
kins' airy, comfortable house, she wrote up her sketches, describing the scenes she had witnessed, the faces she had admired:
"boys' eyes framed by eyebrows in the shape of butterfly wings,"
"the jasmine-colored face of a young girl, caught unveiled," "the
high cheekbones on the face of an old man in the bazaar, prominent and ascetic, like an El Greco." They remained for over a
week, but the magic days had to come to an end. It was time to
leave Isfahan.

To mitigate the horrors of the return journey, George telegraphed his chauffeur to meet them in Qum with the Mercedes.
Until then, they were to travel in the Sultan's spacious, finely up-
holstered landau, a four-wheel closed carriage with front and rear
passenger seats and a detachable roof. All went well until about
halfway to Qum, when for some inexplicable reason the two driv-
ers suddenly rebelled, refused to go any farther and made off into
the desert. Quick as a flash, George pursued them and, with a
mixture of physical force, threats and bribery, forced them to get
back onto the seat. They reached Qum without further mishaps;
there the blessed Mercedes awaited, still functional though with
an ailing carburetor. In no time they were back in Teheran and,
after acquiring some spare parts, they continued on their return
journey to Resht and the frontier. On June 13, a month after
crossing into Persia, they were back in Batum on the Black Sea
and boarded the steamer *Circassia* for Constantinople, stopping on
the way in Trebizond.

The ancient Hellenic city of Trebizond, today's Trabzon, enclosed by Byzantine walls, filled a chapter in Marthe's *Les Huit
Paradis*, the travel memoir that would bring her first literary fame.

"All white, populated by cypress trees, it descends in picturesque terraces to the Black Sea," she wrote. "I found it a melancholic remnant of old glories." Marthe, guided by Emmanuel, visited the ruins of the Great Comnenus Palace, the church of St. Eugenius, the patron saint of Trebizond, and the church of Hagia Sofia, which Emmanuel declared "a poor relation of its Constantinople namesake." In the monastery of Sumelas, built in the early Middle Ages, they reflected on the fate of the little Princess Agnes, daughter of Louis VII and Elizabeth of Aquitaine, who had been brought all the way from France to be affianced to Alexis of Byzantium, "a solemn, eleven-year-old child, dressed in stiff, jeweled robes, riding in a richly decorated chariot at the head of the festive procession."

"Like a string of fine pearls, the historic sights came into view, as we slowly drifted along the coast of Asia Minor," wrote Marthe in *Les Huit Paradis*. "And always at the heart of each place were the gardens, magnificently laid out, overgrown and mysterious, facing the sea and the setting sun . . . they were a pure enchantment to my eye."

At sundown, their steamer docked on the Bosphorus. Marthe was overjoyed. Here at last was the country of her ancestors, the Phanariots, the Mavrocordatos, of whose exploits she learned at her grandfather's knee. She was anxious to see everything and reestablish family links. She remained in Constantinople for two weeks; her cousins, the Phérékydes, had already left for Romania from Teheran. Now it was George's turn. To her immense disappointment Emmanuel also decided to return; his relationship with Marthe was entering a difficult stage, which was undoubtedly the reason for his sudden departure.

What was happening? When the expedition to Persia was arranged by Marthe's father, he had hoped that it would be a second honeymoon for his daughter, more successful than the first. Sadly, it turned out to be the reverse. If anything, Marthe's relationship with her husband deteriorated during the trip and became almost acrimonious. As the journey through Persia progressed, the gulf between them widened. By the time they reached Constantinople, husband and wife were hardly on speaking terms. The trip showed what had already been obvious: the deep incompatibility between the two. George, strong and incredibly fit, often spending as much as twenty hours at the wheel at a stretch, reluctant to entrust his beloved Mercedes to the chauffeur over the atrocious Persian roads, had no time and little inclination to look after his physically more delicate wife. Her frequent bouts of exhaustion annoyed him. Nor did he understand her desire to wander alone in the gardens and the bazaars, gathering impressions for her "writing sketches," or just to sit, quietly dreaming. The tributes paid to her beauty by their hosts failed to placate him; he was also frustrated by her lack of response in the rare moments when he found time to show physical interest in her. During one angry scene in Isfahan, he accused her of being "cold as the marble in the Hall of the Forty Columns." For her part, when Marthe learned of George's visit to one of Isfahan's famous brothels, she erupted in fury, later masking her hurt with contempt. There was constant tension between them. George's cousin Madame Phérékyde, the only other woman on the trip, was not much help. Both she and her husband hated Persia and counted the days before they would return to Bucharest.

In these circumstances it was not surprising that Marthe turned to Emmanuel for solace and moral support. He was blissfully even-tempered, handsome, always immaculately groomed; even after hours of desert travel, he was solicitous of her comfort, invariably ready to protect her from George's sallies. His profound knowledge of history and dry wit made him a delightful companion. Physical proximity on the voyage unavoidably drew them together. During the nightmarish drive to Isfahan, on a road full of potholes, in intense heat, an exhausted Marthe found herself crying in Emmanuel's arms, while George drove on; he held her close, soothing and caressing her, as if she were a small child. Their intimacy grew as the voyage progressed, or such at least was Marthe's feeling. One day they found themselves alone in a room, while the rest of the party had gone in different directions; Marthe, propelled by "an irresistible instinct," as she later described it, threw herself into Emmanuel's arms, kissing him passionately with all the pent-up emotion of thwarted passion and despair she felt at the hopelessness of her situation. She confessed she was in love with him.

We have no way to establish what went through Emmanuel's mind. Very little is known of his personal life and whatever secrets he had he took with him to his grave (he committed suicide in August 1917). But we can guess that his reaction was probably one of embarrassment; his feelings for Marthe, as it became clear in their correspondence, were a compound of brotherly affection and compassion. Her youth, her beauty and her obvious unhappiness tugged at his heart, but his nature precluded the response she so desperately wanted. Marthe's letters to Emmanuel, written while she was alone in Constantinople, are heartrending—if a bit exalted. She passionately longs for the love and the understanding denied to her by her husband; conscious of her physical beauty, she wants to give herself to a man and be cherished. "My heart is full, my mind intensely alive, my body is supple and unused, longing for harmony with another . . . Such riches . . . You are thirty, at the apogee of your masculinity, I am nineteen, we suit each other. Why are you not here with me? I would like to be lying next to you on one of these lovely terraces, overlooking the sea. Your presence makes my perceptions more acute, just as the beauty around me intensifies my emotions . . ." Then, rather wistfully, she adds, "If only I could hear an echo of my feelings in yours."

But days passed without an answer from her cousin. "The post from Romania came this morning, but not even a card from you. My affection however is so great that I will forgive your silence."

Marthe wandered around Constantinople with a heavy heart, visiting its famous landmarks, but depressed by "the number of cemeteries in the city." On her pilgrimage to the family shrines in the Phanar, she found the Mavrocordato descendants disappointing, "unattractive physical specimens, weakened by too many interfamily marriages." The July heat in the city was oppressive, her room in the hotel in Pera stifling; worried by Emmanuel's silence, she decided to return to Romania. As the boat made its way in the Bosphorus and the coast of Asia receded, she composed a long poem in which her love for Emmanuel and nostalgic recollections of Persia intermingled.

When she returned to Bucharest at the end of July, there was a letter from Emmanuel, but it was not the kind of letter she had hoped for. Friendly but cool, he signed it *"avec mes souvenirs affectueux,"* hardly an answer to her passionate outpourings. Though chastened, Marthe did not seem to be discouraged. "No matter what the future brings me I shall always belong to you secretly, for you have altered the face of the world for me," she wrote him.

Back in Posada, she picked up her solitary life. Valentine, her mother-in-law, had not changed; she was as demanding as ever, living on gossip. Little Valentine, now three years old, was adorable with her dark, curly hair, hazel eyes and her mother's beautiful skin. Marthe spent an hour each morning playing with her, but it was "more duty than pleasure," as she ruefully confided to herself. Friendship with Elise Bratiano continued—a source of satisfaction to them both. Yet Marthe was too proud to confide her unrequited love for Emmanuel and the emotional turmoil it caused her. She hid it so well that Elise marveled at her young friend's discipline and sunny disposition. She even wondered sometimes whether Marthe was capable of deep feelings "apart from her undoubted ambition."

Every morning after the obligatory hour with her daughter and a glance at the household accounts, Marthe wrote. "But even my poems and sketches go badly these days," she complained in a letter to Antoine. "Perhaps I am deluding myself in thinking that I could become a good writer." To make matters worse, she learned that George had acquired a regular mistress—beautiful, but very common, whom he flaunted all over Bucharest. In spite of, or perhaps because of, her low spirits, she continued to pour out her heart to Emmanuel, undeterred by the progressively formal tone of his answers, mainly in the form of postcards; soon even these would cease.

On one of her visits to Bucharest that autumn Marthe ran into Claude Anet, their companion on the voyage to Persia. He was preparing a book on the expedition (*A Travers la Perse en Automobile*, Paris, 1908), and was on his way back to Paris now that his assignment as the *Le Temps* correspondent in Romania had run out. Claude Anet had read several of Marthe's descriptive vignettes of

Isfahan and admired some of her poems; he now urged her to develop them into a book for publication in France, offering to talk to Hachette and other publishing houses in Paris about it.

Praise from a professional writer was the very encouragement Marthe needed. She now had a definite goal before her; working on a book would bring her profound satisfaction. She gradually realized that in her relationship with Emmanuel, she had been following a mirage; he was not the man who would compensate her for George's infidelities and for what she then believed to be the complete failure of her marriage. But the world of letters, she believed, would fill that emotional void and it might bring her the success she craved and that her ambition demanded. She returned to Posada to work.

A long winter with much snow and extreme cold made traveling, other than by sleigh, difficult. For weeks on end Posada was cut off from the world, but it did not worry Marthe. Engrossed in writing, she was happy; it was like a balm on her sorrows. Now and then she managed to spend some time in Bucharest, consulting sources and paying visits to family and friends. She dined at the Cotroceni Palace with Ferdinand and Marie, the heir presumptive and his wife, and just before Christmas, was received by the Queen. Carmen Sylva, fey and erratic as ever, wanted to know "the details of their expedition to Persia."

In the middle of March 1907 political developments overshadowed Marthe's concentration on her work. For some time now the Romanian landowners had ignored indications of widespread peasant unrest in the provinces. Warnings of a revolution, like the abortive uprising of Russian peasants two years before, went unheeded, and the long-promised agrarian reforms failed to materialize. In a feudal country like Romania few seemed aware that there was injustice in the boyar landowners holding thousands of acres, some hardly cultivated, and ignoring the claims of those working and sweating on the land. The last traces of serfdom disappeared in the country only as recently as 1848 and only one agrarian reform was enacted (in 1866); the general setup was overwhelmingly feudal. With rare exceptions like the Stirbeys and George Bibesco, who were well liked, the landowners' attitude toward the peasants

was harsh and inconsiderate. There were those who were concerned with solving rural problems, but they were strongly opposed by others who followed the principle: "What was good for
my father will be good enough for me."

As a result, when an uprising began near the Russian border,
few people foresaw immediate danger. But in a matter of days
arson and looting swept the country. Landowners' houses, including those of Emmanuel and Antoine at Corcova, went up in flames.
Stored crops burned like torches; there was much looting; some
hated boyars were savagely murdered. Ten days after the outbreak
the government was compelled to resign and the Liberals under
Ion Bratiano, Elise's husband, came to power. King Carol issued
a proclamation pledging agrarian reform, but he also mobilized
120,000 soldiers, whom he sent to the countryside with orders to
shoot without mercy. The revolt was brutally crushed. The Liberals introduced legislation to hurry the transfer of land from the
boyars to the peasants, whose situation slowly improved.

During the "emergency," with Bucharest under siege and cordoned off, many boyars sent their wives and children to mountain
resorts away from the dangers of the capital. Crown Princess Marie
and her four children went up to the castle of Pelishor at Sinaia.
It was early in the season and the place was isolated and empty;
not surprisingly, she decided to accept Marthe's invitation to stay
with her in nearby Posada, as did her sister-in-law Nadège Stirbey.
The Crown Princess's stay was memorable, for it was in Posada
that her lifelong affair with Prince Stirbey began.

Prince Barbo Stirbey came from one of the great ruling families
of Romania. His grandfather, a prince of the Bibesco clan, reigned
over Wallachia long before the Hohenzollerns ascended the throne
of Romania. Two years older than Princess Marie, Stirbey was tall
and slim and carried himself with great authority. Reserved and
rather elusive, he had great charm and "a hypnotic quality" in his
dark brown eyes, which made him very attractive to women. Educated in Paris, like most aristocratic Romanians, he had studied
law at the Sorbonne, was a brilliant businessman and ran his farms
at great profit, becoming one of the richest and most powerful men
in the country. Prince Stirbey fell in love with Marie during their

sojourn together in Marthe's house. It took her a little time to respond, but she soon fully returned his passion; for both it became the commitment of a lifetime, and their partnership, which had the tacit approval of the monarch, brought immense benefit to Romania.

In the autumn of 1907 the manuscript of *Les Huit Paradis* (*The Eight Paradises*) was finished. A family friend, Alfred Mezières, a member of the Académie Française, suggested, as did Claude Anet, that it be sent to Hachette, the most prestigious publisher at the time. Agreeably surprised, Hachette's editor-in-chief liked the book and informed Marthe that he planned to publish it in February. He also expected her to come to Paris for the launching.

4

❧❧❧

In Proust's Paris

*I*n the spring of 1908 Paris was at the height of what has been
nostalgically remembered as the *Belle Epoque*. The fall of the
Napoleon III Empire, the calamity of the Franco-Prussian War of
1870 and the horrors of the Commune were forgotten; they were
followed by years of determined enjoyment in an atmosphere of
unshakable stability. Visitors who had expected a wake found, instead, an ongoing celebration that was interrupted only by the 1914
war. The city had been transformed by Baron Haussmann, who
destroyed entire neighborhoods to build long, straight thoroughfares like the rue de Rivoli and constructed Les Halles—"the
belly of Paris." Young Marcel Proust, born in 1871, recalled how
he saw the Eiffel Tower go up, "its four perforated iron legs rising
from the green meadow of the Champs de Mars." In 1900, the
Grand and the Petit Palais were opened to the public in time for
the 1900 Exhibition. In the same year, the first line of the Métro
was inaugurated with three wooden carriages proceeding at twenty
miles an hour. Each station had its own original wrought-iron en-

trance with orange lights of insectlike appearance, contributing to what since became known as the "firefly" style. By 1908, the Métro was expanded and transported thousands of passengers to all parts of the city. Automobiles, built by Peugeot, Renault, Panhard and Levassor and Mercedes, were increasing in number, and daring men were testing the possibilities of air travel.

And yet the capital of two and a half million people still resembled a collection of villages. The Champs-Elysées had only recently been paved, but the houses on the Avenue du Bois (today's Avenue Foch) still had private stables. Passy was a rustic suburb. In spite of the Métro and a small number of electric trams, horse-drawn omnibuses provided the bulk of the transport in suburbia. Street lighting by electric arc lights was a novelty used only on the main thoroughfares. Houses, even the houses of the very rich, were badly heated. (In early spring Proust's Madame Swann received her visitors with an ermine wrap over her shoulders and her hands in an ermine muff "like the last patches of the snows of winter, more persistent than the rest, which neither the heat of the fire nor the advancing season had succeeded in melting.")

Dr. Bell's invention, the telephone, had arrived and revolutionized social life.

It was a time of great elegance, corresponding to the Edwardian fashions in England. Women wore high-bosomed, tight-waisted, long, flowing, brightly colored dresses and hats with plumes and artificial fruit and flowers; men attired themselves in bowler hats and dark clothes or white linen and panama hats in the summer, and escorted their ladies to Fouquet's or Maxim's or the Tuesday Gala at the Comédie Française. (Social class was evident in the cut of the beard and shape of the mustache.) The cost of living was stable; it had not varied for the last thirty years—and class distinctions were rigid.

The arts were flourishing; theaters, galleries, music halls, street artists, cafés dotted the city. Franz Lehár's *Merry Widow* was the rage. Writers proliferated: Colette's delicately erotic Claudine books, Paul Bourget's psychological novels, the towering talent of Paul Claudel; in drama Edmond Rostand was the king; his *Cyrano de Bergerac*, first produced in 1897, and *L'Aiglon* with Sarah Bernhardt played to packed audiences. Music lovers flocked to hear Debussy and Saint-Saëns. In painting, Impressionism was giving way to Cézanne, Matisse, Picasso and Gauguin. The air was vibrant with the excitement and novelty of change.

Such was the Paris into which the twenty-two-year-old Marthe arrived in March 1908. She stepped off the Orient Express beautiful, talented, carrying her notebooks and her exotically set emeralds. Fame was waiting for her.

"I am writing to you while resting for a moment on my bed," she penned in a quick note to Antoine, who was in London at the time. "*Les Huit Paradis* has come out. I have a copy right here under my pillow. It seems to me so substantial, so professional, that I am laughing with joy and amusement. . . . But I also feel a certain pity for myself—for all the pain and effort and sacrifice for a year taken out of my youth to produce this fat volume bound in yellow. . . . But no matter, it still is the happiest day of my life. . . . I have tasted success, and pity those who have never experienced this feeling. . . . The book is on its way to you; you will receive it on Monday."

And indeed *Les Huit Paradis* brought Marthe immediate and dazzling success. French literary salons and those of the Faubourg St. Germain that had remained closed to Valentine, her mother-in-law, for the last thirty years opened wide their doors to this girl, so young, so ravishing and gifted. "Paris was stormed in one single season by Marthe Bibesco," wrote Robert de Montesquiou, the literary critic and aesthete, then at his height. Woman and author added up to perfection. Not only her looks, chic clothes and splendid jewels but also her wit, her impeccable French, her talent for skillful quotations and retinue of distinguished admirers who immediately surrounded her made her the marvel of Paris. Envy and criticism were yet to surface, but during that spring her progress was triumphant.

The reviews, headed by Montesquiou's long, enthusiastic article in the *Figaro*, were most complimentary. "An admirable freshness of expression and virtuosity of style," said the influential *Echo de Paris*; "excellent choice of poetic excerpts from the Koran," enthused the *Journal des Débats*; *Le Temps* praised "the power and imagery of expression and the impressionist style of her word pictures," while the *Revue Littéraire* spoke of the birth of a new talent in her masterly descriptions of "the quiescent beauty of decadent places." The *Hamburger Nachrichten* (the book was published in Berlin later that year) called Marthe "the princess of letters"; a Florentine paper in a lengthy profile called her "a delicious and learned writer." Foreign editions of the book soon followed, including one published by E. P. Dutton in the United States.

Emmanuel sent a copy of *Les Huit Paradis* to his friend Marcel Proust. Proust was then thirty-seven, a well-known observer of the Paris scene and about to embark on his life's work, the thirteen-volume masterpiece *A la Recherche du Temps Perdu*. Proust had already been introduced to Marthe at the salon of the Countess Greffulhe, Marthe's cousin, and had "stared at her admiringly" at the opera, which Marthe, being shortsighted, did not notice. He now sent her a letter full of extravagant praise. "You are not only a splendid writer, Princess, but a sculptor of words, a musician, a purveyor of scents, a poet." He praised her "admirably descriptive literary aquarelles," limpidly pure, which "profoundly affected [his] senses." After Marthe's departure for Romania, he sent Emmanuel a short poem, destined for Marthe. "Such clumsy stanzas," declared Emmanuel. "It just proves that a great writer should never attempt to compose verse." Marthe and Marcel Proust did not meet again until four years later at the ball of the *Intransigeant* newspaper, a meeting which gave rise to her 1928 book, *Au Bal avec Marcel Proust*.

In the *Belle Epoque*, the Faubourg St. Germain was the symbolic fortress of an inaccessible caste—less a location than a state of mind. It was not necessarily limited to the fine old houses of the Left Bank; a few of the town houses, like those of Count and Countess Greffulhe, were actually on the Right Bank. But it had everything to do with belonging to the *ancien régime* aristocracy, still royalist, still conscious of its privileges, certain of its superiority and contemptuous of outsiders, surviving thanks to an exclusiveness that made them seem custodians of a rare and desirable way of life and to the rigid enforcement of a complicated social code. Proust's Baron de Charlus declared, "I know nothing outside the Faubourg St. Germain." Like the Forbidden City of Beijing, with which it was sometimes compared, it was a closed, self-contained and self-sufficient society. In the first years of the new century, however, the boundaries of the Faubourg were becoming more flexible. Some "bourgeois" intellectuals were admitted: serious writers, historians and more rarely artists. (This hospitality, however, did not always extend to their wives, for it was widely believed that university professors usually married their cooks.) Proust, like his "Narrator" in *A la Recherche du Temps Perdu*, gained access because he was witty, kind and solicitous, and probably because he so passionately wanted to. After having been its distant admirer, the "Narrator," like Proust, becomes the chronicler of the Faubourg.

George Bibesco's family, as well as their cousins the Branco-vans, were part of the Faubourg St. Germain due to family connections, even though Valentine's scandalous behavior thirty years earlier had forfeited her right "to belong." It was for this reason that Marthe—always loyal to her mother-in-law—declined at first to pay a visit to Countess Greffulhe, the undisputed queen of the Faubourg and a close cousin.

Elizabeth Greffulhe, born Princess de Caraman-Chimay, was the eldest daughter of the Franco-Belgian Prince Joseph de Caraman-Chimay and his wife, Marie de Montesquiou, aunt of the famous aesthete and critic Robert, who became Proust's model for the Baron de Charlus. On her father's side she was a descendant of Madame Tallien. Short of money, Elizabeth's family was delighted when at the age of eighteen she married the enormously wealthy Count Henri Greffulhe of a Belgian banking family naturalized in France. Elizabeth's beauty and her husband's flamboyant style (he was called the "red-haired Jupiter") and his fortune assured them a leading position in society. Contemporary accounts talk of Elizabeth Greffulhe as the "supreme beauty of her time." In fact, her features were rather irregular, but she had splendid dark eyes "like agates," an abundance of chestnut hair and great charm. Everyone liked her. As she entered a drawing room guests could be heard murmuring, "Which way did she go? Did you see her?"

In 1908, when Marthe set off on her voyage to capture Paris, Elizabeth Greffulhe was forty-eight years old and had been reigning over the Faubourg St. Germain for more than twenty-five years. She was one of the few hostesses in whose salon Faubourg society mingled with the literary, political and diplomatic personalities of the time. Her invitations were eagerly sought. Intrigued by this dazzling young cousin who so resolutely held back from meeting her, Countess Greffulhe decided to make the first move. At a diplomatic reception that both she and Marthe attended, she dispatched Prince Gregory Ghika, Romanian Minister in Paris, to tell Marthe that she would be happy to meet her. "Does she know whose daughter-in-law I am?" replied Marthe. Amused by her resistance, Elizabeth Greffulhe sent word that of course she knew and would be happy to call on Valentine Bibesco, if she happened to be in Paris at the moment. "Faced with such charm and goodwill I happily capitulated," Marthe recalled.

From then on, the Greffulhe salon and its circle, which included not only Montesquiou, the Guiche, the Gramont, Chimay, "the beautiful people" who later appeared in Proust's *A la Recherche du Temps Perdu*, but also France's most prominent intellectuals, politicians and scientists, became the natural base for Marthe's frequent visits to Paris.

To the predominantly "*mondain*" personalities, apt to whisper to her during dinner, "I am sitting next to the Ninth Paradise," or express frank disbelief at a ball that someone as elegant and as accomplished a dancer as she could *also* write, she much preferred the company of people like Bertrand de Fénelon, friend of Antoine and Proust, on whom the author partly modeled his Saint-Loup; Elizabeth de Clermont-Tonnerre, nicknamed "the intellectual duchess"; Paul Demidoff, a well-known traveler and authority on North Africa; or Henry Bernstein, the successful playwright. She also spent much time with her cousin Philippe de Chimay, "a thoroughbred, graceful and delicate like a deer with the bluest of eyes, the characteristic blue of the Chimays." George teased her that she had fallen in love with Philippe, but probably the opposite was true. Philippe became her devoted escort in Paris. A conquest that amused George no end—for he had finally come to Paris to

witness his wife's "march of triumph"—was that of the Sultan of
Zanzibar, who, having caught sight of Marthe at a ball wearing a
rose satin gown and her emeralds, fell madly in love with her,
asked for her photograph and next day sent her a huge basket of
roses among which lay a magnificent ruby-and-diamond bracelet.
They debated whether to return the bracelet or to keep it; to
Marthe's joy, Emmanuel, the expert on social code, decided that
she could keep it.

After nearly two months of festivities Marthe decided that it
was time to return to Romania. In spite of her success, she began
to long for the peace and solitude of Posada. An idea for another
book was slowly taking shape in her mind. She promised to be
back in Paris in the autumn.

"I am back in my Carpathian retreat, my dear old Posada, which
is looking lovely just now," Marthe wrote to Antoine in early June.
"My book has been reviewed in most of the Bucharest papers,
quite favorably, am glad to say. Had a lyrical note from the Queen.
Am sending the royal couple a copy, but it will have to be specially
bound in fine leather; they would never open a book in an ordinary
cover. . . . The "Dame Blonde" [Princess Marie] likes my descriptions of flowers. . . . I see a lot of her; she is pregnant again, the
poor thing, and she is *furious*. . . .

"Barbo Stirbey says I have been too nice to the Persians, but
this is not supposed to be a political book after all . . . Elise Bratiano 'quite likes it'; she thinks I will do better in the future. Many
of the Bucharest people we know who have never read it address
compliments to my father, hoping to ingratiate themselves with
him. . . . Have just heard that Violette and Marie Murat and the
Lebaudy are coming to visit me next month. It will be nice having
French people to stay at Posada, but I wonder how the Faubourg
will take to our permissive Bucharest 'beau monde.'

"Simky [Simky Lahovary, a cousin, lady-in-waiting to the
Queen] is about to divorce for the third time and she is barely
twenty-eight. It is bound to be a very small wedding when she
remarries!

"How are you? How is London and how is your 'morale'? Please write."

The French guests who stepped off the Orient Express at the Comarnic station (an unscheduled stop, but the train halted there whenever Prince Bibesco requested) were met by George's Mercedes with its "B.1" license number. A wagon driven by a pair of black horses and a coachman wearing the Prince's livery followed close behind for the luggage. Not knowing what to expect in "Turkish Europe," they were agreeably surprised to find Marthe's house wonderfully comfortable with its English-style furniture, modern plumbing and delicious food.

Violette Murat, an elegant citified Parisian, fell in love with the countryside: "Oh, the gleaming fields of sunflowers spread under the awe-inspiring mountains, the willow trees along the fast-flowing torrents, the primeval landscapes and the perpetual sun that rises in the Ukraine and dies over the Carpathians," she wrote to her daughter back home. There was local sightseeing—monasteries, boyars' houses, picnicking in the mountains and daily visits with the royals at the neighboring castle of Peles. "We produced the King for them two days after they arrived and the Crown Prince and Crown Princess the next day," Marthe recalled.

George was at his most hospitable. He drove the party through the spectacular scenery of Transylvania to visit the lovely city of Brasov, founded by the Teutonic Order in the thirteenth century, then settled by Saxon immigrants; they visited the castle of Bran; and he showed them the castle of Vlad the Impaler of Dracula fame. Stopping to get a paper at the Brasov railway station, they were handed a recent copy of the *Figaro* with another enthusiastic review of *Les Huit Paradis*.

Marthe organized a fancy-dress ball in Bucharest, which turned out to be the event of the season. Soon the French visitors came to know most of the small, inbred Bucharest society. With their nimble and irreverent intellect, honed by years of artful survival under the Turks and the Phanariots, and their love and appreciation of women, the Romanian grandees were great fun. Most of them spoke three or four languages fluently and of course anyone coming from France was imbued with particular attraction. The guests stayed over a month and departed enchanted. On the long voyage home they amused themselves in making careful notes and remembering details of their stay in the "exotic Balkans" to entertain and intrigue the Parisian salons in the autumn.

Marthe went back to work after their departure. With the money from *Les Huit Paradis*, she built herself a "summer house"—a thatched Romanian cottage on the grounds, the perfect hideaway for her writing. In her rustic isolation, *Alexandre Asiatique*, the life story of Alexander the Great, was taking shape; Marthe's thoughts turned toward Macedonia, only a short distance away, where her hero's epic legend had begun. Work was supremely satisfying, but her heart still hankered after Emmanuel, who was spending some time in Bessarabia. Over her desk she pinned an excerpt from Pascal's *Pensées*: "A passion can only be cured by substituting another great passion in its place."

In the autumn Marthe returned to Paris with little Valentine, who had to be operated on for problems with her tonsils. George, temporarily between mistresses, decided to accompany them. His wife's success amused him. Devoid of jealousy and supremely self-confident, he took pleasure in mimicking Marthe's intellectual admirers, particularly the ones of an advanced age in whom, he said, "she stirred ashes of long-extinct fires." They had a tight social schedule drawn up by their summer guests, Violette Murat and Paul Lebaudy. To Marthe's joy, both Antoine and Emmanuel joined them at the Liverpool Hotel, on the rue Castiglione, and Ernest de Caraman-Chimay and the Duke de Guiche called the following day.

To pay respects to her "spiritual father," Chateaubriand, Marthe decided to make a pilgrimage to Brittany. At Josselin, Chateaubriand's former house, now belonging to the Duke de Rohan, Violette Murat's brother, the host presented her with the original of one of Chateaubriand's early letters—a rare honor. After a commemorative walk on the ramparts of St. Malo, where the great writer grew up, they stopped at Le Mans, capital of Brittany, to meet the American aviator, Wilbur Wright. George Bibesco, passionately interested in flying, was anxious to talk to him.

On November 9, 1908, Wilbur Wright in his fragile aircraft rose

several hundred meters over the military training ground of Au-
vours and remained in the air for over twenty-six minutes. Pushing
their way through cheering crowds, the Bibescos, accompanied by
the Duchess de Rohan, arrived to shake the aviator's hand.
George, for whom Wright was a hero, had already spent the previous evening talking to the American; he now presented him to
Marthe and their friends. The Duchess, keen collector of celebrities, rushed to clasp the aviator's hand. "Tell me, Mr. Wright,"
she exclaimed. "You obviously came to France because we are the
country where you can gain glory fastest—*la gloire* matters to us,
as you know." "I am sorry, madame," answered the shy, unassum-
ing Wilbur. "I came here because I was given a contract. No other
reason." "The Duchess was much disappointed," Marthe related
in her journal. "She had hoped for a historic pronouncement with
which to impress her salon guests. How refreshing, this nice American is so modest; he has not yet learned how to cope with
compliments."

Back in Paris the social whirlwind started again. Hostesses vied for
Marthe's presence; dinners, theater and opera parties succeeded
one after another; compliments abounded. "Your eyelashes, madame, are the length of harpoons—and I am hooked," whispered
Maurice de Gheest, Marthe's host at a scintillating dinner party
held in her honor at the Ritz. George complained that he could
hardly find his way to his wife's sitting room through the flowers.

Such success was bound to provoke jealousies. "It is not her
writing, it's her looks they all like," declared a disgruntled society
matron. The Dowager Countess Murat, Violette's cousin, who
prided herself on the quality of her intellectual salon, told Antoine,
"She is pretty and she was wearing a ravishing hat at my lunch—
no wonder men find her intelligent."

Not surprisingly, however, real venom emanated from two of
Marthe's compatriots: the poetess Anna de Noailles and Helen
Vacaresco, the former mistress of Crown Prince Ferdinand. Anna
de Noailles was the daughter of the Romanian Prince Gregory
Brancovan of the ancient house of the princes of Bessarab de Bran-

covan, connected with the Bibescos by multiple family ties. Her
mother, Rachel, daughter of a Turkish diplomat and an avid music
enthusiast, was a close friend of Proust's. Prince Brancovan, who
refused to live in Romania under the Hohenzollerns, emigrated to
France in the 1860s, taking his vast fortune with him. Their apartment on the Avenue Hoche in Paris became the rallying point for
writers and musicians. It was in Princess Rachel's ornate living
room that Ignace Paderewski gave his first piano recital.

Brought up entirely in Paris, "more French than the French,"
Anna was a talented poet and supreme egocentric. Small and dark,
she wore her short black hair down to her eyebrows in a fringe,
which, according to a contemporary description, "she alternately
parted and smoothed down with a tiny hand decked with an enormous sapphire." A few years older than Marthe, she had married
Count Mathieu de Noailles, a member of the distinguished French
family. By the time Marthe arrived on the scene, Anna was firmly
entrenched as a successful poet and popular Paris hostess. Proust
called her "frighteningly brilliant" and put her in *Jean Santeuil* as
the Vicomtesse Gaspard de Réveillon.

For Anna, Marthe's triumph was hard to swallow; for years, she
had lived in fear that one day a new talent would appear on the
scene and overshadow her own. She was devastated when Marthe's
poem "The Poppies," written at the time of her voyage to Persia,
came out in *Le Temps* and was praised by the critics. The success
of *Les Huit Paradis* plunged her into an emotional frenzy. That her
rival should turn out to be a compatriot and a cousin made the
situation even worse.

Carefully advised by Antoine, Marthe decided to avoid a potential conflagration. "Anna is like Vesuvius," she told friends.
"She is splendid, but it is better to look at her from a distance."
When they met, which was seldom, the two women exchanged
conventional pleasantries and mutual compliments. Anna's ani-
mosity was kept at bay for a time, but it changed into hatred after
the publication of Marthe's *Isvor* and persisted until the day of
her death. She never forgave Marthe that so many people in
France preferred the Bibesco prose to Anna de Noailles's poems.

Another compatriot, "insanely jealous of Marthe" (Antoine's

words), was the redoubtable Helen Vacaresco—small and ugly, but also a talented poet, whose acute social antennae and shrewd intelligence, combined with a very thick skin, gave her a certain position in Parisian intellectual, artistic and political circles. Helen Vacaresco was a spinster—an almost unknown species in Romania, where women were intent on marrying no matter what sacrifice it entailed. The one romance in her life—a liaison with Prince Ferdinand, heir to the throne of Romania, whose lack of self-confidence responded to her strong and brash personality—had been shattered by political considerations. Exiled by King Carol, she moved to Paris determined to succeed there as a hostess. Not surprisingly, she viewed Marthe as a threat. "Yes, I do know her," she conceded when asked about her dazzling compatriot. "She is not very bright, but she has talent. Of course, if she wants a position in France, she will have to ask my advice on how to go about it." As Marthe had no intention of talking to the old dragon, Helen Vacaresco's dislike soon turned into open hostility.

While attending soirees and lunches in her honor, Marthe also paid daily visits to the Bibliothèque Nationale to supplement her research on Alexander the Great, her "one great amour of the moment." Her obvious dedication to writing helped calm the fears of the various wives who worried she might have designs on their husbands. Their fears were groundless, for as far as Marthe was concerned, the most important event that autumn was her introduction to the Abbé Mugnier, a man who was to become a central figure in her life—her confessor and spiritual adviser.

The Abbé Arthur Mugnier was the vicar of the fashionable Catholic church of Ste. Clotilde in the 7th Arrondissement—the heart of the Faubourg St. Germain. Small, rotund, in his mid-fifties, with bespectacled smiling eyes and a tuft of unruly gray hair, he was known as the "Apostle of the Faubourg," much loved by parishioners of all classes. He lived in deliberate poverty, walked about in a threadbare soutane, but in the tradition of Catholic worldly priests he also enjoyed good food and fine wines. Immensely well read, he was much concerned with what he called "the state of grace of my literary friends." Edith Wharton, who met him in the winter of 1909, said that she had never known anyone "in whom the keenest intelligence so combined with inexhaustible kindness." Others referred to him as "the witty saint." Once when asked whether he believed in hell, the Abbé replied, "Yes, because it is a dogma of the church, but I don't believe there is anyone in it." For the next thirty-six years, until his death in 1944, the Abbé remained close to Marthe; they wrote to each other every few days and their letters testify to the depth of their friendship (see *La Vie d'une Amitié*).

5

❦

The
German Kronprinz

The year 1909 opened with a series of festivities in Bucharest. At the first court ball of the season, Marthe, dressed
in her latest Paris clothes, danced the cotillon with the heir to the
throne. She looked dazzling, and malicious tongues were quick to
draw comparisons between her and the Crown Princess, eleven
years her senior, who until now was the acknowledged beauty in
the land. "She has a rival," they whispered. The Crown Princess,
radiantly in love with Prince Stirbey, was far above such petty
matters and continued to favor Marthe with her friendship. Indeed, when her sixteen-year-old son, Prince Carol (the future
Carol II), needed a change of air after a virulent attack of influenza,
the Crown Princess asked Marthe whether she could send him to
Posada for a week to recuperate in the mountains. There was little
Marthe could do but agree.

Carol was not a lovable young man. Basically shy, he gave the
impression of being ill-humored and arrogant. In spite of a succession of teachers of various nationalities, his education was at

best sketchy; his manners were notoriously bad. Marthe met him at the door of his car as it pulled into the Posada courtyard and led him into the main drawing room, where her mother-in-law, the Dowager Princess, was waiting behind a table laid for tea. Valentine, as protocol demanded, plunged into a deep curtsy, but the young man absentmindedly extended a flaccid hand. The Princess was deeply shocked. "Monseigneur, it is customary in our country to kiss the hand of an old woman like me," she told him. Carol continued to sulk. "Poor boy," Marthe recorded in her diary, with what proved to be an accurate forecast, "I pity him; he seems to be deeply disturbed; physically he resembles his mother, who is so beautiful, but is more like a caricature of her. He lacks charm and has no discipline. What kind of monarch will he make?"

Much to everybody's relief, Carol's stay at Posada was shortened by a telephone call from the Palace. His return was requested because of the imminent arrival of his cousin Kronprinz Wilhelm, the heir to the German throne, who was paying a state visit to Romania for the purpose of presenting his kinsman Carol I with the baton of a field marshal of the Prussian Army. The visit was totally unexpected and many in Bucharest were puzzled by it. As Marthe's father astutely remarked, the field marshal's baton was probably just a pretext for the Prince and his entourage to survey the Ploesti oil fields. Contracts to exploit them had recently been awarded to the French. George's presence was also requested, for, as the Court Chamberlain explained, the Palace did not possess a suitably representative car and they wanted Bibesco to drive the Kronprinz around in his Mercedes. None too pleased, George remarked that he was not a chauffeur and only consented on condition that he would have young Prince Carol sitting next to him in the front seat, while his own chauffeur would be standing on the running board.

In the brilliantly lit drawing room in the old palace of the Stirbey princes, the evening of evenings was about to take place, for even for this French-loving nation a visit by the heir to the German Empire, who one day would rule over 70 million people, was a memorable occasion. On the stroke of 11 p.m. the great double doors were flung open and through them stepped Crown

Princess Marie, in gold lamé, with Kronprinz Wilhelm at her side. He wore an all-white uniform of the Prussian Guards with the blue order of Carol I blazoned across his chest. Tall and slim with an incredibly tiny waist, blond-silvery hair, a small head perched on an elongated body, thin narrow mouth and aquiline nose, the twenty-seven-year-old Kronprinz was more striking than handsome. Marthe said that he reminded her of a silver fox in the snow. But it was obvious at once that he had his way with the ladies; proceeding down the line at a slow pace, he bent over each Bucharest belle as she curtsied, looking deep into her eyes, while he carried her hand to his lips. The ladies swooned. When the Princess Bibesco was presented, the young Prince stopped, as if he wanted to engage her in conversation. He kept her hand in his a little longer than others, then moved on with obvious reluctance. During the concert which followed, Marthe found herself sitting in the second row, just behind the Kronprinz, who much to the annoyance of the courtiers kept turning to look at her. From the expression on his face it was obvious that he wished they could be alone. He stayed late at the reception and it was noticed that while talking to Prince Ferdinand and his wife, he observed Marthe from a distance. As usual, there was much whispering behind fans and Marthe became the target of countless monocles and lorgnettes, jealous looks from the women and admiring glances from the men.

The next day was devoted to a sightseeing tour of Sinaia, the King's summer residence, with a stop at the Ploesti oil fields. On the way back, George, Marthe and the Kronprinz, accompanied by Prince Ferdinand, piled into George's Mercedes and drove through a rainstorm to a tumultuous reception at the Comarnic railway station, near Posada, where the villagers danced a hora in honor of the visitor. "He was good with our people," Marthe recalled. "The haunting tunes of our songs really pleased him; he went around shaking hands, congratulating the musicians; he wanted to see their primitive instruments and particularly liked our native flute, made of the bark of a certain marsh willow; I promised to get him one next time I go to the Danube delta and send it on to Berlin."

They saw each other again at the ball Ferdinand and Marie gave at the Cotroceni Palace. On this occasion Marthe was commanded to dance the quadrille with Prince Ferdinand, his wife and the Kronprinz. Afterward, as George, bored with the festivities, retired to his car and fell asleep, the German Kronprinz deftly maneuvered Marthe to an out-of-the-way sitting room for "a long, private conversation." General Mavrocordato, Marthe's uncle, anxious to preserve his niece's reputation, stationed himself near the door. Sitting next to each other on a small sofa, chastely holding hands, they discussed politics and her writing. According to Marthe's diary, the Kronprinz asked for her photograph and a copy of *Les Huit Paradis*. If her account is to be believed, the Prince's sudden infatuation got the better of his discretion and he told her of his frequent disagreements with his father, the Kaiser, who "detested both France and England and was building up the strength of his fleet in preparation for a war." To Marthe's surprise and delight he invited her to come to Berlin soon. In the meantime they must write to each other.

The next day, he made a formal request of George: "You are the husband of the most beautiful woman in Romania and the most intelligent—recognized as such in Paris . . . I am an officer in the elite regiment of my army—and so are you. May I have your permission to correspond with your wife? I give you my word of honor to be discreet." He signed himself "Your friend Wilhelm." No record exists of George's answer, but he could hardly have refused this imperial request. Thus started a regular exchange of letters between Marthe Bibesco and the German Kronprinz, which continued until the outbreak of the 1914 war and occasionally thereafter. Malicious tongues, which in the postwar years accused Marthe of having corresponded with the enemy, would have been disappointed had they seen the contents of the Kronprinz's letters. Coming from the pen of the heir to the German Empire, a married man with two children, they appear touchingly naïve and inarticulate. The first letter, which was written in ungrammatical schoolboy English on heavily embossed paper with a gold crown and the letter *W* printed in black, arrived in Posada by courtesy of the German Ambassador to Romania a few days after the Prince's departure.

My dear little Princess,
I have the lovely photo of you and your book. You dont know how
much I like them. Wasnt it a charmink evening in the golden room
of Missy [the Crown Princess Marie] with the musik far off? You
looked so lovely, especially your big eyes, that I pined to give you
a kiss. What you say to this? Well, I was very unhappy when I
heard you could not come to Sinaia to see me off. You interest me
very much and we must be good friends, won't you think so too?
It was such a pitty that our conversation was interrupted that
night. I felt so much in love with you; you are the *person in*
Bukarest. Hearty greetings to G.B. and his Mercedes. You must
come to Berlin on your way to or from that Babel on the Seine
[Paris]. Please do so. Kissing your hand and looking into your
eyes,

                                   Your friend—Wilhelm

Crown Princess Marie, much amused by her cousin's infatuation, told Marthe that King Carol had a message from the Kaiser
extolling the success of his son's visit to Romania. "Relations have
never been better," she teased her friend, "and you are our secret
weapon." This was the kind of talk Marthe relished. She saw herself as a player in international diplomacy, a role to which she had
always aspired. She certainly would not have paid much attention
to her correspondent's boyish effusions and simplistic political talk
had he not been the heir to the German Empire. Given the circumstances, she was elated.

When the Bibescos arrived in Paris in early May 1909, another
letter was waiting, written from Sans Souci, the palace of the Great
Frederick.

Your photo stands on my writing table in a frame and I often
look at your eyes in effigie and think of our little corner in the
golden room. So you are now in Paris. Well it cannot be helped
. . . With my feelings toward France it is like this: I dont hate
French people at all, as some may think, but it is a great pitty the
way a great nation is going to the dogs as they are now [France
was in the throes of a ministerial crisis]. They need a strong man
like Napoleon I to bring order into the whole business. Perhaps

*the time is not far when the old world will have to fight together
against the Eastern Nations? . . . We have very changeable weather
here warm and rain. I had four hours artillery training this morning and came back drenched. I hope you are having a nice time
in Paris and are not forgetting about the promised visit to Berlin.
I wonder when I will get your next letter. I do hope soon.
Dont forget your friend, who kisses your hand*

Wilhelm

On May 6, *Les Huit Paradis* was crowned by the Académie
Française. Congratulations flowed and even George was im-
pressed. Emmanuel gave a lunch in Marthe's honor, Antoine sent
an ecstatic telegram from London. Proust, André Gide and Paul
Bourget all joined in a chorus of praise. Only Anna de Noailles
remained silent. To add to Marthe's state of euphoria, she and
George planned to travel to Berlin on June 14 as the guests of the
Kronprinz and his wife. "I pray for the weather to be fine," wrote
their host, "so that you may get a good impression of my home.
Potsdam is really a very nice place, especially our little marble
palace." He too congratulated her on the prize. "I am going to
reed it now; Cecilia [his wife] has read it and thinks it is absolutely
lovely. Kissing your dear hand, Wilhelm."

Marthe's visit to Berlin remained one of the high points in her
life. Even fifty years later, long after her world had collapsed
around her, the memory of that golden week would evoke a smile
of contentment on her face.

They left Paris on the afternoon of Sunday, June 13, traveling
in great style on the recently inaugurated Mitropa Express. Dinner
was served as the train pulled out of the Aix-la-Chapelle station.
"We have entered the Empire of Charlemagne," Marthe noted in
her diary. Her suite at the Bristol Hotel in Berlin was full of flowers. The Kronprinz was not expected until the next day, but he
arrived unexpectedly about 6 p.m., straight from military maneuvers. George had gone out for a walk and Marthe was alone to
receive him. "I almost died of emotion," she recalled. "My hands
were trembling. Both of us were almost embarrassed by the joy
we felt at our reunion."

The following morning, a day of radiant sunshine, the Kronprinz called for Marthe. He was driving an open-top, cabriolet-type Mercedes, white with black upholstery. A servant, in imperial livery, stood in the jump seat at the rear, armed with a silver trumpet; the three opening notes of Wagner's *Siegfried* warned passersby that the heir to the throne was approaching. As the car glided along Unter den Linden, cheering crowds gathered on the sidewalks. Wilhelm drove his guest at great speed toward the Brandenburg Gate. "At the sound of the trumpet," Marthe recalled, "the great gate, where Napoleon had once passed, opened for us. We drove under the arch—a privilege reserved for royalty and heads of state." It was an unforgettable moment for Marthe. She felt that she had entered history. After visiting the palace, where he grew up as a child, the Kronprinz ushered her into his father Emperor Wilhelm's private study. "I used to come in here as a boy, trembling," he confessed, carrying her hand to his lips.

That afternoon George and Marthe were received by the Kronprinzessin, Cecilia, at the Marble Palace in Potsdam. Taking advantage of the beautiful summer weather, they set off for a drive in the park of Sans Souci, the palace Frederick the Great built and loved. The Kronprinzessin, who was expecting her third child, drove ahead in a landau, accompanied by George and the Court Chamberlain. The Kronprinz, driving a four-in-hand with Marthe at his side, followed in a light equipage. On the way back, Wilhelm deliberately took a wrong turn in order to spend a few moments alone with Marthe. "He vowed eternal friendship—pure alas," noted Marthe. She recalled it as a "deliciously poetic moment, filled with the scent of lime trees." That evening they all dined at the Marble Palace at a party hosted by Kronprinzessin Cecilia, who seemed quietly unperturbed by her husband's obvious admiration of Marthe.

The next three days were spent visiting Sans Souci and its treasures, driving through the Potsdam countryside and watching military reviews, which George found intensely interesting because of the extraordinary precision of the drill. Whenever court protocol allowed it, the Kronprinz arranged to spend a few moments alone with Marthe.

"I found him standing alone on the steps of Frederick the Great's palace," Marthe recalled on June 17. "He was wearing a simple navy and white blazer, like an English undergraduate at Oxford. I had on my rose dress and a black hat. We looked at each other and laughed. 'Aren't we elegant,' he said." They went off for a walk and were caught in a rainstorm. Marthe's hat was totally ruined. Next morning six hatboxes were delivered to the hotel containing an assortment of hats "with compliments and excuses of the Kronprinz."

At the end of the week they visited Kiel to watch the Imperial Regattas; Marthe and George were to be presented to the Kaiser. On the day of the presentation on board his yacht the *Hohenzollern*, Wilhelm II happened to be in excellent humor; like his son, he was much struck by Marthe's beauty and intelligence. While showing them around his private quarters, filled with maps and family photographs, he pointed to a telephone in the main cabin, dominated by a huge writing desk. "I run my empire from here," he told Marthe. Then he added, "Right now my empire can wait —I have a more important duty to fulfill—I want to show you around." Though she knew it was a standard "ready-made" phrase, Marthe could not help but be immensely flattered by the Emperor's words.

The long train journey back to Paris passed in a haze of pleasant reminiscences. Marthe was alone, as George had decided to go to Stuttgart from Berlin to order a new Mercedes. She welcomed the solitude; it suited her mood, as she had many impressions to sort out.

Marthe, in spite of her youth, was too intellectually sophisticated to fall in love with someone as sentimentally immature as the Kronprinz. But the fact that this boyish and earnest young man, who so enthusiastically expressed his admiration for her, was the heir to the German Empire could not fail to make her feel exhilarated. She adored history, she longed to play a role on the international scene—and here she was, entertained by the Kaiser on his yacht, visiting Potsdam on the arm of his son, riding under the arch of the Brandenburg Gate, like Napoleon. The Kronprinz told her on their last evening in Kiel that she "reigned over his heart." "By reigning over him I reign over an Empire," she murmured as the Mitropa Express sped over the flat plain of the Rhineland.

In Paris she found another batch of telegrams from the lovesick Wilhelm. He begged her to meet him in Weimar in two weeks' time; he would be able to stop there for a day on his way back from the military maneuvers in Jena. George, who was to collect his new Mercedes in Stuttgart about that time, good-naturedly offered to drive his wife to Weimar and leave her there for a few days while he dealt with his own business. They left Paris on July 14, as the city was celebrating the annual Fête Nationale. Crossing the German border at Aix, Marthe admitted that she was "quite moved" by the sight of the German eagles. It brought back the happy memories of Berlin.

Kronprinz Wilhelm arrived at her hotel in Weimar in time for dinner. While his faithful adjutant Schenk remained discreetly in the background, the two sat on the hotel terrace, overlooking the enchanting town of Weimar, held hands and talked until late, undisturbed. "*Ich hatte einen Freund gefunden* [I've found a friend]," he told her. "In my life there have only been two people I could trust: Wedell, my aide-de-camp, and Moltzan, my colleague and companion from the military college at Plön. And now I have a third person: you. I hope you will remain my friend, for I need you."

Alone in the car the next day they drove around the lovely countryside of Thuringia; he talked to her of his problems with the new Chancellor (Bethmann-Hollweg), but said how much he liked de Schön, the newly appointed Minister for Foreign Affairs, "who lets me see all the dispatches." He told her he hoped to have more influence on the conduct of German foreign policy from now on. The conversation then veered to more intimate topics: "I love your hands—such a lovely shape, not too soft, not too hard. . . . I would like to kiss your feet . . . just because I like you so much . . . I have never done that to anyone before."

He left her at the door of her hotel in late evening and drove on to Jena to rejoin his regiment. Marthe spent the next day walking about the town of Weimar, visiting Goethe's house, the theater built in 1825 under his supervision; she was moved by the simple wooden cottage with the high pitched roof in which the great man passed his summers. She missed her Prince.

"Goodbye, Weimar," she wrote, when George arrived to drive her to Vienna and then home. "Goodbye, the romantic balcony where we sat, the pyramid-shaped oak tree, the greenery of Goethe's park and the rows of pink geraniums everywhere . . . I will never forget any of it."

In Vienna a few days later she found a charming letter from the Kronprinz and a note from Kronprinzessin Cecilia telling her how much she had enjoyed seeing her. As time passed, Wilhelm's letters became less emotional, though he continued to write to her regularly. They saw each other again the next year at the regattas in Kiel but by then the idyll had run its course.

Though there were no paparazzi in those days dogging their footsteps, the romantic meeting at Weimar and the Kronprinz's infatuation became known in circles of the European beau monde. In Bucharest, Princess Marie chided Marthe that "Cecilia is getting quite worried about you." There was widespread speculation and assumption that Marthe had become the Kronprinz's mistress. This was inaccurate. Marthe, the creative writer, might have liked to exaggerate certain facts or embellish a personal experience, but she always remained rigorously truthful in her journal, to which she alone had access. During the years of the Kronprinz's courtship her journal related pride, elation, excitement, but it also mentioned the lack of physical attraction on her part. "It was *une amitié amoureuse*," she told a journalist many years later, when asked to describe her relationship with the Kronprinz. And in her journal of February 6, 1966, she followed the interview with a remark: "People these days don't understand the term 'courtly love.' How can one explain? It is a romantic notion that has now passed into history. But this is what we experienced—the son of the Emperor and myself. Had it not been for the war he would have become Emperor, but fate decreed otherwise, unfortunately for him and perhaps for us too."

6

Marthe in Love

By July, Marthe was back in Posada. After so much excitement it was a relief to return to the old country routine. "I welcome the first signs of autumn," she wrote in her diary. "The first bunches of grapes on the table, the autumnal flowers in the garden—the dahlias, zinnias and my favorite orange marigolds with their bittersweet smell." Unusual for her, Marthe was now entertaining George's guests. Louis Blériot, who on July 29, 1909, made history as the first man to fly over the English Channel, was an old friend of her husband's. George had helped Blériot to finance some of his projects; in return, the aviator promised to start his European demonstration tour in Romania. Blériot's aircraft, which had been taken apart and shipped by train from Calais, arrived in Bucharest in October, and on October 30 Blériot flew over the Baneasa airfield to the crowd's enthusiastic cheers. George, who had been interested in flying since he was a young boy (at the age of eleven, using his mother's umbrella as a parachute, he threw himself from the second-floor balcony of his house, luckily with no dire results), was now in his element. Convinced that the age of the airplane had arrived, he attended meetings and air demonstrations throughout the country and in Austria. Marthe often accompanied him. As her husband left her free to correspond with the Kronprinz, she was glad to let him indulge in this new hobby; she admitted that it fascinated her too. "I can hardly believe it," she wrote, "each time I see a plane take off and disappear over the horizon."

In early December the Bibescos attended the first International Aeronautical Congress in Pau, during which George received his pilot's license—one of the first ever awarded to a civilian. Present at the meeting in Pau, escorting Marthe while George was busy talking to the aviators, was Prince Charles-Louis de Beauvau-Craon, the man who would fill her life to the brim over the next several years, bringing her delightful companionship, joy and sexual fulfillment—everything she had vainly looked for in her own marriage. He would also become the source of much anguish, as under the restraining influence of her spiritual adviser, the Abbé Mugnier, she struggled to find a way between her growing love for Beauvau, her reluctance to divorce George and the ever present demands of her overwhelming ambition.

Marthe was nearing her twenty-fourth birthday; intellectually she was far ahead of her years, but she had not really lived as a woman. She may have been the idol of Proust's Paris, but she did not interest her husband. "He finds me boring," she often confided to Antoine. She was the proverbial sleeping beauty waiting to be awakened by a man.

Charles-Louis de Beauvau-Craon, whom she met at a ball in Paris earlier that year, came from an old aristocratic French family which could trace its ancestry back to the sixteenth century. Thirty years old and unmarried, he was tall, blond and blue-eyed, with a slender figure, beautiful hands, a soft-spoken voice and a charming manner—a product of centuries of good breeding and healthy open-air living. His clothes, made by the best London tailors, gave him an air of casual elegance. Well educated and widely read, adept in three foreign languages, he would have made an ideal husband for Marthe—if only she had not already been married.

It was Emmanuel who introduced them, as they were going up the palatial staircase to the Princess Lucien Murat's ball. Marthe was looking particularly beautiful that night, flushed with her recent triumph; she had just been told that she would be awarded the Prix de l'Académie Française for *Les Huit Paradis*. Her effect on Beauvau was immediate. But Marthe's thoughts at the time were centered on the German Kronprinz, the excitement of the forthcoming visit to Berlin, the prospect of the regattas at Kiel, being received on the Kaiser's yacht, on "entering history," as she saw it. No admirer could compete with such a dazzling scenario. But Beauvau was waiting for her when she returned to an empty Paris in July—charming, cultivated, immensely rich, unencumbered by wife or mistresses and determined to pursue his courtship. Though her mind still harked back to her "German idyll," Marthe had to admit to herself that she enjoyed Charles-Louis's company.

She stayed with him at Haroué, his palatial property in the Lorraine near Nancy, where she befriended his sister Henriette d'Harcourt, and allowed him to accompany her on various errands in Paris; together they attended exhibitions and went for drives in the country. Beauvau loudly proclaimed his love. He was more enterprising in his advances than the Kronprinz, and slowly Marthe began to respond to his passion. He turned up at the aeronautical meeting in Pau, and after George's departure for Bucharest, he and Marthe traveled back to Paris together. Three months later, in the spring of 1910 he arrived at Posada, much to George's amusement. "At last you have found yourself a good-looking and relatively young admirer," he told Marthe. Busy with his own turbulent love life, George viewed his wife's involvement with detachment. He did not realize how serious this affair would become.

Charles-Louis was determined to marry Marthe. "Because of you I love life more than I could ever have imagined," he wrote to her in March 1910. "The same thought runs through my days, like a prayer in a rosary, and it is you and you always." He wanted her to divorce George and come to him.

It was not an easy situation. By the spring of 1910, Marthe had come to know Charles-Louis very well and was happy in his company. The prospect of marrying the most eligible man in France and becoming the mistress of two magnificent country homes, one of which "almost equaled Versailles," was tempting. George's infidelities had finally taken their toll. In spite of the superficially relaxed atmosphere between them, conjugal relations, never satisfactory, ceased abruptly when Marthe was told by her doctor that George had acquired a case of syphilis "almost as bad as a trooper's." (He was eventually cured by a course of mercury tablets.) Convinced that he had caught it from his longtime mistress Victoritza, Marthe sadly confided to her father that because of this "disreputable liaison" the Bibesco line would become extinct. No one could expect her to have children in such conditions. Though she still remained fond of George—"force of habit"—this was the one period in her life when she came close to leaving him. A visit to an eminent Paris gynecologist reassured her that she was in perfect health and could bear children, if she chose to marry again. Should she then go ahead and obtain a divorce from George, as Beauvau so passionately urged her to? His arguments were persuasive; his masculine attraction was growing. Gradually, Marthe's emotions veered his way, yet her cool analytical mind prevailed. After much agony, she refrained from a temptation which might have been catastrophic.

In these days of marriage, divorce and remarriage, it may be difficult to sympathize with Marthe's reluctance to follow her heart's command. But in pre-1914 France, divorce, unlike love affairs, was rare and carried a social stigma, which was passed on to one's children. This was particularly true in the aristocratic circles of the Faubourg St. Germain, where succession and hereditary titles were involved. The example of her mother-in-law Valentine had shown Marthe that divorce would not be tolerated in Beauvau-Craon's world. Married to Charles-Louis, no matter how happily, she would become a social outcast—and so would their children. What was the point of inhabiting a palatial residence if she held no place in the social hierarchy, if the people whose company she embraced rejected her invitations and shunned her? Paradoxically, being Charles-Louis's mistress would only enhance her glamour. It was a difficult decision, and neither of them found a satisfactory solution in the years to come. The only person who breathed a sigh of relief was Charles-Louis's mother, the Dowager Princess, who had watched—with understandable alarm—her only son's growing attachment to an "exotic" Romanian princess. The old lady even went to the extreme of calling on Marthe at her Paris apartment to upbraid her for "usurping" her son. "It was like the worst boulevard farce," Marthe recalled, "and it made Charles-Louis very angry."

"How do you break off a love affair with a man who is absolutely determined to keep you and to whom you are irresistibly attracted? Just as it takes two people to fall in love, it takes two to break off the relationship. What do I do? Tell me," Marthe begged in an agonized appeal to Antoine.

The charming, erudite cynic, well experienced in the affairs of the heart, wrote from London: "*Ma pauvre petite Marthe.* Why is it always the wrong people who suffer?" He advised her to go on a trip and leave it all behind for a while. "You talk about Algiers— solitude and the beauty of Arab burnooses will do you good." Marthe's idea of going to Algiers was a desperate measure to escape the pressures and complications of her affair. The prioress of the Carmelite convent in Algiers was Jeanne Bibesco, George's cousin, who would receive her for a long stay in her convent. There, among the orange groves, the peace and quiet of the white-walled priory, she would be able to restore her "inner self" and complete work on *Alexandre Asiatique*, the manuscript of which had been languishing on her desk.

In the meantime she continued to see Charles-Louis. "She remains his mistress in order to console him for not being his wife," remarked her mother-in-law, Valentine, who at the same time begged her not to divorce George, the son she had so outrageously spoiled. George, Charles-Louis and Marthe attended the annual regattas in Kiel, from where George again departed to inspect the new Mercedes models in Stuttgart. Charles-Louis stayed on in Kiel, torn between his desire to be with Marthe and his dislike of the Kronprinz and the Germans in general. He refused to be presented to the Kronprinz—"German annexation of Alsace-Lorraine makes it impossible for me to shake his hand"—thus enabling his German rival to spend a whole day alone with Marthe on the Kaiser's yacht. But the Kiel episode was only a passing cloud. Marthe stayed with him at Haroué and St. Assize, the Beauvau properties in the country; he accompanied her to Florence; and they spent some idyllic moments together in Venice before Marthe's departure for Posada. Knowledgeable and articulate, with a delightful sense of humor and a mental acuity which went hand in hand with an almost feminine sensitivity, Charles-Louis was the ideal companion for a woman of Marthe's intellect and worldly tastes. "Our minds are so alike—I love you and I hate myself for causing you pain, when we could be so blissful together," she wrote to him from Posada.

Throughout most of 1911 the pendulum swung back and forth: they were to run off together and live abroad; they were to give each other up forever; Charles-Louis was to get married to a girl of his mother's choice, beget an heir, but continue to remain Marthe's lover; Marthe was to enter a convent and retire from the world . . . the permutations were endless. The Abbé Mugnier, whom Marthe consulted almost daily, advised restraint. At one point, when Beauvau, overcome by frustration, threatened suicide, the wise priest wrote to Marthe, "Don't forget, dear Princess, that Monsieur de Beauvau is French—he will not kill himself." The Abbé also took time to discuss the problem with George. They got on unexpectedly well. In spite of his infidelities and selfishness, George became quite concerned about Marthe. He realized that she was passing through a deep crisis and was thoroughly miserable. "How can I help?" he inquired. The Abbé's correspondence does not reveal his advice, but notes George saying of his wife, "Her character is infernal, but I admit that she is adorable."

To calm the impetuous Beauvau ("If you don't want to have my death on your conscience, obtain George's permission to meet me for the last time") Marthe agreed to meet him in Lemberg, an attractive small town in what used to be southern Poland but was part of Austria at the time. Her sister, Jeanne Vacaresco, and her husband accompanied her. Much was said, emotions ran high, but they failed to arrive at a compromise. The two met again in Graz on September 15, 1911. This time they were alone and unchaperoned; the autumn weather was perfect, the woods and forests of Styria all golden: arm in arm, they strolled around the picturesque eighteenth-century town, climbed the steps to the citadel where lookouts were once posted to watch for approaching Turks and dined in small local restaurants, serenaded by gypsy bands. "My love for you is immense," Charles-Louis wrote to Marthe a few days after they parted. "It is luminous like the lovely countryside you and I have been discovering together. Do not let me sink into a night of despair."

Marthe returned from Graz deeply shaken. The ten days she spent alone with Charles-Louis were among the happiest in her life. Their minds and bodies were not only marvelously well attuned to each other, but she realized again that he was her intellectual equal—an attribute she had always craved in a man. Yet she could see no future for them, as no conventional solution was possible. Surely this was the moment for her to withdraw. She drove back to Romania through Hungary and the mountain landscape of Transylvania engrossed in thought. A period of calm and reflection was what she needed.

On her desk in Posada lay the unfinished manuscript of *Alexandre Asiatique*; her emotional turmoil had made writing virtually impossible and she felt guilty for betraying her craft.

On November 5, 1912, Marthe left Bucharest for Algiers followed by distressed appeals from Charles-Louis, who called her decision to spend time in a convent "an immolation." At the hotel in Marseilles where she stopped before sailing, she was surprised to receive a telegram from her husband, telling her that he had just bought the property of Mogosoëa from his Brancovan cousins and was presenting it to her as a gift. It was an inspired move on George's part. Mogosoëa, a former Byzantine-style palace a few miles from Bucharest, was built in 1702 by Prince Constantine Brancovan, the reigning Prince of Wallachia, as his summer residence. Twelve years after its construction, it was invaded by the Turks. Sultan Ahmed III demanded that the Prince and his family renounce their Christian faith; when they refused, they were killed and the palace destroyed. It remained a picturesque ruin for the next 180 years. Marthe had always loved Mogosoëa: its romantic setting on a lake, surrounded by woods and tranquil waters, the beauty of the old stones, the crumbling Byzantine palace and the terraces and Venetian arches. She longed to bring it back to life. Nothing could have been better calculated to rouse her from her depression and to strengthen her ties with Romania. It was exciting news, though at the moment she received it, Marthe was too emotionally depleted to appreciate its ramifications and rejoice.

Tired as she was, Marthe nevertheless presented an arresting picture on the boat during the sea crossing, as she reclined on a deck chair swathed in a blue veil, wearing a gray traveling cape with a leopard-skin rug over her knees. But disappointment awaited her in Algiers. Her cousin Jeanne Bibesco, the prioress, was leaving her Carmelite convent, throwing off her nun's habit, breaking her religious vows and returning to Paris to sample the delights of lay life. The reason—as Marthe learned to her astonishment—was bizarre. At the age of forty and after twenty-two years spent in a convent, her saintly cousin had fallen desperately in love with the sixty-five-year-old Emile Combes, the anticlerical left-wing French Prime Minister, under whose government the separation between church and state in France was taking place. The improbable romance between the "Diable"—"the Devil" as he was known to Catholics throughout France—and the "defrocked Carmelite" provided much merriment to the public in years to come.

When Marthe arrived in Algiers, the eccentric "Holy Mother of God" (Mère Bénie de Jésus), the name Jeanne Bibesco had taken when she made her vows as a nun, was intensely preoccupied with her own problems, planning to organize her "reentry into civilian life," sorting out her financial affairs, writing innumerable letters to Combes. She had no time or desire to take care of her cousin. Faced with a distinctly cool reception and depressed by the unseasonably bad weather ("all I saw of Algiers were rain-soaked orange groves and a few Roman ruins"), Marthe decided to return to Paris. "It had all been a dreadful mistake," she confessed to Antoine, as she happily settled back in her rue du Faubourg St. Honoré apartment.

Marthe's unexpected return delighted Beauvau-Craon. He took

it as proof that "nothing could detach them from each other." Passion again was rekindled. In time Marthe found that Charles-Louis was an excellent sounding board for her writing. "*Lui* arrives," reads an entry in her diary. "We read *Alexandre Asiatique* together aloud, correcting certain words and expressions. He said to me before leaving, "It is quite unbelievable this attraction that exists between us."

Each morning she awoke to a fresh bunch of flowers: "violets to keep next to your bed," roses, tulips, carnations, mimosa from the Côte d'Azur. In between Charles-Louis's visits. Marthe tried to spend occasional afternoons working, lunched with friends and saw Emmanuel and his constant companion, Jean Cocteau. She also took religious instruction from the Abbé Mugnier, as she was thinking more and more of becoming a Catholic. Antoine, who came over from London for a visit, did not approve of her change of religion. "I don't know how much spiritual discipline it will give you, but it certainly will make your life much more complicated, my dear cousin." While recounting London gossip and his own affairs of the heart (he had just fallen in love with the Duchess of Westminster), Antoine observed that he had never seen Marthe look more beautiful. "She has fulfilled the promise of her early youth," he told his brother. And indeed, if viewed from the outside, Marthe—loved by the German Kronprinz and by Prince de Beauvau-Craon, dressed by top Paris couturiers, painted by Boldini, admired by the French literary elite and about to be published by the prestigious Maison Hachette to more acclaim—seemed to epitomize success and glamour. But happiness eluded her. She was torn to pieces by the "Beauvau problem," for there seemed to be no conventional solution to their love. It was obvious that her duty was to leave him. Could she, however, bring herself to do so?

All this time the Dowager Princess de Beauvau-Craon was busy scheming. Determined to push her son into marriage, she cast her net far and wide and finally presented Charles-Louis with her choice. The young lady was neither beautiful nor rich, but she came from an impeccable background. She had hardly met Charles-Louis and must have known of his involvement with

Marthe, which was an open secret in Paris. But none of it seemed
to matter either to her, to her family or to the old lady; arranged
marriages were the norm in those days. "Being a princess will
compensate her for my son's lack of enthusiasm," the Dowager
told her friends, many of whom were skeptical about this particular
matrimonial venture.

After talking it over with Marthe, Charles-Louis finally decided
to please his aging mother and go ahead with the sham engagement. It was duly announced in the papers and soon after he reluctantly agreed to accompany his fiancée and her mother on a trip
around Corsica. It turned out to be a disaster.

Bored to tears, missing Marthe, to whom he wrote "delicious"
letters every day, irritated by the "immature and overenthusiastic
girl" and her "unbelievably pushy mother," Charles-Louis left
them abruptly in Ajaccio and fled back to Paris, determined to
break off the engagement. In his absence Marthe finally managed
to complete *Alexandre Asiatique*, a gemlike little volume, written in
luminous prose. It is more a series of vignettes, illustrating the
various episodes of Alexander's life, than a proper biography, but
the style is so poetic, the writer's admiration for her subject so
genuine, her use of the French language so exquisite, that it stands
as a monument to fine writing. Not surprisingly, it met with immediate success. The reviewers launched into paeans of praise.
Proust, who professed disliking the person of Alexander the Great,
praised the style of the book: "the beautifully balanced sentences,
the evocative atmosphere." He promised to "try to revise" his
opinion of the great conqueror to please the author and ended his
letter extolling "the supreme talent of the gifted and beautiful
Princess."

The success of her book did much to compensate Marthe for
her worries. "I wanted it to be a success," she noted in her diary,
"so that Charles-Louis would be proud of me." It also helped to
ease the pain of their imminent separation. For Charles-Louis,
having caused a scandal in Paris and a rift with his mother by
breaking off his engagement, decided to go to Canada and stay
away from France for at least six months. Perhaps it was just as
well that he was leaving, for their relationship would have been

further complicated by Marthe's recent conversion to Catholicism. On April 18, 1912, in a simple ceremony, with only the Abbé present, Marthe left behind the Orthodox religion of her ancestors and was received into the Catholic Church. Being a Catholic imposed obligations. The Abbé, in spite of all his worldly forbearance, made it clear that she had been living in mortal sin. Unable to give up Charles-Louis while they were both in Paris, Marthe now almost welcomed his departure. Worn out by the maelstrom of emotions, she returned home to supervise the rebuilding of Mogosoëa.

Emmanuel was waiting for her as the Orient Express pulled into the Bucharest Central Station. He carried a large bunch of irises and an envelope with letters from Charles-Louis written before his embarkation for the New World. After calling on the Lahovary parents at Balotesti, they drove on to Mogosoëa. It was to be Marthe's first night on the place—spent camping! George arranged for a small pavilion in the grounds to be made habitable, while the restoration was completed. The place's sheer beauty, slowly emerging from ruins, filled her with joy.

During most of the summer Marthe traveled between Mogosoëa and Posada, supervising work in progress and entertaining visitors. Crown Princess Marie and Prince Stirbey came to call; Elise and her husband, Ion Bratiano, now Prime Minister, also stopped by; the future King Ferdinand paid a special visit to Mogosoëa, intrigued by the process of bringing this historic residence back to life. Valentine, Marthe's little daughter, now nine, was happy to be home in Posada. Thanks to the steadying influence of her governess, Miss Chatfield, her mother's peripatetic existence did not seem to unduly upset the child. She adored visiting Mogosoëa. "Mummy, I so admire you," she whispered to Marthe as they were rowing on the lake one morning and Marthe was describing to her the projected color scheme for the gardens. Always in awe of her mother and overshadowed by her in her youth, Valentine was nevertheless beginning to develop a personality of her own; a lonely child, fond of reading, she adored animals and flowers. Though Marthe, preoccupied with her own life, often failed to devote a sufficient amount of time to her daughter, she nevertheless went out of her way to ensure that the child was well educated and looked after and protected her from gossip about her father's adventures. Even in the Paris apartment, Valentine and Miss Chatfield had their own independent quarters; everyone's privacy was respected.

The publication of *Alexandre Asiatique* continued to evoke praise from many quarters. At a meeting of the Council of Ministers in Bucharest, King Carol complimented Jean Lahovary on his daughter's achievement and announced that he was presenting Marthe with the much coveted Medal of Merit. Letters arrived from everywhere, including an enthusiastic message from the Kronprinz. "Congratulations—I am proud of you, my little friend." But the letters she most eagerly awaited were those from Charles-Louis, sent through the intermediary of her French secretary in Paris, Mademoiselle Meyer. In a series of daily letters to Marthe, Charles-Louis described his lonely progress across Canada. He was overwhelmed by New York, delighted with Boston, thought Montreal "deadly provincial," found delightful company in Quebec and was looking forward to crossing the continent to Vancouver.

Conscious of the many compliments that had been raining on his daughter, Jean Lahovary thought it wise to try to "redress the balance in the marriage." Taking advantage of his close friendship with the King, he asked that George Bibesco be awarded the Romanian Legion of Honor "for services to aviation." To celebrate the occasion, Marthe held a festive dinner at Mogosoëa in her husband's honor, with most of the cabinet and a number of ambassadors present. The occasion, however, was marred by George's sudden departure after dinner for Bucharest, where he said he had "a late-night appointment." "I shall always be lonely while married to him—and humiliated," Marthe wrote in her diary the next day.

More rewarding than either her husband or her absent lover was Mogosoëa, the reconstruction of which absorbed most of her energy. Under the brilliant direction of the Venetian architect Domenico Rupolo and the famous decorator Fortuny, the main building—the Spring Palace—was nearing completion, its balconies and terraces overlooking the waters of the lake. A field of newly planted blue irises stretched all the way to the water's edge. The Crown Princess Marie, who was enchanted with Mogosoëa, often came to see Marthe. She loved to paddle a canoe through the reeds on the lake, watching the colors of the sunset and listening to one of Marthe's "magical short stories," which she could conjure up at a moment's notice and recite in her distinctive low-pitched voice, "the voice of Scheherazade," as Emmanuel called it. During one of her visits that autumn, "a day of brilliant sunshine and flaming trees," the future Queen, pregnant with a child by Prince Stirbey, took Marthe into her confidence, discussing the difficulties of court life, and talked of the "great love between her and the Prince."

That autumn the political situation in Romania was darkening. A shifting of power was taking place among the Balkan nations, reflecting the struggle for Eastern Europe by the Russians, Austrians and Turks, which Germany and England closely observed. But trouble really began when Serbia declared its independence from the Austro-Hungarian Empire in 1903. To teach the Serbs a lesson, the Austrian Emperor ordered the immediate annexation of Bosnia and Herzegovina, a move which deeply disturbed the Romanians, for the Serbs were that country's natural allies against their traditional foe, the Bulgarians. When King Carol expressed his disapproval to the Austrian Emperor, the Archduke Franz Ferdinand, the ill-fated heir to the Hapsburg throne, was dispatched on an official visit to Sinaia "to soothe Romanian feelings." A liberal, concerned with the welfare of the people in his empire, and above all sympathetic to the lot of Romanians living in Transylvania who suffered under the Hungarian yoke, Franz Ferdinand was warmly received in Sinaia by Carol I and his family. The visit was a success, but of course did nothing to prevent future conflicts.

In the autumn of 1912, Bulgaria, Serbia and Greece, emboldened by the growing belief that Turkey, "the sick man of Europe," was heading toward terminal decline, declared war on the Sultan, hoping to divide Turkish holdings. Known as the First

Balkan War, it was a defeat for the Turks and resulted in substantial territorial gains for Bulgaria. The Romanians, who had not taken part in the war but who watched closely from the sidelines, were incensed and demanded that Bulgaria cede a slice of Dobrudja, a province on the Black Sea formerly annexed from Romania by the Turks. "The Bulgarians have gone out of their minds and want to be the dominating power in the Balkans," Crown Princess Marie wrote to her American friend Pauline Astor in January 1913.

As the Balkan cauldron continued to boil and war fever raged in Romania, Bulgaria suddenly changed sides and launched a surprise attack on her former allies the Serbs and the Greeks, who retaliated by joining with their old enemies the Turks. King Carol and his government, unable to resist popular pressure for war, issued a call for mobilization and swiftly declared war on Bulgaria. The Second Balkan War was short and inglorious and resulted in a total defeat for Bulgaria. The much larger and well-equipped Romanian Army marched through the fertile countryside of Bulgaria, meeting hardly any opposition.

It was all over in a month. Romania's victory, however, had its price. A cholera epidemic broke out in the wake of the retreating forces; according to existing accounts, it spread because the Bulgarians themselves threw corpses of cholera victims in the wells in order to poison the water that would be used by the advancing Romanians. Though there were comparatively few wounded, the cholera casualties were huge. Camps had to be set up on both sides of the Danube to care for the sick soldiers. The Crown Princess Marie, assisted by Elise Bratiano and a number of ladies of her court, organized hospitals and quarantine camps, equipped ambulances and, oblivious to the threat of contagion, tirelessly nursed the sick soldiers. In her memoirs the Crown Princess described how "this sudden contact with cholera" became the turning point in her life, as it brought her in direct touch with her people. "It enabled me to sacrifice myself for their sake."

Prominent among the ladies on the Crown Princess's team was Marthe Bibesco. She joined the Corabia (the Romanian Red Cross), bought and equipped an ambulance at her own expense and took up work in one of the field hospitals. George was already at the front. He was one of the first to enlist and departed in command of a squadron of airplanes. Valentine and her governess, Miss Chatfield, were sent to safety in France to stay with Marthe's friend Berthe de Ganay at Courrances. As the frontiers were closed, the Austrian Ambassador, Prince Fürstenberg, volunteered to drive the child and her governess to the frontier at Predeal, where they could board the Orient Express for Paris.

As the brief war was concluded, King Ferdinand of Bulgaria (Foxy Ferdie) came to Bucharest to sue for peace; a conference of the five Balkan nations—Romania, Bulgaria, Serbia, Greece and Montenegro—was convened to arrange the terms of the peace settlement and the division of Turkish spoils. Bulgaria was forced to cede southern Dobrudja to Romania, Albania was granted independence from Turkey, while the Serbs and the Greeks were awarded chunks of territory formerly controlled by the Turks. But more than anything else, the Treaty of Bucharest spelled the end of the rule of the Ottoman Empire in Europe. The treaty did much to enhance Romania's international prestige as well as that of King Carol. It impressed even his arrogant nephew Kaiser Wilhelm, who sent a warm telegram of congratulations.

It was hot and stifling in Bucharest that August when the peace conference was taking place, so the delegates were delighted to accept Marthe's invitation to transfer their deliberations to the cool gardens of Mogosoëa. Eleutherios Venizelos, the Greek Prime Minister, who nursed visions of a "Greek-Latin Oriental Empire" at the time, with Romania and Greece at its center, was enchanted by the peaceful setting of Marthe's palace. "We have come here to make peace," he declared, "but we have found it already in this beautiful garden."

On August 10, the day when the Treaty of Bucharest was formally signed, King Carol and Queen Elizabeth, who also were suffering from the heat, sent a message to Marthe expressing their desire to spend the afternoon at Mogosoëa. "It was too hot to take tea on the terrace," Marthe recalled, "so I received them in a vast underground room, admirably cool, furnished with wicker chairs and simple matting. They arrived about four in the afternoon in their old-fashioned convertible, covered with dust. The King, for whom this had been one of the happiest days of his reign, wore his usual old infantry general's uniform; he held himself erect in spite of his advanced age. The Queen, dressed all in white, was swathed in motoring veils, as in a cloud. With her snow-white hair, equally white aging face and gold spectacles perched on her prominent nose, she looked like one of the benevolent German fairies, straight from Grimm's tales. The old couple stayed all afternoon and most of the evening. After the heat had subsided, I walked in the gardens with the King; he was in a very relaxed mood, smiled frequently, which for him was quite rare. . . . None of us realized at the time that this was the old King's last visit."

Now that the peace treaty had been signed, Marthe planned to travel to France to fetch little Valentine and Miss Chatfield. A telephone call from Emmanuel changed her plans. "The Enthusiast" (Emmanuel's nickname for Charles-Louis) had arrived in Bucharest and Emmanuel was bringing him to Mogosoëa in the morning. Marthe and Beauvau had been out of touch for a while, as postal communications were disrupted by the war. After a lonely weekend at Haroué, his country property, Charles-Louis, who sometimes liked to do things impulsively, boarded the Orient Express at Nancy and turned up two days later at Emmanuel's house in Bucharest, certain he would know Marthe's whereabouts.

Charles-Louis's absence in the New World did not alter their relationship. Their reunion that December was as passionate as their last farewell. Marthe's diary for the first part of 1913 records the pattern of previous days spent together: visits to Charles-Louis's properties, friendship with his sister Henriette and agonizing arguments about their future—with Charles-Louis, as always, determined to marry and Marthe reluctant to face the long, unpleasant process of divorce. It was not that she hesitated to leave George; his dissolute life had become the scandal of Bucharest before the war. Even his mother, who took his side in most matters, sadly advised her "to forget George and get on with your life." The overwhelming consideration for Marthe, even stronger than her newly acquired Catholicism, was the prospect of social annihilation in France. Time and time again she returned to the dismal conclusion that she could never marry Charles-Louis. But suddenly here he was at Mogosoëa, on her own ground. Charles-Louis had visited Posada but he had never been to Mogosoëa and was unprepared for its exotic beauty.

Marthe's Byzantine palace, at the edge of the water, with its graceful terraces, fields of flowers, the statues, the Venetian interiors designed by the master hand of Fortuny stunned Beauvau. Though himself brought up among beautiful things, he was unfamiliar with the Oriental style of the house and its decoration. Here was a new facet of the woman he loved, a side of her he did not fully appreciate in their Paris surroundings. "I understand now why you hesitate," he told her. "How could I blame you?"

Charles-Louis's stay at Mogosoëa was brief. With George still away with his air squadron, Marthe did not want to risk unnecessary gossip. They left together for France, stopping at Ragusa (today's Dubrovnik) for a few blissful days of sightseeing, then continued on to Trieste, where they parted. Marthe went on to Paris and Courrances, the Ganay château near Paris, to collect little Valentine and her governess. After a short visit to England, probably with Charles-Louis, she found at Courrances an urgent telegram from George, summoning her back to Romania. Her mother-in-law, Valentine, had suffered a serious stroke and was asking for her. The next day Marthe boarded the Orient Express, narrowly escaping a serious accident near the Austrian frontier. Because of intense fog, which covered most of Central Europe on that day, several carriages went off the rails; the train driver was killed and a number of passengers were rushed to the hospital with injuries. Marthe was badly shaken but unhurt. Responding to an alarmed telegram from Beauvau, which was handed to her at the Vienna station, she lightheartedly replied, "*Je vis encore. Tout est bien.*" Arriving at Bucharest after an eight-hour delay, she found her mother-in-law partially paralyzed, attended by Catholic nuns. Sensing that death was approaching, Valentine had decided to return to the Catholic Church.

For the rest of the year, Marthe spent most of her time nursing her mother-in-law, supervising work at Mogosoëa and dealing with business affairs in Posada. The cement factory at Comarnic was booming, producing large revenues for the family, most of which went to sustain George's lavish lifestyle. But the business suffered a serious setback when in early December their faithful manager Aronovici was murdered by a disgruntled accountant whom he had fired a few days before. Between old Valentine's sickroom and the bereaved man's family in Posada, whom she did her best to help, Marthe had her full share of pressing worries, and it was with a sigh of relief that she welcomed the end of 1913. "A war, a cholera epidemic, a train accident, illness, murder . . . it has been a violent year," she wrote to the Abbé Mugnier in December 1913. She prayed that 1914 would be different, but her instinct warned her that the violence she deplored was only a mild prelude to the catastrophe that was coming.

❧❧❧

7

The End
of Old Europe

*E*arly in 1914, Marthe found herself a key player in an important diplomatic venture. Taking advantage of a temporary
improvement in her mother-in-law's health, she spent a few days
in Paris and at her friend Berthe de Ganay's house at Courrançes.
It was a few months before, during her last stay at the Ganay
château, that her old friend Alexander Izvolsky, the Russian Ambassador to France, searched her out for what he called "a confidential talk." Izvolsky was a friend of the Lahovary family; he had
served in Bucharest as a young man and had known Marthe since
she was a small child. While walking in the Ganay formal gardens
he explained to her how important it was at this time for Romania
and Russia to draw closer. He did not believe that the peace
following the Second Balkan War would last; Austria would end
up by attacking the Serbs and supporting Bulgaria, Romania's traditional foe. "To cement the relationship between our two countries," he told Marthe, "it is necessary to arrange a marriage
between one of the Tsar's daughters and Prince Carol. Will you
please talk to your father about it?"

Since her childhood Marthe had been familiar with discussions about treaties, alliances, the concept of the balance of power, the movement of diplomatic pawns on the European chessboard. Her father and her two uncles had at one time or another served as Foreign Ministers; all three had been in the government all their lives. At an age when little girls were concerned with their dolls, Marthe worried about the fate of the province of Bessarabia and listened with interest to her father's plans for political reform. She immediately understood the importance of the Ambassador's idea and continued to discuss it with him during subsequent meetings in Paris, usually at some social function. Friends teased her that instead of dancing, she spent her time "talking to the old Ambassador." Izvolsky was well aware that the Tsar and his family could not be persuaded to visit Bucharest. He believed that the best plan, in these circumstances, would be for the two families to meet casually on their yachts at the time of the Tsar's annual visit to the Crimea in the spring. The Romanian port of Constantsa on the Black Sea was only a short sail away from the imperial family's residence at Yalta. Thus an informal visit could take place and a meeting arranged between Prince Carol and the Tsar's daughters. With luck, it would lead to a marriage.

Marthe duly reported the conversation to her father, and in the ensuing weeks the Izvolsky plan began to take shape. It was helped by Crown Princess Marie's enthusiasm for the project. As granddaughter of Tsar Alexander II, she had for years nursed the hope of a family alliance with the Romanovs.

What had started as a suggestion from Ambassador Izvolsky, taken up by Marthe with her father, now turned into a definite state project. In spite of the Tsarina's well-known remoteness, Crown Princess Marie found a way to discuss the idea of a possible marriage between Carol and one of the Grand Duchesses. They agreed that as parents they would make no promises in the name of their children, but would "create an occasion" during which they could meet. But it would have to be a love marriage—not a union arranged for dynastic considerations. The imperial couple appeared to the outside world as a model of conjugal felicity; they desired the same happiness for their daughters. As the projected meeting at Constantsa was to last only fourteen hours, what in fact was required and hoped for was an instantaneous *coup de foudre* between two adolescents.

On June 14, 1914, Marthe was on board King Carol's yacht *Carolus Primus* anchored off the port of Constantsa, awaiting the arrival of the Russian visitors. A special pavilion had been constructed in the port in which the Romanian royals were to entertain the Tsar and his family. There was to be a church service, a state banquet and a military review. Like the rest of the Romanian entourage, Marthe wondered whether there would be sufficient time for the romance to blossom. In her book *Images d'Epinal*, Marthe described the events of that day. "I was at my observation post on the captain's bridge when the firing of guns signaled the approach of the imperial yachts. At this moment a squadron of three airplanes, commanded by my husband, took off into the sky to meet them. Somehow I had been expecting the boats to be white and I was not prepared for the sight of the two huge ships—all black and gold, like some gigantic toys made of Chinese lacquer, slowly making their way into the Constantsa harbor, gold eagles glistening at the mastheads. The *Standart* with the imperial family on board came first; the equally magnificent *Polar Star*, carrying the Tsar's entourage, followed closely. They solemnly made their way to the quay; all other ships in the harbor appeared puny by comparison, like a flock of ducklings in a pond into which two great swans had just set sail. The crowds, stupefied by this splendor, burst into spontaneous acclaim. A small man, dressed all in white, stood in the prow of the *Standart*: Nicholas II, the 'Emperor of all the Russias.' Next to him was the Empress, tall and slim like a poplar, towering over her husband, looking remote; she was holding the nine-year-old Tsarevitch by the hand. Behind them loomed four white dresses and four summery hats: Olga, Tatiana, Marie and Anastasia. . . . Which of the four would turn out to be Carol's fiancée?"

As the imperial guests disembarked and proceeded to the cathedral between serried ranks of Guards for the traditional "Te Deum," everyone tried to catch a glimpse of the Grand Duchesses. Which was the prettiest of the four? Which one is going to be our Queen? But soon the public became disappointed and their initial enthusiasm subsided. Under the light summery hats the girls' faces appeared deeply tanned, almost the color of mahogany, "like some gypsies." They thought them common-looking and plain ugly, unlike their little brother, the Tsarevitch, who was blond and cream-faced.

The day passed in a round of festivities. Politically, the visit appeared to have been a success. George Bibesco was warmly congratulated by King Carol, for his air squadron turned out to be a sensation, much enjoyed by the children of the Emperor, who had never seen airplanes at close range. "The June night was soon upon us," Marthe recalled. "As the clock on the town hall tower struck ten the *Standart* and the *Polar Star* cast off their moorings and, to the accompaniment of the two national anthems, slowly veered away from the quay. The Tsar and his family's last voyage outside Russia had ended."

And what about the projected love match? It was reported that during the banquet given by King Carol at the Constantsa town hall, young Prince Carol, who sat between Olga and Tatiana, appeared sulky, while the two girls remained silent most of the time. Only later did it transpire that the four Grand Duchesses, reluctant to leave the home and the family they adored, decided to make themselves as unattractive as possible for young Carol. By mutual consent they remained outside on the deck all the way from Yalta to Constantsa. The Black Sea sun in mid-June gave them instant sunburns—a look that upper-class ladies avoided. They certainly looked unattractive as they stepped off the boat at Constantsa, but they were happy and carefree when they departed that night, delighted to have avoided what seemed to each of the girls a dull future. They could not know what awaited them four years later.

"Izvolsky's plan had collapsed," Marthe concluded her account of the visit. "There would be no Russian bride for King Carol, but I shall always remember the approach of those two gigantic ships, symbols of an empire that was to sink into one of the greatest cataclysms of modern times."

⁕

On June 28, 1914, less than two weeks after the Tsar's visit, the assassination of the heir to the Austro-Hungarian Empire and his wife at Sarajevo shocked governments throughout Europe. In Bucharest the members of the royal family were at the races; they immediately returned to the palace. King Carol, in a somber mood, told the assembled diplomats that the murder would lead to a world war.

Marthe heard the news while keeping vigil at the bedside of her mother-in-law. Valentine Bibesco, herself a relic of the nineteenth century—Belgian by birth, then French, German and Romanian by marriage—had had a long and eventful life. As Marthe said to the Abbé Mugnier, "It was fitting that Valentine would depart at a time when the old Europe that she represented was also dying."

And indeed Europe was at war a month later: Germany and the Austro-Hungarian Empire (the Central Powers) against Russia, Serbia, France and Great Britain (the Entente—or Allies, as they were called). In the first week of August, Kaiser Wilhelm's armies invaded Luxembourg and marched through neutral Belgium. In the general conflagration, Romania remained neutral. Crown Princess Marie and the majority of the country were on the side of the Allies; King Carol, a Hohenzollern, and his wife, a German princess, were pro-German. It was an awkward position for King Carol: some twenty-five years before, he had concluded a pact of mutual assistance with Germany and the Austro-Hungarian Empire, but had kept it a secret from his government and his people. Now he was being pressured by both the Kaiser and the Austrian Emperor to enter the war on their side. ("Honor obliges you to unsheath your sword, Your Majesty," he was told by the Austrian Minister, Count Czernin.) Trained in the Prussian Army, the King genuinely believed that Germany would be the victor in the conflict; it was obviously in Romania's interest, he reasoned, to be on the side of the Central Powers. But he was well aware that he would be unable to carry his government and his country with him. At a meeting of the Crown Council he was warned that a decision to support the Central Powers might well provoke a civil war. In the circumstances, neutrality, with all its drawbacks and loss of valuable friendships, seemed to be the best available solution, though it ran much against the desire of his people, who wanted to fight Austria in order to regain the disputed province of Transylvania.

Marthe's first thought when Britain and France entered the war was for Charles-Louis. As a reserve officer, he had been called up in July and was now waiting to be sent to the front with his regiment. The war, she reflected philosophically, provided a temporary solution to their problem. But their problem now seemed small when weighed against the scale of events. Though most of her world was centered on France, whose culture she had absorbed and where most of her friends and relations lived, Marthe—the true European—was determined to rise above "the suddenly unleashed nationalistic hatreds" and remain faithful to individual friends, no matter to which camp they belonged. A few days after Germany's declaration of war, Marthe wrote a personal letter to the Kronprinz in which she vividly described the general atmosphere of hostility toward Germany in her country. In reply, he told her to remember that Russia was their mutual enemy and that "it would be tantamount to suicide for Romania to side with the Allies, for there is no doubt at all that we shall win."

A few weeks after the death of the Dowager Princess Bibesco, it was King Carol's turn to leave forever the country he had governed as an autocrat. Lunching with him on October 9, Marthe noted that "the old King looked very tired." On the night of October 11, while Crown Princess Marie was staying with her at Mogosoëa, Marthe was telephoned with the news that the King had just died. She was the first to inform the Crown Princess of his death and the first of her subjects to address her as "Your Majesty." Before leaving for Bucharest the new Queen signed the Mogosoëa visitors' book—it was the first signature of her reign. When Prince Stirbey arrived to escort Queen Marie to the palace, the new Queen, looking radiant, leaned out of the car window and asked, "Will you like me even better now that I am Queen?" to which Stirbey replied, "Yes, providing you hold on fast to your throne."

In November 1914, George Bibesco was sent on a mission to Paris concerning the purchase of airplane parts. Air reconnaissance was widely credited for helping the Allies win the Battle of the Marne that September, and Romania wanted to build up its Air Force. In a rare display of marital unity, Marthe decided to accompany her husband. Expecting to be plied with questions about the current policy of Romania, Marthe shrewdly asked her father to "give her a thorough briefing." Jean Lahovary explained why at the present time Romania's neutrality was of real service to the Allies. Neither the British nor the French statesmen realized, he told her, that Bulgaria had just concluded a secret treaty with the Central Powers. If Romania entered the war on the side of the Allies, Bulgaria would instantly mobilize and openly join the Central Powers, thus establishing a common front with Turkey and cutting Allied communication lines.

Although the French Minister of Foreign Affairs, Théophile Delcassé, was familiar with the "Balkan conundrum," it was nevertheless interesting for him to get the information from a source so close to the government of Romania. He sent his deputy, the Marquis de Breteuil, to the Hotel Meurice as soon as the Bibescos arrived, suggesting that Marthe call on him at his office at the Quai d'Orsay. Marthe refused such an official visit, which would have been inappropriate in view of George's government mission, but she took pains to explain thoroughly to Breteuil the complexities of the current situation in the Balkans, laying particular stress on the well-known duplicity of the King of Bulgaria, who detested Romania as much as he hated the Serbs. As a Cobourg prince, his sympathies were on the side of Germany and of Austria, where he had substantial financial interests. The Allies should not count on his cooperation. In a letter to her father Marthe complained that Western European chancelleries and the Quai d'Orsay in particular tended to lump all the Balkan countries together and find the whole lot of them a "perfect nuisance"—a feeling familiar to Western governments in our day.

Marthe's one diplomatic success was the interview she obtained with Aristide Briand, a member of the French War Cabinet and soon to become Prime Minister, in which she asked that Charles-Louis de Beauvau-Craon be transferred from the Quartermaster Corps, which he hated ("an unsuitable place for a descendant of a marshal of France"), to serve as military attaché in Madrid, a position well suited to his diplomatic talents. To give him his due, Charles-Louis had asked to be sent to the front lines—an ambition he eventually achieved—but had been turned down on account of his age (he was thirty-five at the time).

After the Battle of the Marne, which halted the German advance toward Paris, life in the capital resumed its nearly normal rhythm. But it was no longer the Paris of the *Belle Epoque*; those who could, retired to the country with their families, and social life was nearly at a standstill. The great ladies who had entertained Marcel Proust were now vying to join the Red Cross and the ambulance service. Marthe, who had been so much a part of that set, "French to her fingertips" in mind and language, was now regarded with suspicion. Why wasn't Romania in the war? Why haven't they become martyrs, like the Belgians? What was Marthe doing, traveling between Paris and Bucharest, talking to politicians? Was she gathering information? If so, for whom? Malicious gossips, Anna de Noailles in particular, remembered her friendship with the German Kronprinz. "It is odd how women who adored entertaining international celebrities have suddenly become xenophobic," she remarked in a letter to the Abbé Mugnier. "All Germans are now supposed to be monsters." Patriotic fervor was sweeping through the Parisian beau monde. *"Quand est-ce que vous marchez?"* ("When will your country join us?") Marthe was constantly being asked. Someone sent her a book inscribed "To Princess Bibesco, daughter of Romania, to make her country join us," as if Marthe could achieve that objective single-handed.

Marthe's diary for the end of 1914 has been lost, but it is possible to reconstruct her various moves from scattered references in her letters to Antoine. She probably returned to Romania with George in time for Christmas. In February 1915 we find her again in Paris, meeting with Charles-Louis, who was on a short leave from the Army, dining with Jean Cocteau in a spectacular blue velvet dress and attending an elegant soiree at the Duchess de la Trémoille's escorted by Aristide Briand and Paul Claudel, the most distinguished intellectual of the day. The eminence of her escorts quelled the malicious rumors for a while, but they surfaced again due to an unfortunate incident on the eve of her departure for London.

Marthe was about to leave Paris when she received a message from an old family friend, Count Primoli, telling her that the former Empress Eugénie, widow of Napoleon III, who was living at Farnborough Hill near London at the time, would welcome a visit from her. The exiled Empress had been a friend of Marthe's father-in-law, George Bibesco, when he was an officer on the staff of Napoleon III. At a moment's notice Marthe decided to go to London. Because of wartime restrictions, additional permits and photographs were needed. As photographs in those days took a long time, Jean Cocteau suggested she borrow two snapshots of Lantelme, the famous actress and beauty of the day, to whom she bore a striking resemblance. The deception passed unnoticed. On the eve of her departure for London, Marthe innocently expressed the hope that Paris would not be bombarded by German Zeppelins in her absence. There must have been some hostile people around when she said it, for her words were misquoted and construed as a message she secretly had received "through enemy channels" from the Kronprinz. Her friend Jean Cocteau, without meaning to hurt her—or so he said—composed a witty poem describing "Little Willy's" frustration at not being able to "visit Paris on Marthe's arm." Reprinted in a popular weekly, it contributed to the campaign against her, in which only the Abbé Mugnier and Marcel Proust would remain reliable allies.

Oblivious to what was happening in Paris, Marthe took the slow, blacked-out train to Calais, arriving in Dover in the middle of a Zeppelin alert. Antoine met the boat train at Victoria. Councillor at the Romanian Embassy in London, he lived in a lovely house on the Thames at 114, Grosvenor Road, where he entertained politicians and intellectual friends. They talked until late in the night. Antoine was pessimistic about the current progress of the war. "The French seem to confuse their wishes with reality," he told Marthe in what turned out to be a prophetic observation. "They rely too much on trench warfare; in the last three months Joffre [the commanding general] advanced about fifty centimeters—no more."

Wartime London impressed Marthe more than ever before. "This capital of the greatest modern Empire in the world," she wrote in her diary of March 13, 1915, "reminds me of a gigantic spider's web, controlling vast armies drawn from immense distances."

Visiting Farnborough Hill was like being back in the nineteenth century. The Empress, now eighty-nine, a small figure dressed in black, looking amazingly similar to Valentine during the last days of her life, was sitting in a small armchair facing the garden beyond. Behind her on the wall was the Winterhalter portrait Marthe had always admired. Nothing was left of the radiant beauty, but her mind was as alert as ever. She had no doubt about the outcome of the war: the Allies would triumph. The disaster of Sedan, which cost her husband his throne, would be avenged. As Empress, she liked to influence politics; even now she still spoke like a consort of the Emperor, taking pleasure in reshaping the postwar map of Europe, predicting the breakup of the Austro-Hungarian Empire, awarding the disputed Transylvania province to Romania, creating new independent nations in Eastern Europe. In an astonishing flash of foresight she told Marthe, "The first country to sue for peace will be the one threatened with a revolution, and it will most likely be Russia." As she talked, her face filled with life, traces of former beauty reappeared. "I looked up," Marthe remembered, "and saw a sudden resemblance to the portrait on the wall."

Shortly after the end of World War I, Empress Eugénie left Farnborough Hill to return to Spain, her native land. She died there on July 20, 1920, at the age of ninety-four, a remnant of the nineteenth century's old order.

In Boulogne, on the way back to Paris, the movement of troops delayed the train's departure. Marthe spent the night sitting on a packing case on the quay, wrapped in her blue traveling cloak. All around her were ambulances carrying wounded from the trenches back to England. A flotilla of ships spread out as far as the eye could see in the Channel, guarding the approaches to the British Isles. She was reading a small volume of poems by a young—yet to become famous—poet, Siegfried Sassoon.

Arriving in Zurich three days later, Marthe found the newspapers full of anti-Allied propaganda. *Die Woche* carried pictures of French soldiers being marched to prisoner-of-war camps, German troops happily sunning themselves in a Belgian village, Kaiser Wilhelm being "enthusiastically" received in a recently conquered town in northern France; there was even a faked sign of the grocery store Félix Potin in the background. On her arrival in Vienna, she was handed a personal letter from the Kronprinz, which she found deeply embarrassing. Besides pointing to the advantages that would accrue to Romania if she declared war on Germany's side, the Kronprinz was suggesting the conclusion of a separate peace between Germany and France in which France would retain a part of Belgium with the rest of it going to Germany. "They could then jointly wage a war against the British Empire, made easier by the establishment of a German military base on the Channel." The Kronprinz stressed that the proposals were his own and did not necessarily reflect the views of his government; nevertheless, he *was* asking Marthe to "unofficially transmit them to the French government through Aristide Briand, her old friend."

After the desolate plains of Hungary, which the heavily blacked-out Orient Express crossed at a snail's pace, it was a relief to behold the awesome sight of the Carpathian Mountains, covered in snow. The general atmosphere in Bucharest was very tense. Britain's continuing lack of success in the Dardanelles confirmed the worst fears of the uncommitted. Czernin, the eloquent and persuasive Austrian Minister in Bucharest, was deploying a range of arguments in favor of Romania's joining the Central Powers. London and Paris, on the other hand, wanted it to side with the Allies. To this end, Lord Kitchener, British Minister of War, dispatched to Bucharest one of his ablest and most politically experienced staff officers, Lieutenant Colonel Christopher Birdwood Thomson, a thirty-nine-year-old veteran of the Battle of Ypres, familiar with conditions in the Balkans and, unusual for a English-man, fluent in Russian, German and French. His mission as military attaché in Romania was simple: bring the country into the war on the Allied side as soon as possible.

8

❧

The Knight-Errant

*C*hristopher Birdwood Thomson was an unusual man. Brought up in India in a family distinguished for its service to the British Empire, Thomson was educated at Cheltenham and the Woolwich Military Academy near London, joined the Army at the age of seventeen and was commissioned as an officer a year later. A commanding figure—one of the tallest officers in the British Army—dark-haired with merry blue eyes, he was energetic and articulate, qualities that endeared him to Romanians. As British representative in Serbia in 1913 at the time of the Second Balkan War, he became fascinated by the seemingly insoluble complexities of the Balkan scene, its handsome people and lovely landscapes. Yet years in the Army did not suppress his romantic and idealistic nature; rare for a soldier, he remained a thoroughly unconventional man.

Colonel Thomson arrived in Bucharest in early March and took up his post at the Legation under the British Minister, Sir George Barclay. On March 24, at the invitation of King Ferdinand, he attended a concert at the Cotroceni Palace. Marthe, recently returned from abroad, was dining with King Ferdinand that evening "to brief him on the mood prevalent in French political circles." As Queen Marie was temporarily indisposed, the King himself escorted Marthe to the concert. She entered the candlelit drawing room on the King's arm, wearing a long black velvet dress and her emeralds. To the newly arrived Colonel, she appeared like a vision straight out of the fairy tales of his childhood. He thought he had never seen anyone so beautiful; he could not take his eyes off her face and her figure, much to the amusement of Elise Bratiano, who leaned over and whispered to Marthe that this "handsome British Colonel was rapidly getting cross-eyed." When, after the concert, Sir George Barclay introduced him to the "vision" and they talked, he was swept off his feet by the force of Marthe's personality and her erudition. A lesser and a less well-educated man would have probably withdrawn—overwhelmed—but Thomson had enough personality to meet Marthe on her own ground. He fell in love with her, and his devotion, not always reciprocated by Marthe, lasted until the end of his life.

That particular evening at the Cotroceni Palace, Marthe was in a receptive mood, ready for a "knight-errant" in her life. She was lonely. It was wartime and she felt unprotected. Charles-Louis, though he continued to write, was far away in the Army; the majority of her friends were cut off from her by the war; George, for whom the war turned out to be an unexpected bonanza, providing an outlet for his adventurous spirit and love of flying, spent all his time in aviation circles.

The day after they met, Thomson rode over to Mogosoëa, as if by chance. According to Thomson's recollection, they spent the afternoon walking in Marthe's gardens, "a beautiful and remote place on the banks of the Cotentina River, surrounded by woodlands and sleeping waters, a chapel and a Venetian Palace on three sides of a courtyard." "I have found a name for the châtelaine," Thomson wrote in his book *Smaranda*, which was dedicated to Marthe, "a name which suggests some of her attributes—I will call her 'Smaranda,' which means 'emerald'; it was once the name of a Byzantine Princess, whose effigy appears on a stained-glass window in Constantinople; she is always represented with a rose in her hand." And he went on to say, "I don't think I have ever come across a brain and a mind more elegantly furnished than Smaranda's. Her memory is prodigious, her knowledge of art varied and profound, of French history and literature amazingly complete. She knows more about the exhibits in the British Museum and the Victoria & Albert than most curators I know."

Thomson soon realized that Marthe evoked as much envy as admiration on her home ground. "Smaranda is not popular with the women," he noted after a few months in Bucharest. "Her admirers are legion, but it does not help with her own sex. She possesses too many advantages: wealth, beauty, brains and social position combined in a single person are never forgiven by the jealous." He shrewdly put his finger on Marthe's current problem: "She has a truly European mind. In ten years' time this kind of mind may be Europe's salvation—today it brings reproach."

During late spring and summer the relationship progressed; the Colonel fell deeply in love. Marthe let herself be adored without commitment, and it is hard to judge from her diary to what extent she reciprocated his feelings. It was a wartime romance in Ruritanian surroundings. She called him Kit, his family nickname, and he addressed her as Smaranda. There must have been occasional tender moments. "This evening Kit and I alone at Mogosoëa," reads an entry in her diary that summer. "Red roses . . . One day perhaps I will be the wife of an Englishman?"

Marthe's question must be taken with a grain of salt. Even assuming that the war lent a different perspective to Marthe's feelings, it is impossible to imagine her as plain Mrs. Thomson. They belonged to different worlds, and it was only years later, when they were both middle-aged and Thomson had assumed high office and a title, that their lives might have merged. But in the summer of 1915 the distant Beauvau-Craon still held her heart.

For the time being, however, Thomson's masculine presence filled a void in Marthe's life, particularly after her father's recent death from a heart attack. In Constantsa one day George suddenly appeared before her, looking grave. "A misfortune happened to your father," he told her. She guessed immediately: "It is not to him—it's to me."

Her father had been her hero; she had adored him ever since she was a child and was proud of the position he occupied in Romania. He was the only person in the world whose advice she followed without hesitation and whose company she cherished at all times. Jean Lahovary was given a state funeral, with King Ferdinand himself leading the mourners. Afterward, Marthe retired to the solitude of Posada. For days, she remained there alone, discouraging all visitors except Thomson, whose strength and devotion seemed to soothe her.

In the meantime, however, life in neutral Romania continued at a relatively normal pace. The harvests of 1914 and 1915 yielded excellent crops that sold at very high prices. Bucharest was a speculator's paradise, with the Allies and the Central Powers bidding up prices to keep supplies away from each other's hands. Corruption and blackmail were rife, but this was the way it had always been in the Balkans. Thomson had to play a lonely hand against the heavy weight of German influence and intrigue. Though Queen Marie and most of the government were pro-Allies, King Ferdinand and some of his ministers were not; the failure of the British attack on the Dardanelles gave a powerful argument to the pro-German faction, waiting to enter the war on the winning side. When in October 1915 Bulgaria declared for the Central Powers, the odds seemed heavily stacked against Thomson's mission.

Throughout Marthe played a key role as a hostess. In the relaxed atmosphere of Mogosoëa, representatives of hostile countries mingled on neutral ground to thrash out ideas, to discuss the latest news, even to form temporary friendships across political and military lines. Russian generals conferred with Italian diplomats and all mixed with Turkish envoys and representatives of the King of Greece. King Ferdinand or Queen Marie, accompanied by Prince Stirbey, dropped in occasionally for a neighborly visit to Marthe, who reigned over her political salon, skillfully keeping passions at bay. As a place to gather information and influence local politicians, Marthe's salon was of inestimable value to Colonel Thomson. For once pleasure and duty concurred.

In times of war, a neutral country is a perfect terrain for belligerents and even allies to spy on each other; needless to say, there was much activity of this sort in Romania, with the government spying on both camps. Rightly or wrongly, Thomson decided that the security arrangements at the British Mission in Bucharest left much to be desired. On his return from a short trip to London that August, carrying confidential documents and memorandums from Lord Kitchener, the War Minister, Thomson conceived what in retrospect seems like an odd idea—to ask Marthe to store the bulk of his secret documents at Posada, "far out of harm's way." The procedure was as unorthodox as it was naïve, and it is hard to imagine why his Chief of Mission ever authorized such a step. Marthe was, after all, one of the best-known personalities in Romania; her friendships were international; she traveled widely and entertained diplomats and politicians from both camps. It was natural that she would have been kept under surveillance and perhaps spied upon. The thought did not seem to have occurred to Colonel Thomson, for on September 15, 1915, according to his wartime diaries, Thomson and Frank Rattigan, First Secretary at the British Mission in Bucharest, drove to Posada with a huge load of cardboard boxes, containing the precious documents. They were unloaded openly and stored in a small attic room above the library in the main house.

On Saturday, September 25, Christopher Thomson was returning home to Bucharest after dining with Marthe at Mogosoëa. As he entered his house he heard the telephone ringing; it was Marthe telling him that her house in Posada was on fire. "Within minutes I was in the garage, had roused my chauffeur Virgil and we were racing along the empty streets," he recalls. "Smaranda in her car was waiting for us at the corner where the side road from Mogosoëa joins the Great North Road to the mountains. We sat together in silence while her high-powered Daimler sped on. For about twenty miles along the plain the road is broad and straight, then it begins to climb among the foothills. The night was clear and very still; in the far distance we could see a red glow in the sky." As they drove through the gates, they realized the extent of the devastation. The villagers had done their best to save the building, but the fire-extinguishing appliances were scanty and the old woodwork burned with astonishing rapidity. Some pictures and a few pieces of furniture had been saved, but soon the roof fell in and the thick stone walls enclosed a roaring furnace. Valuable paintings, priceless Persian rugs, china, but above all personal papers, letters and family photographs went up in flames—as did the British government's secret documents. Day dawned upon a scene of desolation; a group of badly scorched birches loomed like skeletons in the morning mist; from the distance came the lowing of cattle and the patter of sheep coming down from the mountain.

Marthe was too shaken to cry. Thirteen years of her life had vanished in the inferno: memories of her youth good and bad, her first literary efforts, the writing of *Les Huit Paradis*. She had loved Posada—her retreat from the world—and was proud of the house and the garden she had created. A sobbing Outza, the village maid, led her to the charred remains of Pat, the Siamese cat she adored. He lay next to a large bottle of Houbigant's Hyacinth, Marthe's favorite scent, which had exploded in the heat and was now burning with a yellow flame exhaling a beautiful fragrance.

Nothing more could be done on the mountain; Marthe thanked the assembled villagers, comforted the wailing Outza and let herself be driven away to Mogosoëa. In a few years she would start rebuilding Posada, she vowed, assuming the world had not collapsed around her. Thomson sat silently in the car, guilt weighing heavily on his mind. As they drove into the Mogosoëa courtyard, he asked whether she preferred to be left alone. Marthe said, "No—I am glad of your presence."

It was later established that German Intelligence had set fire to Posada.

The winter of 1915–16 was particularly depressing for Marthe. She spent a great deal of time alone at Mogosoëa, waiting for events to develop. She missed her father. After his death, Marthe's mother and younger sister Marguerite (born a few years after her brother's death) left Romania and settled in Geneva for the duration of the war. Marthe's relations with her mother improved after her father's death, and as the eldest in the family and the one with money, she now felt an obligation to look after her. It was not easy, for Madame Lahovary, emotional and high-strung at the best of times, now entered upon a period of mental instability, which ended with her suicide three years later.

As the political situation grew tense and Romania remained stubbornly neutral, its relations with the Central Powers grew acrimonious. Encouraged by their victories in the Balkans, Germany and Austria treated the Romanian royal family and the government with increasing disdain. As it was obvious to all that the Queen controlled King Ferdinand, both the Austrian Count Czernin and the German envoy von dem Büssche concentrated on convincing her that it was to Romania's advantage to shed her neutrality in their favor. The Queen remained unmoved. She never had a moment's doubt that England would win, but Thomson had misgivings where Romania was concerned. An experienced observer, he was aware that the involvement of an unprepared and ill-armed country in a war on three fronts—against Austria, Turkey and Bulgaria—would invite disaster, and Romania would then become not an asset but a liability to the Allies. His misgivings were overtaken by events.

Finally, in the spring of 1916, the long-awaited "great Brusilov offensive" materialized. Russian forces started attacking Austrian troops in the East and pushed on to the Carpathian Mountains. To the Allies this looked like a propitious moment to have Romania enter the war, for it would draw Austro-German detachments away from the battlefields of the Somme.

It was thus with a heavy heart and dire forebodings for the country he had come to love that on August 13, 1916, Thomson —on behalf of the Imperial General Staff—signed an agreement to "supply and support the Romanian armies on all fronts." His colleague Colonel Henri Berthelot signed on behalf of France; both of them realized that the agreements could never be implemented. Two weeks later, Romania declared war on the Central Powers. Queen Marie was jubilant, though she knew "that we are coming into terrible times." For King Ferdinand it had been a painful decision, for it meant going against his upbringing and his family wishes. To a pro-German courtier, who argued that the Hohenzollerns had never been defeated, he answered sadly, "You have just seen one who has."

Marthe was in Paris on the day her country finally entered the war. To ensure little Valentine's safety in what she imagined would be a protracted and dangerous struggle, she decided to take her daughter and Miss Chatfield to Switzerland, where her mother and sister were staying. "Geneva, safe, boring Geneva," Marthe confided to her diary on August 11. "The air is filled with the smell of international money . . . banks, banks everywhere . . . a glass cage suffused with the pink gray light of the Lake." She settled her daughter and governess at St. Cergue, a charming village just above Geneva, then left for France. Even the long passport controls at the border and the crowds of soldiers filling the corridors of the train did not spoil her anticipation of returning to France and to Paris. "Dear France, I love you," she whispered as the train at last gathered speed after crossing the frontier.

The apartment at 71, Faubourg St. Honoré, kept immaculate by her Swiss butler Zufall, was strangely quiet. No buses or taxis, which usually filled the Faubourg, could be heard. They were all at the front, requisitioned for transport by the Army, defending the line of the Somme; and so was Charles-Louis, whose presence still filled the rooms. She walked across the Place de la Concorde to the Seine, contemplating the lovely panorama of the bridges, thankful that this beautiful city so far had remained untouched by the war.

The Abbé Mugnier came to lunch the next day—"witty, affectionate and full of the latest political gossip." That same evening Emmanuel came to call, greatly changed. The splendid-looking young man, "la belle Aimée," who had so enchanted Proust in years past and had been Marthe's great love in her adolescence, was suffering from clinical depression. He was thin to the point of emaciation, his movements were jerky, his speech slurred. He complained that his French friends were "getting on his nerves" and said he planned to go to London to be near Antoine, as soon as necessary travel permits could be obtained.

The mood in Paris was somber. Every day brought news of heavy casualties on the Western Front. Marthe had hoped to see Charles-Louis, but it turned out to be impossible, as all military leaves had been canceled.

On the afternoon of August 27, 1916, while working on her diary, Marthe received a telephone call from her cousin Alexander Lahovary, the Romanian Minister in Paris. "*C'est fait,*" he exclaimed, "we are in it—at last." Romania had declared war on the Central Powers. Like Queen Marie back at the Cotroceni Palace, Marthe was elated; she dismissed the opinion of a French politician who predicted that "the Germans would be in Bucharest in a fortnight." Many people congratulated her on the outcome. "I felt like a bride, receiving bouquets and telegrams from well-wishers," she noted on August 29.

But how was she ever to get home? With Romania now a belligerent, the only way for Marthe to return to Bucharest was to take the boat train to London, a ship to Norway, a train across Scandinavia to St. Petersburg—recently renamed Petrograd—and another train across Russia to Kiev and Bucharest, a formidable journey which she dreaded. Still, there would be compensations: a chance to see Antoine in London, renew contacts with the Russian imperial family in Petrograd and gather information about the Russian military and political goings-on, which were of such vital concern to Thomson and members of the Romanian government. A cable to her old friend Maurice Paléologue, the French Ambassador to Russia, produced an invitation to be his guest at the French Embassy in Petrograd. Armed with a "special exit visa" signed by Jules Cambon of the French Foreign Office, Marthe set off for Boulogne to board the cross-Channel boat, on which, she noted with some satisfaction, "I was the only woman traveling."

Antoine met her at Victoria Station, driving his open 1911 Bentley. Just back from a diplomatic reception, dressed in a perfectly cut morning coat and gray spats, immensely good-looking and distinguished—"unique, mocking, staccato, affectionate and impatient"—he swept Marthe into his arms and announced that they were off to a reception at the Rutlands' for Sir John French. Marthe pleaded for time to change clothes, but this was brushed aside with a curt "There is a war on, no one cares." Hours later, settled in Antoine's charming guest room with flowery chintz, Marthe tried on her gas mask and went for a stroll by the river, "to rediscover the little rose-colored houses on the Chelsea Em-

bankment I so loved." There was a Zeppelin raid that night.
Marthe woke up suddenly at 2 a.m. hearing the bombs fall
"amidst the solemn silence of the river." She lifted her head on one
elbow and listened. "London closed around me like a huge quiet
lake," she recalled. "I went back to sleep unafraid." Next morning she heard that the Zeppelin had been shot down somewhere
north of the London Docks.

On September 10, Marthe embarked on the *Jupiter* for Norway.
Bergen did not impress her. "Rows and rows of little houses, all
painted green—and no newspapers anywhere . . ." She crossed
Sweden in pelting rain, noting the "lugubrious soggy pine
forests—and again not a single newspaper in any language except
Swedish. . . . How very dull are the northern neutrals." After seven
days on the train, she arrived at Petrograd, where Maurice Paléologue received her in his sumptuous embassy on the Neva, an
island of luxury and comfort amidst the revolutionary upheaval of
the Russian capital. Her room overlooked the great river, full of
barges, all bathed in autumn sunlight. She walked along the pink
granite quays, admired the pastel-colored palaces—a rainbow of
pinks, yellows, pistachios and blues. Paléologue drove her out to
the islands and took her to visit the dazzling Fabergé shop on the
Nevsky Prospekt. "Ducky," Queen Marie's favorite sister, married
to Grand Duke Kirill, the Tsar's first cousin, was particularly
delighted to see her; together they visited Tsarskoe Selo and
Ducky's mother-in-law, the "supremely well-informed" Grand
Duchess Vladimir, who talked to her about Rasputin and his sinister influence on the Empress. Marthe recalled her father's sense
of foreboding at the time of the imperial couple's visit to Constantsa, and after a day spent in Petrograd the same feeling of
doom communicated itself to her. "The city is very tense," she
wrote in her diary. "It is a charged, neurotic atmosphere; in contrast to the opulence of the shops, the streets are filled with un-
collected rubbish. I am told that there is practically no firewood in
St. Petersburg and not much to eat either. Every day there are
demonstrations of some kind. . . . All sorts of rumors abound.
Where will it all end?" Six months later, the Tsar abdicated and
the Revolution was in full swing.

Anxious to get out of Russia before the services stopped functioning, Marthe spent only one day in Moscow, then continued on to Kiev—a long, cold, uncomfortable journey in a train filled with disorderly soldiers. In Kiev, she ran into a French military delegation, on their way back from Romania, who warned her that the situation there was dangerous and the government was moving to Jassy, the old capital in Moldavia, as Bucharest was too close to the front line. "Let them go"; Marthe resolved to remain at Mogosoëa and continue her hospital work in Bucharest, no matter what.

As the train approached the Romanian frontier, the war came nearer and nearer. The engine slowed down to a snail's pace; a German Zeppelin flew over but did not drop any bombs. After a day and a half's delay, the train finally pulled into the Bucharest Central Station while German planes dropped bombs on the city. Towering over the crowds on the platform was Christopher Birdwood Thomson. He had been waiting sixteen hours.

"I drove her straight to Mogosoëa," Thomson recalls. "She was in a state of complete exhaustion, combined with an exaltation of spirit that casts out fear. She is proud of her country and full of hope and ideas of glory. This, of course, is the atmosphere of Paris and all very well in its proper place, but here she will be running frightful risks, as the situation is deteriorating rapidly and the Germans are bound to walk in. . . . The absence of fear is admirable, but most undesirable in a charming woman. . . . The hospital in which she is going to work is right in the very center of the city and faces the royal palace . . . a great target for bombs." The Colonel became even more depressed after Marthe related to him her conversation in London with Sir John French, Chief of the Imperial General Staff, who had told her, "I think Romania came in too early for her own good." It only confirmed the fear that had been haunting him for a long time, that the Romanian Army was being sacrificed in the cause of the Allies and that he, Thomson, was one of the instruments of its destruction. But there was nothing he could do at this stage—not even give adequate protection to the woman he loved.

9

The Hospital

*I*n spite of the exhaustion of the journey Marthe refused to rest for more than a day. Living at Mogosoëa, she returned each morning to Bucharest to work in Hospital 118, which she had helped Queen Marie to organize and equip. There was certainly plenty to do, as each day more casualties arrived from the front. The Romanian soldiers, though brave fighters, were no match for the superbly trained and equipped German Army. To make matters worse, their Allies, the Russians, failed to support them; Brusilov's much touted offensive became mired in the mud and stopped just as the Romanians were counting on the Russians to keep the enemy occupied in the north of the country. Heavy German bombardment created a sense of panic in Bucharest, and "all this during the most beautiful September weather on record —what irony," noted Marthe. On September 26 a bomb landed in the garden of Colonel Thomson's house, wounding him slightly. "The first British blood spilled in the defense of Romania—don't worry your pretty head about it," he told Marthe over the telephone.

In the face of the rapid German advance, families started to leave Bucharest. Some decided to travel to the Crimea, not realizing that they would be engulfed by the Revolution. The Romanian national treasure and Queen Marie's crown jewels were sent to Petrograd, from where they never returned. Marthe, more cautious than the Queen, deposited all her valuables, including the famous Bibesco emeralds, in the care of the French envoy to Bucharest, Count de St. Aulaire, who dispatched them via diplomatic bag to Ambassador Paléologue. Locked in the French Embassy safe, they were later taken to Paris and given back to Marthe in Geneva.

Bombardment now became part of a day's pattern. If German planes failed to appear, people wondered what had happened to them. Does it mean we are not worth bombing anymore? Do they take us for dead? But worse was still to come.

Each day Marthe arrived at the hospital at 8 a.m. to work alongside the doctors, assist with the operations and comfort the unfortunate amputees, whose limbs had to be severed using only chloroform as an anesthetic. "Don't the scenes remind you of Dante's Inferno?" she asked Elise Bratiano, who was working with her. Every night she left the hospital nauseated, unable to sleep because of the nightmares she had witnessed during the day.

As the promised Russian offensive failed to materialize the Germans had ample time to occupy the mountain passes of Transylvania and spill down into the plains of Wallachia eastward toward Bucharest. Queen Marie, who had been valiantly visiting soldiers' camps, distributing food and words of comfort, was ordered to go with her children to Jassy, the temporary capital and headquarters of the Army. On the eve of her departure from Bucharest the Queen paid an unexpected visit to her friend at Mogosoëa. It was late in the evening, and Marthe, exhausted by the day's work in the hospital, had gone to bed. Queen Marie later described the visit. "Marthe looked very beautiful in her bed under a red brocade baldachin, surrounded by icons and vases of flowers, arranged with faultless taste, her abundant red hair spilling over the lacy pillows, her huge eyes luminous in the candlelight. Yes, she was quite beautiful that night, our unique and fascinating Marthe, but *why* was she staying behind?"

The two women had an uneasy relationship of late. Queen Marie, in mourning for her youngest child, exhausted by the strain of the little boy's illness and the ever worsening military situation, built up an exaggerated picture of Marthe's influence on her husband. A weak man, overshadowed by his wife, Ferdinand liked to visit Mogosoëa, where he found an oasis of peace, a welcome change from the turbulent atmosphere of the palace. It is true that in later years their relationship went deeper, but in the autumn of 1916 they were just friends. However, Queen Marie, though not overly fond of her husband and rarely begrudging him his ladies, suddenly became jealous of Marthe and possessive of her husband. She disapproved of Marthe's courageous decision to remain with her hospital in Bucharest, and in a much quoted remark, unworthy of a queen, she suggested that Marthe was staying in the capital under the Germans "in order to gather exciting material for a book and to profit from her friendship with the Kronprinz."

Nothing could have been more unfair. Except for the usual notes in her diary, Marthe never wrote a book about the occupation; she spent her days and nights tending to the wounded and warding off German efforts to remove them into captivity. To remain at her post was for Marthe a matter of dignity. She believed it her duty to protect Mogosoëa, just as it was her duty not to abandon the hospital she directed. When Thomson suggested the evacuation of the hospital by special train she refused, because the majority of "her wounded" were in no condition to be moved.

In the third week of November, the German Army, under General August von Mackensen, crossed the Danube River; German, Austrian, Turkish and Bulgar troops began to converge on the capital.

On the evening of November 24, the "day of destiny," as she noted in her diary, Marthe had just returned from the hospital and was sitting upstairs in her bedroom at Mogosoëa, while Outza was massaging her feet, when she heard a car driven at high speed turn into the courtyard. Christopher Thomson was announced. He was wearing his uniform and carried a pistol in a holster. Marthe dressed hurriedly and went downstairs to receive him. Thomson's usual calm had temporarily deserted him. "You must leave at once," he told her. "German armored patrols might be here at any moment. Move into the hospital—it is safer. Have you got a car? I will drive into Bucharest with you, but for God's sake let's clear out of here as soon as possible."

Standing by the Venetian fireplace, with the fire blazing merrily behind her, Marthe looked at the beloved room she had created. She thought of all the people who had leaned against the same mantelpiece in the past months, of the conversations and the arguments that had swirled around it. She picked up her treasured visitors' book and ordered the maids to pack it together with family photographs, manuscripts, a few pictures and one or two precious sculptures. She calmly said goodbye to her household, explaining that she was going into Bucharest to be nearer her work at the hospital and would visit them in a few days. The gardener gave her a huge bunch of carnations from the hothouses; she thanked him and, stifling tears, got into the car next to Thomson. Virginie, the Swiss maid, followed behind with the luggage. The avenue of poplar trees was all black—there was no moon and no light shone on the waters of the lake. "If we are surrounded by the enemy," said Thomson, "I shall have to take the other car to escape. For tomorrow I have an important mission to carry out."

They arrived at the hospital in the early hours of the morning. Leaving her at the door, the "Knight-Errant" kissed her hand and drove off in a great hurry.

Marthe was to learn later that Thomson had been entrusted with a secret British government mission to destroy the Ploesti airfields and oil installations to prevent them from falling into German hands. Coincidentally, the man who assisted Thomson in this complex and highly dangerous operation turned out to be Marthe's own husband, George Bibesco. As soon as Thomson received the orders from London, he arranged for the cooperation of the Romanian Army and the Standard Oil people who worked the fields. In view of the Germans' rapid advance they had to act instantly. Thomson had the overall responsibility for the operation, but its execution was entrusted to a special Romanian Air Force commando unit led by Captain George Bibesco. The two men, united in a common cause, met at Ploesti as the Germans marched toward Posada. It took two days to destroy the installations and ignite the reservoirs, an operation fraught with danger in which George and his men risked their lives. As columns of black smoke rose into the air and reservoirs became a sea of fire, German tanks entered the outskirts of Ploesti. George, who carried an injured Standard Oil operator on his back, escaped, and so did Thomson and his people. George found time to telephone Marthe at the hospital: "Nero did nothing compared to us. What a sight." (For this heroic exploit George was later awarded the Distinguished Service Order by the British Army; Thomson himself wrote the citation.)

After George hurriedly departed for the Army HQ at Jassy, Colonel Thomson, who by then had a price put on his head by the Germans, secretly sneaked into Bucharest to say a last goodbye to Marthe. The Ploesti operation haunted him. He had come to protect this country and was now leaving it as a destroyer. "How can I ever make it up to you?" he asked Marthe. They were not to meet again for several years.

All night long columns of cars passed under the hospital windows: the government was moving out of the capital, but the people were staying behind. And Marthe was remaining with them. Her room, to which she moved a few precious possessions from Mogosoëa, now resembled a corner of the Louvre: a bust of Canova, one of Coustou, a lovely Winterhalter portrait, three precious Louis XV armchairs, one Empire desk and odds and ends saved from the impending wreckage of her home. It was a soothing background to retire to after a day of dismal scenes at the hospital.

"Seventeen wounded," records an entry in her diary; "one lost his arm. . . . We wash their feet, burn all their clothes covered with lice. . . . Two operations. . . . Young Dimitri dies holding my hand. . . . The lights fail. . . . Prepare the candles. . . . More casualties as our retreat gathers momentum." And later: "Where are the Germans? They have taken Ciconesti. . . . They are in Chatila. . . . Expect them here any moment. . . . Matila Ghika [a cousin] arrives with a huge bunch of flowers. . . . He is taking the last train out of the capital. . . . 'I admire you,' he says, 'for staying here.' "

There was no more time for the diary. Now that the evacuation was completed, Bucharest lay defenseless; a foreboding silence descended. It started to snow.

At midnight on December 6 the street arc lights suddenly came ablaze, as did gas lanterns everywhere. "The town has thrown its mask away," Marthe recorded. "No need to worry about air attacks any longer . . . we have been conquered." The next morning German detachments arrived on the Palace Square directly under the hospital windows. "We hear their voices and their loud cheers, then the national hymn—the song of the regattas in Kiel—a world away now. I forbid the auxiliaries and the servants to look. No hanging out of the windows in my hospital. . . . I go back to my patients. . . . Many of the soldiers are crying."

The following day five wounded Germans were brought into the hospital, escorted by a medical officer, who demanded dressings, medicines, disinfectants. He shouted at the Romanian doctors to be quick. Marthe's stony face calmed him down; he saluted and left abruptly, announcing the arrival of another consignment of wounded the next morning.

Later that week, as she came out of the operating room, Marthe was handed a note from her old acquaintance von Waldburg, a member of the German Embassy in Bucharest and former frequent guest at Mogosoëa, asking her to receive Prince Schaumburg-Lippe of the German General Staff, who would like to meet her. "I did not know what to answer," Marthe recalled. "I finally sent a message that the doors of a Red Cross hospital are open to all."

Schaumburg-Lippe, of an ancient German family, was polite and reassuring. He told her that a civilian administration under the command of the Duke of Mecklenburg was taking over the town and that the hospital would be protected. Later that day eighteen more wounded Germans arrived, filling every bed in the place; Romanian soldiers were relegated to straw mattresses on the floor.

On Sunday, December 10, as Marthe was returning from church, a message arrived at the hospital that Mogosoëa had been ransacked by German soldiers. The officer who brought the news offered to drive her there to survey the damage. She went, accompanied by Sister Julie, one of the Catholic nuns at the hospital.

Mogosoëa, Marthe's Venetian jewel on the lake, admired by

visitors from all over Europe, presented a heartbreaking scene. The long poplar drive, along which a battle must have taken place, was strewn with the decomposing bodies of farm horses. Inside, the house was in shambles: pieces of antique furniture, some stacked in the fireplace to be used as firewood, curtains torn from the windows, a sea of valuable china littering the floor, carpets stained with soldiers' excreta. The Byzantine chapel of the Brancovan princes, where Orthodox services were conducted, had been turned into a stable. "I am deeply ashamed of my men," said the local commander, von Diergard, "and I apologize—poor Princess." Whereupon a young German soldier, looking at Marthe's lovely face, exclaimed with a sudden surge of regret, "We had no idea that the owner was a young and beautiful woman—we would not have done it had we known." "Should I have put a notice on my house advising that I was not an old woman?" Marthe remarked bitterly to herself.

In the village, her peasants had suffered the same fate; most of their meager belongings had been seized, yet they all lamented the calamity that had befallen their mistress. Later, as Marthe visited their houses, distributing money and whatever was left of sugar and flour on the estate, she told them, "I would have been ashamed had they not pillaged my house, when you yourselves lost so much."

The sack of Mogosoëa was only the beginning of the misfortunes that Marthe had to bear that fateful year. Ten days later came the news that both Balotesti, her parents' home, and Posada, her beloved retreat in the mountains, had also been looted. At Posada, soldiers of a Hungarian regiment found family portraits that had been stored in an attic and, lining them up in the courtyard, peppered the pictures with shots and then set fire to them. In an old-fashioned twist of courtesy, they decided to save the portraits of the ladies; the men, however, went up in flames. Thus perished a famous family Renoir, bought by George's father in Paris, entitled "Guide to the Emperor."

At other times, Marthe would have been devastated by her losses, but somehow they did not seem to matter anymore. The human misery she witnessed at the hospital every day was so enormous that any material losses seemed puny. Her days were now overshadowed by the constant fight for supplies. As the German occupation set in, the inhabitants of Bucharest were ordered to turn in their stores of food and fuel to the Germans, depriving them of basic necessities for survival. The winter of 1916–17 turned out to be the coldest in fifty years and the suffering of the people was intense. There was no fuel for heat and no means to obtain it. Houses abandoned by their owners were stripped bare by the soldiers (only the royal palace was left undisturbed out of respect for the late Carol I, "a friend of Germany"). As winter progressed, people began to die of starvation.

The hospital lacked everything, but the most pressing need was for food and warm blankets. Marthe spent days making the rounds of the city, trying to obtain donations from store owners, but their inventories too were depleted. Determined to get help for "her wounded," she even tackled the German Military HQ and persuaded the medical officer to allocate medicines and some flour to the hospital. "After all, we are treating your soldiers as well," she told him.

Mogosoëa was now under the administration of an Austrian officer-farmer and a semblance of order was being restored in the house. The "farmer," a stocky, blond soldier of about forty, presented himself to Marthe at the hospital one afternoon proudly carrying a large pot of azaleas from her own greenhouses. Marthe thought it a curious gesture, "but I could hardly send him away —he meant well."

Marthe fared better than her sister-in-law Nadège Stirbey at nearby Buftea, where a Prussian regiment was stationed. Having looted the house, the officers turned over the contents of Nadège's cupboards to their wives, newly arrived from Berlin, who paraded all over the village in her clothes. They also managed to dig out the Stirbey silver, carefully buried under an oak tree at the edge of the park. Marthe complained to Headquarters and a senior officer was eventually dispatched to put a stop to the senseless plunder.

One day in late January a high-ranking German officer, a Baron Stolzenher, called at the hospital. He had come, he said, on orders of His Imperial Highness the Kronprinz to inquire about Marthe's well-being. The Kronprinz sent his regards and stood ready to transmit news to Marthe's daughter in Switzerland, which he did. The visit of the emissary impressed the local command, and Marthe took advantage of it to obtain permission to visit the prisoner-of-war camps outside Bucharest, where epidemics of typhus, smallpox and other diseases were raging and soldiers were dying like flies. She was able to distribute whatever food and medicine she could lay her hands on and—more important—to prevail upon camp administrators to free dozens of convalescent soldiers and return them to their families. At a village outside Ploesti she came across a handful of Romanian women who had been forced into a brothel by the occupying forces and managed to set them free, much to the annoyance of the local military commandant. She went on with her mission in spite of mounting exhaustion. "I am falling down with fatigue," she wrote on February 17, 1917. "I have lost my voice after talking to several hundred men in the camps."

A few days later as she watched a soldier die in front of her, she admitted, "I can't even feel compassion anymore, I have given my all . . . my cup is full."

In spite of the exhaustion, little sleep and little food, Marthe still managed to look beautiful. Even the unbecoming nurse's uniform of the period could not detract from the radiance of her face; she exuded a spiritual energy and a commanding force which defeated the German bureaucrats and military. Her hospital patients adored her. One of them, upon hearing her cough, sent a bottle of Linctus syrup, a rare treasure, with a note saying, "Am protecting my enchantment."

Marthe had hoped that she would be allowed to remain at her post for the duration of the war or "at least as long as I have the strength to carry on." The knowledge that she was desperately needed gave her enormous satisfaction; each morning her patients' greeting renewed her depleted energy reserves. What she missed was solitude and her writing routine, but there was a war on—the hospital and her wounded had to come first. "One day," she repeated to herself, "there will be time for writing again. . . . Pray

God make peace come soon before our world is irrevocably altered."

Immersed in her duties, Marthe did not realize that there was a conspiracy to unseat her and indeed to do away with the hospital altogether. Her enemy was a Dr. Woolf, the newly appointed director of the German Red Cross in Romania. When he took up his duties in February, Dr. Woolf, a gruff and arrogant man, decided that Hospital 118, which occupied a prime site across from the royal palace, should be moved to the outskirts and the building turned into a casino for the troops (some said brothel). Horrified, Marthe appealed to Prince Henry von Preussen, Inspector of Prisoner-of-War Camps on the Eastern Front. Von Preussen was a cultured, aristocratic German of the old school, a former diplomat, whose wife, Princess Victoria von Preussen, was one of Marthe's prewar friends. After looking into the matter von Preussen overruled Dr. Woolf; the hospital was to remain where it was. Dr. Woolf was incensed. A determined and vengeful man, he painstakingly built up a case against Marthe for "administrative transgressions." Taking advantage of von Preussen's absence in Berlin, Dr. Woolf obtained an order to arrest Marthe. She was to be deported to a camp in Bessarabia together with Elise Bratiano and two religious nurses on the staff. On March 15 a detachment of German military police stormed into the hospital; Marthe was ordered to retire to her room under guard and relinquish all hospital duties. Only the sudden return of von Preussen saved her from being deported to some distant village. Armed with a letter from the Kronprinz threatening local authorities with his displeasure, he arranged for Marthe to be interned at Mogosoëa while her request to rejoin her mother and daughter in Switzerland was processed.

There were emotional scenes during Marthe's farewell to her patients. She went around the soldiers' wards, slipping each man a gift of money, calm and smiling, trying to alleviate their distress. "No woman likes to watch grown men cry," she recalled. "These farewells affected me very much." Marthe herself ended by bursting into tears, while German officers looked embarrassed. Defiantly wearing her Red Cross uniform and escorted by her faithful maid Virginie, she was driven to the station under guard for the short train journey to Mogosoëa, where a couple of rooms had been made available for her by the German tenant.

Days went by, cut off from the world. Marthe learned of the Romanovs' abdication and the revolution in Petrograd, of the typhus epidemic in Jassy, where the King and the government had taken refuge. There was no news about George, nor did she expect any; the hero of the Ploesti raid had to remain out of sight.

Will they grant me permission to leave Romania? she wondered. Luck followed Marthe. In the freemasonry of the aristocratic European network, which even the war failed to disrupt, Count Czernin, her old friend and admirer, the former Austrian Minister to Bucharest, occupied a prominent position. He had just become Foreign Minister of the Austro-Hungarian Empire and it was to him that von Preussen addressed Marthe's request to leave for Switzerland.

Permission arrived on May 1; Marthe and the three Red Cross nuns she insisted on taking with her were issued permits to travel to Vienna. After the obligatory two-week quarantine in Bohemia they would be free to go on to Switzerland. Good as his word, Czernin even sent two officials to escort the party through the frontier. "The friendship of a great man is a gift from the gods," noted Marthe. She arrived in Vienna on May 3 and left almost immediately for the castle of Lautchin in Bohemia, the property of her friends the Thurn und Taxis family.

In the last week of May she arrived in Geneva, where Valentine and her mother had long been waiting.

✥

10

In Exile

The war changed Marthe, as it changed an entire generation of writers. She was deeply and permanently affected by the scenes she had witnessed at Hospital 118, by the deliriums, hallucinations and continual nightmares of the patients traumatized by shell shock, by the terror of those destined for an amputation and the madness and curious flights of fancy of the soldiers whose lives were drawing to a close. It was reality as seen by Rimbaud and Apollinaire—far away from the world of Proust, which now seemed to exist on a different planet. In her imagination, galvanized by the war, images of Romania were taking shape; she belonged there in her "land of the willows," of mountain streams and strange folk tales. She longed to be back in Posada among her own people and to share their suffering. As days went by, she came to resent her comfortable Swiss exile and the company of moneyed expatriates.

"We have three rooms on the fourth floor," Marthe wrote of her apartment in the Villa Rochefoucauld in Geneva. "My room is spacious with three windows, a view of the lake and landing quays. I have installed a vast working table facing the windows; I write all morning and throughout a good part of the afternoon. My new book is multicolored and quite different from anything I had written before. . . . Valentine and Miss Chatfield are in the adjoining room. . . . They dash in and out to tell me the day's news. Valentine has dispensed with her canary, which kept her company while she and Chatty were alone here. She says I provide enough entertainment to replace him. . . . Virginie, our maid, occupies the third room. She is Swiss, back in her own country, but she misses Mogosoëa and our life in Romania; she complains of the dull routine of our days. . . . The hotel is full of foreigners: there are Egyptian princes, South American diplomats, Russian aristocrats and a number of Russian government officials, unsure of their future and wondering how long their funds will last. Also a few Canadians, recuperating from wounds received on the battlefields of Flanders. In the evenings we dine among a forest of potted plants in the dining room with the orchestra playing 'neutral' tunes of indefinite provenance, so as not to offend anyone. It is all very dull and expensive and we try to keep within a budget. . . . No more hired cars or taxis. . . . For the first time in my life I have taken to using trams, which I find perfectly adequate and even exciting, as you never know where they will take you."

It was all a long way from Posada, from the old Baba Outza and her folk tales and the villagers Marthe left behind. Alighting from a train at the immaculate Montreux railway station one summer evening, she recalled with a sudden ache in her heart the local Comarnic railway stop near Posada, half station and half village market, where local girls in striped yellow-and-orange skirts ran along the trains offering fruit and flowers from the Valley of Prahova. At the first sign of spring came the snowdrops, like "little fingers of white wax peeking from among tender green shoots," then the violets, white or mauve, interspersed with hazel branches, gold-eyed narcissi followed by fragrant wheels of forget-me-nots interwoven with tiny branches of fir trees. In June, passengers on the Orient Express would be offered baskets of wild strawberries arranged in earthenware pots, covered with sage leaves. One used

to lift the leaves slightly and breathe in the incomparable aroma
of the fruit; later there would be garlands of cherries—black and
yellow, plaited like tresses—then raspberries picked on the mountain slopes and gathered in long cone-shaped baskets, woven out
of the branches of young willows. Later still, baskets of blackber-
ries would be brought to the travelers, and then the first hazelnuts
and mushrooms, ending with luscious red apples in October.
"They earned little, the girls of my village of Isvor," Marthe recalled. "They preferred to wander picking fruit in the woods,
weaving willow baskets by the stream, rather than work in some
dull factory in Comarnic. . . . I can still hear their laughter and
their chatter. Isvor was always alive—in tragedy or in joy—in all
seasons."

She dreamed of being back in Posada, waking up in the night,
listening to the patter of hundreds upon hundreds of sheep. It was
spring, the time of the annual migration of flocks from the plains
of the Danube delta, where they spent winters, to the high plateaus of the Carpathians for the summer. "The patter of their feet
was like rainfall," she recalled, "hitting the soil lightly, at regular
intervals. . . . A bleating sea coming down from the mountain at
great speed. . . . The dogs guarding our sheep look like wolves,
and rightly so, because they have to defend their charges against
them. The rams, walking ahead of the flock, are magnificent with
their aquiline profiles and spiral horns, like the figures reproduced
on antique vases; certain breeds have black faces, which gives
them an expression of diabolical cunning. . . . And the shepherds
. . . all our shepherds are handsome. At their passing women and
girls rush out of their houses to greet them. They wear hats of
caracul lamb in the shape of a tiara, floating felt capes, which are
impervious to rain; they carry crooks, like pastoral batons, and like
good pastors are often seen with a stray lamb draped round their
necks. To be a shepherd is a proud occupation in our country; it
goes back to ancient times, to the days of King Priam, whose three
sons were all shepherds. . . . They are like hermits, lost in the
desert marshes of the Danube delta throughout winter and on high
mountain plateaus in the summer, spending most of their lives
without seeing a human face or hearing a human voice, conversing

only with the ewes and deriving comfort from them. Music and song come to the rescue when melancholy becomes hard to bear. In a country where most children are born musicians the sound of the flute is ever present, but their songs are sad; it is the voice of the marshes, of the high mountains and of great distances."

Isvor: The Land of the Willow, Marthe's next book and her Romanian masterpiece written in Geneva, conveyed brilliantly the everyday life and customs of her people, the extraordinary mixture of superstition, childlike philosophy, resignation and hope, and the unending struggle between age-old pagan beliefs and Christian faith. In the early days of her marriage, old Baba Outza was her link with the villagers of Posada and her guide through the fantasy land of make-believe. Now memories came flooding back. "What is a Crasnic, Baba Outza?" Marthe used to ask. And Outza would solemnly explain that a Crasnic, which always looks like a black piglet but cries like a baby, is the product of a union between the devil and a woman (usually the wife of an Orthodox priest). Such a creature brings bad luck and must be immediately done away with; first roasted in the oven, then drowned in the river. A Crasnic is surprisingly agile, more than most piglets, and it is sometimes hard to catch, but misfortune will overtake the village unless it is quickly disposed of. Baba Outza had seen two Crasnics in her life and remembered that after one got away an earthquake immediately followed.

And the vampires? On the eve of the feast of St. George, the patron saint of the cows, the entire village keeps watch against the milk-sucking vampires, who come out of their lairs on that night and attack cows, goats and sheep, the wealth and livelihood of the peasant. "No one ever sees or hears them," Baba Outza used to tell Marthe. "They creep up and steal the 'manna' [the milk] of our animals, which as a result of their visitation go dry and become infertile. Neither prayer nor magic will keep a vampire away, though tall hedges of thorns might deter them."

There were flashes of wisdom in Outza's world of fairy tales, Marthe often thought, drawing analogies between the vampires and certain human beings on this earth, who are born evil and become destroyers of happiness. If one did not succeed in keeping out of their way one paid for it—every time—with much suffering.

"How well they walked, the girls of my village of Isvor," Marthe recalled, looking disapprovingly out her window at the passersby hurrying on the quay by the Lake of Geneva. "They walk tall and proud, used to carrying wooden pitchers of water on their heads from the river. 'My proud one' is the term of endearment from a boy to his girl in Romania. In England she would be 'my sweetheart,' in France he would be calling her '*ma belle*,' Italians would address her as '*mia bella*,' the Germans would call her '*mein Schatz*,' but it is only in Romania that the supreme compliment is '*mandra mia*'—'my proud one.'

"And proud they are the girls of the village of Isvor, proud of their youth, splendid bearing and dark beauty, short-lived like the flowers in the field before marriage, motherhood and hard work ruin their looks before their time. And how they dance! No one could forget the hora of Isvor!"

On May evenings, just before sunset was the hour of the hora, performed barefoot on the village green. The dance, in which only single people take part, is like a religious ritual, a kind of rhythmic invocation of love. There are two circles: men on the outside, women facing them on the inside, and the circles turn round and round; couples form, but the rondo goes on and on to the sound of cymbals and gypsy violins.

"I recall Profira—the Proud—Isvor's most beautiful girl, who arrived one night while the hora was in full swing. She turned up late, as was her due, for in the hearts of the village men she came first. For a time she stood on the edge of the circle looking on. How beautiful she was: dark-eyed and slender with her small pointed breasts under a finely woven shirt embroidered with silver and gold bird motifs, a crimson skirt, a bunch of lilac in her hair. She waited for the moment to join. Whom will she choose? In this dance it is the girls who decide on the man. Will she choose Ghitza, the shepherd—master player of the flute? Or Ion, the carpenter's son, rich and handsome, or Nicholas, the soldier, smart in his military uniform, or Petar Comana, the village dandy, who wears his hat at a rakish angle? Profira enters the circle; the music surges; she lightly taps the shoulder of Dragomir, Outza's nephew;

twice round and round, holding hands; the music now becomes solemn and sweet; they leave together and are seen walking toward the bank of the river."

Writing *Isvor*, moving between the reminiscent and the legendary, isolated Marthe from events. But there was no getting away from the fact that she was living in historic times and the news intruded. On August 13 she heard that the Tsar and his family had been moved from the palace of Tsarskoe Selo to Tobolsk in distant Siberia. Kerensky, the liberal but powerless Prime Minister, was about to be overthrown by the Bolsheviks led by Lenin and Trotsky. News from Romania was tragic. Romanian soldiers, recently armed and trained by the French, fought brilliantly against the combined forces of Germany and Austria, but had to abandon hard-won gains to send reinforcements to the north, where their so-called Russian allies, prey to Bolshevik propaganda urging immediate peace, had stopped fighting. In the face of the Russian collapse Romania was left undefended. At Jassy, the provisional capital, King Ferdinand and Queen Marie feared they might be taken prisoner and were looking for ways to fight their way out through enemy lines. "Misfortune pursues us; we can be invaded in a few days—the Russians have cut our throats," Queen Marie recorded in her diary.

And George? He was at Headquarters in Jassy; what would happen to him?

But bad news was to strike closer to her temporary home. On August 27, while Marthe, anxious to escape the "stifling" atmosphere of Geneva, was spending a week in St. Moritz with her daughter, a telegram arrived from Antoine: "Emmanuel died yesterday—I have lost everything." It was a cry of despair, without explanation or details. She later learned that he had hanged himself on a curtain loop at a house in Marlow, near London, on the afternoon of August 22. It was a shattering blow. The beautiful, enigmatic Emmanuel of the days of *Les Huit Paradis* and Isfahan was the first man she had loved, who later became a close friend; he was her youth. She had worried about him since he returned from Japan, much altered, three years before. Always mysterious, he had kept the nature of his illness a secret, gradually withdrawing from the world. (Emmanuel had creeping paralysis.) He even refused to accompany Antoine on a visit to Proust, much to the latter's chagrin.

Marthe's first impulse on hearing the news was to be with Antoine. She knew what Emmanuel meant to him. Lighthearted about love between himself and women, Antoine had loved his brother with a "losing frenzy"; losing, because he knew that Emmanuel would one day escape his surveillance and "win." But there was a war on and travel to London was out of the question. All Marthe could do was send her beloved cousin a long telegram expressing her boundless affection. She decided to leave St. Moritz the next day, as "I could not bear to remain any longer in the place where I heard this terrible news."

In November came the long-awaited letter from George. It described the horrors of Jassy and the desperate situation in Romania. He was naturally critical of the Allies, who had encouraged the Romanians to enter the conflict but failed to assist them materially. The tone of his letter to Marthe was affectionate and there was a separate page for Valentine, full of amusing drawings and snatches of verse. The child, who adored her father, was elated. The letter also mentioned the arrival of a handful of soldiers from Marthe's former Hospital 118. "They were full of praise and admiration for you," George related. "Their testimony, much discussed in Jassy, gave me pleasure."

Her husband's letter did much to restore Marthe's spirits, undermined a few days before by a six-page communication from Queen Marie, which sent her into a paroxysm of fury and indignation. Its arrival is noted in her diary by a series of exclamation marks interspersed with angry comments. "Crownie," as Marthe referred to the Queen in her notes, wrote in English in a mood of "unabashed immodesty." After dwelling at length on her charity work in the field and how much she was "loved by the Army for her courage," she talked about her newly discovered passion for writing, which resulted in two volumes of war memoirs, currently being serialized in England and the United States. She then came

to the core of her letter—the question of Marthe's alleged cooperation with the enemy. "A certain amount of indignation was
raised by the fact that you owed your evacuation from Bucharest
to a special favor, and especially the fact that you spent your 'quarantine' in the house of a wealthy enemy," referring to Marthe's
stay at the Thurn und Taxis castle in Bohemia. "Personally I cannot judge your actions from so far," the Queen continued, "but I
simply do not understand what made you accept an enemy's hospitality. Towards all of us here it did put you into a difficult
position, therefore I cannot encourage you to come back, whilst
people are feeling thus towards you. . . . Also, as you may have
heard from George, the conditions of housing in Jassy are incredibly difficult."

Marthe's answer is a model of dignified calm. She contemp-
tuously rejects accusations made against her by court gossips in
Jassy and reminds the Queen of her work in Hospital 118, "where
it was my duty to remain," and quietly lists the numbers of Romanian prisoners of war freed through her intervention. She also
points out that the decision was taken out of her hands by the
closing of the military hospital where she worked, her arrest and
the subsequent order of expulsion. Furthermore, she chose to
spend the obligatory "quarantine" in secluded Bohemia on the
estate of a member of an international family, far away from "contacts with the enemy."

Opinion was to veer again in Marthe's favor in the course of
the next year, when more and more prisoners of war and former
patients drifted back and testified on her behalf, but relations between the two women—though later cordial—never fully recovered from the effects of these wartime accusations. The same
stories, fanned by gossip from Helen Vacaresco and Anna de Noailles, soon reached Paris, creating an atmosphere of hostility toward
Marthe. "I warn you they are on the rampage," the Abbé Mugnier
wrote from Paris. "I advise you to forgo your visit for the time
being. It is all most unfair . . . and it will change."

Dear Abbé Mugnier! How Marthe wished he could be at her
side in Geneva! She felt very much unprotected and alone; there
was hardly anyone she could talk to. Her mother, more and more

immersed in her own world, was no help; there had been no news from Christopher Birdwood Thomson since he left on a military mission to Palestine earlier that year; Charles-Louis was in Madrid, and war had somehow disrupted their close relationship. She missed Emmanuel and Antoine. Only writing was left. "I suffer from these accusations, but I slip my contempt under my pillow and sleep on it, dreaming of the book I am writing."

In the West the war seemed to be dragging on and the slaughter in Flanders continued. "France is tired," Marthe noted in her diary, "but we are coming on slowly but surely, 'inch by inch' as Antoine has predicted. The burden now rests on the shoulders of Great Britain, France and the United States."

A week later Marthe received a letter from the Kronprinz, stationed with the German Headquarters in Flanders. Coming, ironically, so soon after Queen Marie's letter, she found it unwelcome, even embarrassing. Her "admirer" assured her of his continuous devotion—"no war could ever destroy it"—complained that America's entry into the conflict would only prolong that "bloody struggle we are bound to win in the end" and told her, with a schoolboy's naïveté, that he was doing everything possible to be kind to the French population in occupied territories, so "they will keep *un bon souvenir* of us Germans and myself in particular."

In mid-November she heard that on November 6 Lenin and his followers had overthrown the Provisional Government in Petrograd, were negotiating peace terms with the Germans and were threatening to imprison the Romanian government and the royal family if they did not agree to lay down their arms. "What will happen in Jassy?" That Sunday both mother and daughter went to church to pray for husband and father's safety.

It was now obvious that Romania must soon capitulate, for its effective participation in World War I had ceased with the collapse of the Russian armies and the Allies' inability to send reinforcements. The country was like an island surrounded on all sides by the enemy: Austrians and Germans to the north and west, Bulgarians and Turks to the south. Remarkably enough, the Romanian peasants did not succumb to the Russian revolutionary propaganda; they remained faithful, encouraged by King Ferdinand's promises of agrarian reform and Queen Marie's popularity. As the peace negotiations between Russia and the Central Powers opened in Brest Litovsk—with Trotsky representing the Bolsheviks—and as the German pressure increased, Romania was finally forced to lay down its arms. On December 9 an armistice was signed with the Central Powers; fighting ceased, but the country was at the mercy of its occupiers. The Allied military missions departed, the enemy took over the telephone and the telegraph, the royal family was forced into isolation and the Romanian oil fields were turned over to an Austro-German company. For the next seven months, until the tide of victory was reversed, an iron curtain separated Romania from the rest of the world.

Marthe spent the remaining days of 1917 in Lausanne with her mother and the now fourteen-year-old Valentine, working on the Committee for Aid to Romanian Prisoners of War, which she founded that year. The family spent a subdued Christmas in Lausanne. Though the jewels she had sent to Ambassador Paléologue for safekeeping two years before were returned to her in December, Marthe worried about the family's finances, as the war seemed to be dragging on indefinitely.

The beginning of 1918 coincided with the onset of a deep depression for Marthe. Writing *Isvor*, which until recently she had relished, suddenly ceased to interest her. She kept on with her work routine, however—three or four hours each morning—but she found the results unsatisfactory. She was drained by constant quarrels with her mother, whose mood oscillated alarmingly from day to day. To add to the complications in her life, Marguerite, her twenty-one-year-old sister, who had recently returned from London, where she had been working for the International Red Cross, became infatuated with a young Englishman in Geneva, who, it appeared, had no desire to marry her. Impetuous and self-willed, dependent on Marthe for money, Marguerite strained at the leash, resented her sister's advice and made herself as unpleasant as possible. And yet they loved each other very deeply. Their complex relationship was later described by Marthe in *Le Perroquet Vert* (*The Green Parrot*), the most autobiographical of her books.

On April 4, 1918, after a shopping expedition in Montreux, and as Marthe, her mother and her other sister,* Madeleine Quaranta, were preparing to have lunch at the hotel, Marguerite quietly went up to her room and shot herself. It was a devastating blow for Marthe; Marguerite, ten years younger, had been her favorite sister, more like a daughter, in fact. They resembled each other: both red-blond and rosy, unlike the rest of the family, who were dark. Marguerite had Marthe's hair and eyes with the long, curly lashes. As Marthe grew up and married, Marguerite inherited her room in the family house, her textbooks and her governess. She was like a replica of Marthe at her age: a mirror that revealed the changing image of her past.

Marguerite was buried in the cemetery at Clarens, above Montreux; Marthe retired to the solitude of a convent, from where she dispatched a desperate letter to the Abbé Mugnier in which she brooded over the family's tendency to suicide. The Abbé hastened to answer: "I beg of you to remain on this earth. You are needed to record its tribulations."

It took time for *Isvor* to reclaim her, but Marthe did go back to work, inspired by a travel memoir, *Reminiscences from Romania*, which she came across in a Lausanne bookshop. The book was immensely evocative; suddenly the Valley of Prahova rose before her and the full panoply of its spring rites; familiar colors and smells assailed her. The writer's block disappeared; *Isvor* won.

Throughout the spring and summer of 1918 Marthe worked quietly in Switzerland. The war was slowly drawing to a close and cautious hopes of Allied victory were filtering through to the neutral Swiss press. For the time being, however, Romania remained isolated. Only occasional, brief, but affectionate messages from George managed to get through the German censor to Geneva. Queen Marie, however, in her own spectacular gestures of defiance, contrived to send out dramatic messages to the president of the American Red Cross and to "cousin Georgie" (King George V of England), begging them not to forget Romania and her royal family, whom the Germans "are so anxious to depose." The Ger-

---

* Two more sisters were born after George's death, Madeleine in 1893, Marguerite in 1897. And all in all, there were three Lahovary girls, but Jeanne died before 1914.

mans saw to it that she never got an answer. Had the Queen been able to peer into the future, she would have been much comforted to know that before the end of the year the Hohenzollern Reich would collapse; Kaiser Wilhelm would abdicate and flee to Holland, leaving her husband the only Hohenzollern left on a throne.

As the day of Allied victory drew near, the German armies occupying Romania began to retreat. It was the moment for King Ferdinand to proclaim universal suffrage and land reform. Then, in early November, a few days before the Armistice, the King ordered the "remobilization" of his Army, disbanded a year before; he gave the Germans twenty-four hours to leave the country.

The war was over.

꧁✦꧂

A New World

*M*arthe's diaries for the latter part of 1918 are sketchy, but judging from her letters to Antoine she was back in Romania in mid-November, as soon as a modicum of train service was restored. Leaving Valentine and her governess in Geneva for the time being, accompanied only by the intrepid Virginie, she arrived in devastated Bucharest after a journey lasting more than three days. Not knowing what she would find at Mogosoëa, she went straight to her Bucharest house in the Chaussée Kisselev, badly pillaged and freezing, but livable, where she was joyously greeted by the servants. Next morning, as she was sitting in bed sipping a cup of ersatz coffee, a change from her luxurious Geneva breakfasts, and listening to the woeful tales of the cook, the door opened and in walked her husband, George—cheerful, fit, slightly thinner, but with the same old swagger about him. Alerted by the telegram she had sent from the border, he had managed to drive to Bucharest from the Military HQ in Jassy, a lengthy and difficult journey, as the Germans had blown up most of the bridges near the capital. Almost two years had passed since they parted, since George had heroically destroyed the Ploesti oil fields with Thomson's help.

It was an affectionate reunion. He thought his wife looked "beautiful and serene"; Marthe in turn was immensely reassured to see him. It did not take George long to confess that he had just acquired a new mistress, called by the improbable name of "Gongu," which threw Marthe into paroxysms of laughter. She had been expecting news from that quarter, and it did not diminish her affection for her errant husband; the war had—if anything—enhanced his energy and old attitude of *carpe diem* she knew so well. "She takes a lot of my time," George remarked of his mistress; then, turning to Marthe, he announced, "*Mais je t'aime bien quand même toi tu le sais*" ("But I also like you very much, as you know well"). "And so we were exactly where we left off when the war started," a resigned Marthe reported to the Abbé Mugnier.

In spite of Gongu, who fortuitously was residing in Jassy at the moment, husband and wife planned together how to rescue the family fortune. Its basis was the cement factory at Comarnic, near Posada; it had been run by a German administrator, who had now fled, and it was essential that it be reactivated as soon as possible. They drove up to Mogosoëa in George's battered military vehicle and found it "habitable." The German farmer who had lived there (the one who had brought Marthe azaleas from her own hothouse as a present when she was at the military hospital) obviously loved the place, which did not, however, prevent him from stripping the house of most of its furniture. But Marthe's bed with the baldachin, obviously too heavy to remove, was still there and so were a supply of linen and some china and kitchen utensils. She decided that as soon as fuel became available, she would move to Mogosoëa and camp out there, where it would be easier to supervise the gradual rebuilding of the beloved house. As George had to return to Jassy the next day, she remained in Bucharest to await the sovereigns' triumphal reentry into the capital.

December 1, 1918, a day of low clouds and intermittent snow flurries, was indeed a memorable day for the royal couple of Romania and their subjects. After two terrible years of occupation,

Romania emerged from the war doubled in size with a population of 16 million; four new provinces were added to the realm, including the beloved Transylvania, which had been annexed after the collapse of the Austro-Hungarian Empire. As she watched the colorful procession winding down the Chaussée Kisselev, Marthe's thoughts went to King Ferdinand, her old friend, who a few days before had sent her a reassuring "welcome home" note and expressed his desire to see her shortly. She rejoiced in Ferdinand's hour of triumph. More than most people, she knew what it had cost him—a Hohenzollern—to wage war against Germany. His brother and the rest of the family he so loved declared him a traitor; the German Emperor took away his decorations and struck his name from the family tree; he had gone through personal hell for Romania. And now here he was, two years later, the only Hohenzollern left on a throne—wildly cheered by his subjects, proceeding in triumph through the streets of his capital, decked with national flags, interspersed with the Stars and Stripes, the Union Jack and the French Tricolor. At his side rode the Queen. Marthe, whose personal anger at Crownie had not abated, nevertheless had to admit that Queen Marie looked superb. Mounted on a splendid gray horse, which she rode with expert grace, dressed in a military tunic, a fur-lined cape and a gray astrakhan bonnet, tied under the chin, holding a bouquet of yellow chrysanthemums, her beautiful face wreathed in smiles, she radiated happiness. Flanked by General Berthelot, the French Chief of Mission, who reorganized the Romanian Army during the war, and Prince Nicholas, the younger son, followed by their daughters in a carriage drawn by four horses, accompanied by dozens of generals and officers of the staff, the sovereigns advanced under Marthe's windows, down the Chaussée and into Calea Victoriei to the Metropolitan Cathedral for a thanksgiving service. It had been a great day for Marthe as well as for the royal couple; after almost two years of exile from Bucharest they had come home.

"My dear Marthe," wrote King Ferdinand, "it is good you are back. . . . The malicious gossip spread at Jassy was an aberration, which I deplore. When I tried to defend you, it was said that I was being partial . . . I know about your work at Hospital 118 and with the prisoners of war and I commend you for it."

Royal favor was one thing, but feminine jealousy was another. Though Marthe's immediate family welcomed her, most of the former Bucharest beau monde was hostile, accusing her of committing treason by spending the required "quarantine time" in enemy-occupied Bohemia while the war was still going on. As if Marthe had had any choice in the matter! And though she had now lived with these accusations for several months, they continued to hurt every time a poisoned dart flew in her direction. During those painful days Marthe found unexpected support in her husband. "They'll forget and move on to other things," George assured her. "I give it a few weeks; after that you will not be news anymore." He was right. By the end of the year all topics of conversation were pushed into the background due to Crown Prince Carol's conduct. It was now public knowledge that Queen Marie and King Ferdinand's willful and undisciplined eldest son had deserted his regiment in wartime to marry (with the connivance of the German military authorities) a young Romanian girl—a commoner—named Zizi Lambrino, had sired a son and had applied to renounce his succession to the throne. (The marriage was rapidly declared unconstitutional by the courts and annulled, making the child illegitimate.) For Ferdinand and Marie, celebrating the triumphal end of the war, the affair was a devastating blow, undermining the foundations of the monarchy. For Marthe it was not a surprise. She had always been critical of the Queen's educational methods, "the inevitable result of the sort of permissive upbringing the boy received," she declared.

Now that peace had arrived Marthe was able to resume her correspondence with Antoine, who was in London. Everything in Romania reminded her of the brothers; she could not get used to Emmanuel's absence and missed him more than ever before. She also longed to see Antoine again, look out of his windows at the Thames, hear his acerbic comments on life and take part in the wide, cosmopolitan world he inhabited. Marthe wondered why he had not answered her letters. She was soon to find out. On February 9, 1919, while Marthe and George were entertaining guests at their Bucharest house, a message came from Prince Stirbey. He had just heard from London that Antoine was about to announce his engagement to Elizabeth Asquith, the daughter of former British Prime Minister Herbert Asquith and the formidable Margot Asquith. It was quite a sensation. Marthe had never met Elizabeth, but she recalled vividly a conversation with Emmanuel two years before. At that time Antoine had barely met his present fiancée, but Emmanuel, an admirer of Margot, had told Marthe, "She is a bit like her mother; she would be able to cope with you and Anna de Noailles if she ever became part of the family."

A telegram of congratulations was dispatched to Antoine and an enthusiastic letter to Elizabeth, welcoming her into the family, was sent through the diplomatic post, as ordinary mails were still uncertain. Marthe was pleased. "Let me know immediately the date of the wedding and whether you want George and me as your witnesses and Valentine as your bridesmaid," she cabled. The answer to both questions was "yes," and Marthe began her preparations to travel to London via Paris. It was the very change that she needed and the kind of grand marriage of which she approved.

Marthe arrived at her apartment at 71, Faubourg St. Honoré in Paris in late March, but stayed only long enough to get clothes; she had to replace her prewar outfits to shine at her favorite cousin's wedding. She saw the Abbé Mugnier and probably Ambassador Paléologue; the others could wait until her return from London in late April. Being back in Paris was happiness; she walked for miles, revisiting the familiar sights, reliving her memories. It was in this mood of euphoria that she answered a call from Queen Marie requesting her to visit her at the Ritz, where she was installed with her daughters. Queen Marie was in Paris as the official representative to plead the cause of Romania with the Peace Conference delegates. Romania's territorial expansion was in danger of not being approved by the Supreme Council, and Queen Marie was dispatched, as a measure of last resort, to "try her philtres" on old Clemenceau and Lloyd George. It was the sort of assignment the Queen relished, and so far her lobbying had turned out to be very successful. It was said that Clemenceau had fallen under her spell and completely reversed his stand on awarding Romania the province of Banat since the Queen had given "a face to her country." In the midst of her triumphs it occurred to Queen Marie that Marthe, so familiar with the French political scene, might have some grains of experience to contribute. Marthe's reference to their meeting is very brief: "Crownie dressed in new Parisian clothes, imbued with self-importance, looked beautiful—and different from the woman I used to see back home. I warned her that Allied statesmen, and particularly the English, are not very well up on the geography of the Balkans, hence false impressions arise." She thought the Queen had been well coached by Bratiano and would do well.

There might have been traces of Marthe's own coaching in Queen Marie's subsequent talk with Clemenceau, when she asked him about the province of the Banat. "Your Majesty wants all of it up to the river Tisza? But this is the lion's share—impossible!" exclaimed the French Prime Minister. "That's why I came to the Tiger to ask for it," answered the Queen. Romania got the Banat province.

Antoine's marriage to Elizabeth Asquith was the high point of that year's London social season. Celebrated on April 28 at St. Margaret's, Westminster, it was attended by Queen Alexandra and the entire roster of distinguished personalities from England's political and social life, including George Bernard Shaw. Herbert Henry Asquith, who had been Prime Minister for over ten years until he was replaced by Lloyd George, was still one of England's most beloved statesmen. "It was raining as we came out of St. Margaret's after the wedding," recalls Marthe. "The first car in front of the steps was Asquith's; he took me by the arm and swiftly shepherded me in to protect me from the rain and the crowds. Mrs. Asquith and two of the bridesmaids joined us. As the car started, a cheer rose from the multitude massed in front of the church—a spontaneous acclamation from the people for their old chief on a day so emotional for most fathers. I found it touching."

Gossip had it that the Asquiths had misgivings about marrying their daughter to a diplomat from a faraway country, and a well-known seducer. But Elizabeth was in love, and Antoine's charm, looks and intelligence won the day; he was also supposed to be very rich, as indeed he was at the time. "I understand that you have substantial landholdings in Romania," Herbert Asquith is reputed to have inquired of his prospective son-in-law. Antoine cogitated for a moment and then said, "Yes—just to give you an idea—the Orient Express takes a day to go through *me*."

Though George soon became bored with the unending round of festivities and left for home, Marthe enjoyed her visit to England, which seemed to her totally untouched by the war. "No one here talks of the conference at Versailles—such a relief," she wrote to the Abbé Mugnier from London. She stayed with the Asquiths at the Wharf, their country residence near Oxford; Asquith himself, with whom she struck up an immediate friendship, based on their mutual love of history, took her on a tour of Oxford and conducted her around his old college, Balliol. On her last night in London the Asquiths took her to the Coliseum to see the Diaghilev ballets, of which Margot Asquith had become an enthusiastic promoter.

Marthe bade farewell to London with regret, but the Paris to which she returned in late May was the center of the political universe. All the representatives of the victorious nations had gathered there to sort out the ruins and the war's carnage and attempt to rebuild a world that lay in fragments. The task was formidable. Out of a total of 65 million men mobilized in the war, 8 million were dead; 20 million were wounded; millions of civilians had been killed or mutilated; thousands upon thousands of farms and dwellings had been devastated and runaway inflation was destroying the countries of Central and Eastern Europe. Four great empires had fallen: the German, Austro-Hungarian, Russian and Ottoman Turk. It was their collapse that caused the political drama being presently enacted at Versailles.

The United States was represented by President Woodrow Wilson, billed as "the savior of the civilized world." Marthe, who keenly followed the newspapers, decided that he looked and dressed "like a Presbyterian minister with a three-piece suit, firmly buttoned, silver-rimmed pince-nez and a ready-made toothy smile." She admired Clemenceau, whom she had met in Paris many times. Prime Minister Clemenceau was a short, powerful man with a solid square body, short legs, a barrel chest, prominent high cheekbones, dark eyes, a gray mustache, short neck and rounded shoulders; now seventy-eight, he had been known for decades in French politics for his fierce patriotism and single-mindedness.

"You will be meeting Lloyd George in Paris," Henry Asquith told Marthe when she was staying with them at their country place near Oxford. "Yes, and he is enormously proud of his large head," chimed in one of his political opponents.* The British Prime Minister, as Marthe was shortly to see, had indeed a large head and a great shock of white hair that he wore in a flowing mane, which fell below his collar. Quicksilver sprang to her mind when she later thought to characterize him, for he was shrewd and witty at the dinner table and she imagined that he would be a quick and ruthless opponent in debates.

Besides the heads of state and armies of frock-coated officials who accompanied them, the generals, maharajahs, gossip columnists, representatives of the arts and social matrons had also returned to Paris and were now keenly stalking celebrities to adorn their salons. Everybody was there from Walter Lippmann to Sarah Bernhardt—now old and grotesque in a golden wig—to Ho Chi Minh, working as a pastry cook in a Paris restaurant and vainly trying to obtain an audience with Clemenceau.

Among the British delegates to the Versailles Peace Conference there was one of particular interest to Marthe: Christopher Birdwood Thomson, fresh from his successful mission in Palestine. He was now a brigadier, decorated for his services in the Middle East and considered a "high flyer" by his superiors. Marthe had last heard from him just before she left Geneva for Bucharest. They had not seen each other for two and a half years.

"Smaranda has arrived," Thomson noted in his diary. "She is looking lovelier than ever. Paris agrees with her; it is her spiritual home and she loves every inch of it, especially the part around the

---

* Lloyd George liked to measure his contemporaries by the size of their heads. He dismissed Neville Chamberlain, for example, as "a pinhead."

Cathedral of Notre Dame. I don't think that by nature I am a jealous man—and I am not of other men, of whom there seem to be many around Smaranda. By the grace of God she enjoys my conversation, for she has got that supreme ability of drawing out the best I have; we get on fine as long as we are alone together. But here in Paris I sometimes feel like an accessory, not a presence; indeed my predicament is painful."

Poor Thomson. His attempts to recapture the intimate relationship they enjoyed in wartime Bucharest were doomed to failure. Paris in the spring of 1919 was an incredibly exciting place to be in and Marthe was in her element. She moved from one distinguished gathering to another, lunching with British Foreign Secretary Arthur Balfour on one day, seeing her old friends Aristide Briand and Raymond Poincaré on another, discussing the future with Maynard Keynes, dining with the painter Vuillard or sipping tea at the Ritz with Marcel Proust and his latest admirer, Harold Nicolson. Her schedule was indeed crowded, as Thomson rightly complained; what he did not realize, however, was that his most serious rival for Marthe's time was Charles-Louis de Beauvau-Craon, who had recently returned to Paris from Madrid.

After serving on the Western Front for two years, Charles-Louis spent the rest of the war in Madrid, where he served as military attaché. Gossip had it that he had formed a "close friendship" with Queen Ena, wife of the reigning monarch, Alfonso XIII. Whatever the truth of the rumor, the intimate link between him and Marthe had been weakened—a casualty of the war. Like many men before him, who had survived the horrors of trench warfare, Charles-Louis now felt a desire to settle down to domestic life and a family. He was approaching forty and since his return to France had again come under the influence of his mother, who insisted it was "the very last moment" to get married and produce the long-awaited son and heir. Recently, while visiting friends in Bologna, he met Maria Gregorini, an attractive, wellborn girl of twenty-three, who to his astonishment and pleasure fell for him. Yet Marthe still mattered; she had been the axis around which his life had revolved all these years; it was a past that he cherished and always would. But where in it was his future?

We will never know what transpired that May evening when they met alone at 71, Faubourg St. Honoré, the apartment which held so many memories of their love. Marthe makes no mention of it in her diary; she simply records "a long meeting"; nor did she write about it to the Abbé Mugnier, which is surprising. We do know that she continued to meet Charles-Louis at social functions in Paris, but a decision had been made and this time there was no going back. Ten months later, on March 27, 1920, Charles-Louis married Maria Gregorini in Bologna.

No one seeing Marthe in those days, as she shone on the Paris social scene, would have guessed that she was undergoing emotional turmoil. In the course of the following years she often tried to convince herself that "perhaps she had never loved Charles-Louis," that what she had loved in him was France, which for her he personified. But Charles-Louis would not go away. Many years later, one July evening in Paris, she heard under her window on the Quay a long-forgotten song. "Charles-Louis came back to me that evening," she wrote, "and I realized what so many of my friends had always known, that he was my *real* love and that he—in turn—never got over the loss of me."

On Saturday, June 28, 1919, Marthe was lunching with Antoine and his bride, Elizabeth Bibesco, in Antoine's Ile St. Louis apartment, when they heard cannons boom. Peace had been signed in the Galerie des Glaces at Versailles. "*C'est fait—ils ont signé*," exclaimed Antoine. "I regret it," said a journalist friend, Joseph Reinach. "It is a bad treaty—vindictive and a prelude to the next war." He was voicing the prevalent feeling of the time. Christopher Thomson, who also was present, shared the general unease. And so did Marthe. She was too European and too loyal to rejoice in the humiliation of her many friends now among the vanquished. She thought of William, the Kronprinz, exiled to a little village in Holland, separated from his wife and three children, "depressed and dying of boredom here among the fishermen," and of Ottokar Count Czernin, the delightful and brilliant "Kerry," the former Austrian Minister in Bucharest and then powerful Minister of Foreign Affairs of the Austro-Hungarian Empire, who wrote to Marthe, "I live in hiding in Vienna, for I am unpopular with the masses, who only two years ago worshipped me. Since the dismemberment of Austria, Bohemia, where my home is, has become part of the new state of Czechoslovakia. All my properties have been confiscated. . . . I have nothing and am not even allowed to return home. But I have six children and I must fight. . . . At this moment everything depends on Great Britain. If the British government indicated to Prague that their conduct toward me makes a bad impression in London, the Czech government would listen and I might be allowed to keep my fortune, or part of it."

The letter upset Marthe, for she knew that there was little she could do to help her old friend. A word with Balfour or Churchill in London? They would listen politely and express their regret, but now that the treaty had been signed they certainly would not intervene. She recalled the words of Izvolsky, the former Russian Ambassador to Paris: "To abolish the Austro-Hungarian Empire would be like breaking a beautiful piece of machinery."

As always in moments of stress, Marthe found release in her writing. *Isvor* was almost completed, but it needed some finishing touches. Suddenly she felt a desire to leave Paris, to get out of the social whirl, made even more intense by the presence of Antoine and Elizabeth Bibesco, inveterate partygoers. The weather was getting hot and Valentine needed a holiday from her lessons. On July 27 she left Paris accompanied by Valentine and her new governess, Mademoiselle Viaud. They traveled through Orléans and Le Mans to Trestrignel, a small resort town on the Brittany coast, where Marthe rented a simple, unpretentious villa overlooking the Atlantic Ocean. She remained there for five weeks, writing, walking and resting. In mid-August, Christopher Thomson arrived, taking rooms in an adjoining hotel. He too was working on a book, *Old Europe's Suicide*; it was laden with doom and was to express his misgivings about the Treaty of Versailles and the dire consequences that would follow.

Thomson too was undergoing an emotional struggle, for he had come to a decision that would change the direction of his entire life. At the age of forty-five, having spent the preceding twenty-eight years as a soldier, he planned to retire from the Army and enter the political scene in England as parliamentary candidate for

Labor. Having witnessed the horrors of war, distrusting the politicians, who had just concluded what—to him—was a disastrous peace treaty, he was attracted to what he called "the Messianic side" of the Labor movement. It was a brave choice—even more so as he must have realized that by joining Labor he would be distancing himself from Marthe and her world. "Smaranda was surprised," he notes in his book of reminiscences. "She had hoped that I would end up as a successful general, one of the heroes of the war; it will—I am afraid—require an effort on her part to remain a loyal friend if I turn out to be a failure in politics."

Marthe returned to Paris on September 11 to welcome her new "cousins" the Asquiths, with whom she was going to visit Venice and Ravenna. After bidding them farewell in Venice, Marthe boarded the inevitable Orient Express and arrived in Romania at the end of September. She was glad to be back in her "land of the willows." It was autumn, the willows in Posada were turning gray, but the Carpathian hillside was a riot of color. Garlands of red peppers, hung to dry, decorated every house in the village; wooden carts, drawn by oxen, filled with corn, squeaked up the hill. The harvest festival was in full swing. In the Valley of Prahova, autumn is the most beautiful season of all and it lasts longer than either the spring or the summer. The days are of brilliant sunshine and blue skies; at night a huge white moon hangs over the mountains, making it as clear as day. It is an age-old custom in the villages to lend one's labor to a neighbor, who in exchange pays for music and drink. Marthe recalled one such gathering. "Baba Outza told me that, as it was full moon, they would be shucking corn at Anika's house this evening. I went off quietly and stood by the wall to watch them. They were sitting in a circle, boys and girls around a huge mountain of corn, pulling off leaves and roots and singing the old traditional songs of Wallachia. Two swarthy tziganes—one with a violin, the other with a guitar—accompanied them, adding on improvised ditties:

I'll marry you, Kiva, my darling, but you must wait.
Oh, oh, when will it be?

Oh, not before a fox in velvet slippers is put in charge of
  the geese,
Not before the blind hare agrees to count the grains of
  the corn;
Not before duck perch in the trees, or turkeys swim;
Yes, I'll marry you when the willows bear apples and
  poplars bloom with violets.

"It was a jolly gathering held under the full moon; wine and
local brandy flowed, all paid for by the owner of the corn plot.
This is the way of life in our country—labor in exchange for laughter, music and drink."

A few days later Marthe was sitting on the terrace at Mogosoëa,
basking in the autumn sunshine, watching a couple of black swans
on the lake, when her husband's white Mercedes came roaring up
the drive. George, handsome in his elegant London clothes, sporting a panama hat they recently bought together in London's St.
James's Street, greeted her affectionately, but appeared decidedly
uncomfortable. "I have come to ask you for a divorce," he announced as soon as he settled down in a chair. "*She* [Gongu, his
mistress] insists on marriage; otherwise she will leave me. Of
course I like you too, but not enough to spend the rest of my life
with you." He offered "a river of money" as a settlement.

"So like George," Marthe wrote to the Abbé Mugnier that
evening. "Ever since the day he was born he has been spoiled
and indulged by his doting parents; he believed that it was enough
for him to exist to be loved; it never occurred to him to give
anything of himself in return. Adored by women, he spent money
on them, but was incapable of returning their love. Young, handsome, scion of a great family, he was perpetually searching and
getting frustrated. . . . 'You must forgive me,' his mother once said,
'I brought him up very badly'; she then made me promise not to
leave him."

Supported by Antoine, advised by Elise Bratiano and Jon Duca,
a Romanian statesman and friend of George's, and with the authority of Barbo Stirbey behind her, Marthe refused to grant a
divorce. "It is for your own good," George's friends explained to

him; "the lady in question is a figure of fun in Bucharest—she does not even know how to spell in French—and would render you ridiculous." They pointed out that divorce would be a disaster for their daughter and might interfere with her marriage prospects. It was also well known that his mother had extracted a promise from Marthe on her deathbed that she would never leave him: her wishes should be respected. In Bucharest's easygoing society, divorce was certainly not a problem and George was taken aback by the powerful allies his wife had marshaled. When he counterattacked, citing her affair with Beauvau-Craon, he was briskly reminded by Marthe's lawyer that he had written a number of affectionate letters to his wife during the war years and had been seen frequently with her ever since. It would be useless, therefore, to bring up Charles-Louis; George would only put himself in the humiliating position of a cuckold. "Why insist?" Prince Barbo Stirbey told him. "You will only stir up a lot of dirt, make lawyers rich, and the result will be nil." "I have been fighting all those weeks," Marthe wrote to the Abbé in November. "But it now looks as if I have circumnavigated the 'Cape of Storms'; victory appears on the horizon."

George, feeling that he had been vanquished, pretended to commit suicide, shooting himself through the sleeve of his coat, a farcical gesture he later explained as an accident that occurred while he was cleaning his gun in preparation for a pheasant shoot. The divorce drama was over. To placate his inconsolable mistress, George dispatched her to Paris with a fat check to buy clothes— "a trousseau for which she would have no use," Marthe commented.

The whole drama, in spite of its comical overtones, resulted in strengthening the marriage. From then on there would be no more question of a divorce. Marthe and George continued to lead separate lives, but a constant bond of affection remained between them.

The year ended in relative peace; Marthe, though shaken, went back to her writing and the task of rebuilding Mogosoëa.

12

❧❦❧

Fame

*T*he twenties were a good period for Marthe. She finally
achieved what she had dreamt of since the days of *Les Huit
Paradis*, universal recognition as a distinguished writer. First *Alexandre Asiatique*, then *Isvor*, then *Le Perroquet Vert* and finally *Catherine Paris* met with wide acclaim and not only brought financial
independence but made her rich. Just as well, for Mogosoëa, the
"dream palace," was turning out to be an insatiable consumer of
funds. At the same time Marthe was rebuilding Posada, destroyed
in the 1915 fire, the origins of which remained mysterious. An
admirer of the English country style, she proceeded to turn the
Posada staff quarters into a rather grand cottagelike dwelling with
colorful linen chintz, comfortable sofas, some well-chosen pieces
of English eighteenth-century furniture and modern bathrooms, a
rarity in that part of the country. Local pottery, antique Bibesco
silver, handed down from the seventeenth-century hospodars, and
Oltenian rugs gave it a local touch. The main sitting room featured
a huge open fireplace; large windows framed the spectacular sce-

nery of the mountains. Even George was impressed and agreed that it was a tremendous improvement on the old house. Nadège Stirbey called it "an oasis of civilization in the Carpathian wilderness." Baba Outza took longer to convince, and it was only after the house had been blessed by the local bearded Orthodox priest that she agreed to go back to work there, confident that no vampire would bar her path.

Leaving the workmen behind, Marthe set off for Switzerland to visit her mother, whose health was deteriorating. Madame Lahovary, having refused to return home after the war, was leading an aimless existence, moving from one Swiss hotel to another. Conscious of the "suicide streak" in her mother's family, Marthe arranged for a companion and settled Madame Lahovary in a new house in Lausanne, which she seemed to like very much. But the change did not help. On April 18 she committed suicide in the ladies' room of a hotel in Lausanne. Marthe buried her next to Marguerite in the same cemetery of Clarens, adding another cypress to the joint grave. "I have now lost most of my family," Marthe wrote to the Abbé Mugnier. "My father, my mother, my two sisters and my young brother. You are the only one left. I need to see you."

Her spirits were indeed at a low ebb when she reached Paris. Her mother's suicide unleashed an avalanche of guilt. They had never been very close, but should she have done more to prevent it? Shown more affection? Remained with her? She felt emotionally drained and very lonely. The news of Beauvau-Craon's wedding in Bologna, splashed over the Paris newspapers and much commented on by her friends, did nothing to allay her depression. Nor did the general mood in Paris, where everyone criticized the peace treaty. "Bad as the pre-1914 Europe was and full of injustice," her friend Paléologue kept repeating, "it was better than what we have now—a continent torn to bits, ugly and financially ruined."

As many times before in her life, an invitation from Antoine came to the rescue. His wife, Elizabeth, had just delivered a daughter, Priscilla; would Marthe please come to the christening in June? "It will do you good to visit England," wrote Antoine.

And it did. She felt her spirits revive at the sight of the beautiful green countryside, basking in unaccustomed sunshine. And it was delightful to watch Antoine at the baby's christening in the role of a proud father and English gentleman.

On her return to the Ritz Hotel that afternoon, Marthe was handed a message from a "Duke of Toledo," alias King Alfonso XIII of Spain. "Georgette!" (He mischievously called her by her husband's name.) "Could we meet? I long to see you again!" They had met before several times, but always at official functions. The admiration of a king is not to be treated lightly, particularly one as attractive as Alfonso of Spain. What added piquancy to the encounter was his wife's—Queen Ena's—reputed infatuation with Charles-Louis at the time of his tour of duty in Madrid. Marthe's diary reveals that "they saw a lot of each other *alone*" those two days. She later accompanied him to a polo match in Roehampton, which he won, laying the trophy at her feet. "A charming interlude with no future," she recorded, "but it left me exhilarated."

As a couple, George and Marthe had comparatively few mutual friends, but one George wholeheartedly approved of was Sir Philip Sassoon, politician, millionaire and aesthete, whose hobbies were entertaining and airplanes. Sir Philip was in his late twenties, a slender, good-looking man with a pale thoughtful face and a touch of aristocratic hauteur. He had inherited a large fortune in banking—from his father, Edward Sassoon, of Indian-Jewish descent—together with a mansion in London's Park Lane and estates in the Home Counties. In his favorite house, Port Lympne, he entertained a glittering assortment of guests from cabinet ministers to writers and members of the aristocracy. The house, with murals painted by the fashionable José María Sert, was supremely comfortable, and delicious food was served by an assortment of French chefs. Sassoon had served in the Army as military assistant to General Haig and, while carrying out cross-Channel errands, had developed a passion for flying. The moment the war was over he bought himself an Avro, which he used for ferrying friends to Paris and for visits to his constituency. But besides being a sportsman Sassoon was also an intellectual and a fervent admirer of Proust, whom he had met in Paris with Antoine. During Marthe's visit to Port Lympne he often spent hours discussing the fine points of *A la Recherche du Temps Perdu*, a book he kept at his bedside at all times.

Among the guests at Philip Sassoon's house that first weekend in August when Marthe visited was Winston Churchill, then Minister of War in Lloyd George's cabinet. "I was walking in Philip's gardens early that morning," Marthe recalled, "when I came across Mr. Churchill sitting in a chair on the lawn in the sunshine with several canvases and a box of paints around him; he was painting the landscape in front of us—the famous view of cliffs and coastline unchanged since the days of Julius Caesar. He waved amicably and I settled by him on the grass, watching in silence. Suddenly he turned toward me, removed his sun hat and asked, 'Is it the first of August today?' I said, 'Yes,' and wondered why he asked. Then I remembered. Of course—this was the anniversary of the day in 1914 when Winston, then First Lord of the Admiralty, realizing that war was about to erupt, ordered the British fleet out of the Channel and into the North Sea." No wonder Marthe was a success with prominent statesmen; she had a superb knowledge of history and a gift for drawing out famous men's reminiscences. "You saved the British fleet on that day," she told him. Winston's face lit up with a smile. " 'Yes, I was haunted by the thought that we would find ourselves strangled by the German submarines in the Channel. That night, six years ago, I ordered the fleet to sail under cover of darkness—eighteen miles of warships, all lights out. Next morning they were safe in the deep waters of the North Sea. If I hadn't done it the war might have taken a different course.' He smiled at me and picked up his brushes again. We had become friends."

George made a brief appearance at Port Lympne, long enough to discuss the latest aviation news with Sir Philip; husband and wife then drove back to Paris together. George had just acquired a new car and planned to drive it all the way back to Romania from Paris. He asked, in a spirit of reconciliation, whether Marthe would care to accompany him. "Aren't you getting bored with the Orient Express?" he asked. Brushing aside the protestations of her maid ("It is too far, the Prince drives fast—he is going to kill the Princess"), Marthe agreed.

They traveled through Switzerland, Liechtenstein and Innsbruck to Vienna. A year after the Hapsburgs' departure, revolutionary Vienna presented a pitiful sight. Driving through the outskirts past the once lush and romantic Vienna Woods, which used to be full of cafés, carriages and happy burghers enjoying their afternoon walks, they were struck by the ravages brought about by the revolutionary takeover. The woodlands had been brutally decimated to provide fuel for the winter; as they drove, they passed groups of old people carrying bundles on their backs, barefoot children dragging carts filled with dry wood, a long procession of the city's poor collecting provisions against the coming cold. "I could hardly bear it," Marthe recalled. "There we were driving alongside in our gleaming yellow Mercedes, chromium-plated and rather vulgar, raising a huge cloud of dust, and these people were so heavily laden that all they could do was turn their heads away and close their eyes so as not to be blinded by the dust. . . . Oh, Vienna, what happened to you?" The next day, Marthe walked around the familiar streets, visiting her friends' palaces, now boarded up, their owners departed, the buildings occupied by crowds of squatters. Only the Sacher Hotel, where they stayed, though a shadow of its former glory, retained some of its prewar atmosphere. It had become the rallying point for what was left of the former aristocracy and disparate right-wing elements. It was all due to Frau Sacher, the owner, who, having entertained royalty all her life, ended up by looking like a royal herself. In a city full of revolutionaries, Frau Sacher loudly proclaimed her reactionary opinions; she refused to admit Communist functionaries into the hotel. "*Kein Bolshevik*," she insisted, and somehow got away with it. "They ought to make her President of Austria," George remarked.

They were back in Romania in September. *Isvor* was almost completed, but before sending the manuscript to her editor at Plon in Paris, Marthe decided to devote the next few months to a project in memory of her mother-in-law, Valentine.

It was on the morning of her wedding day that Marthe was first told of the link between her mother-in-law's family, the Chimays, and Napoleon Bonaparte. Prominent among her wedding presents was an exquisite bracelet of different-colored golds, ornamented with rubies and emeralds, which had been presented to Emily Pellapra, grandmother of Valentine Bibesco, née Chimay, by Emperor Napoleon at the time of his return from Elba. To this were later added other mementos: a blue enameled watch, decorated with pearls, with the imperial eagle at the back, which had once belonged to Marie-Louise; a large diamond, one of several sewn into the Emperor's belt by Hortense, Josephine's daughter, at the time of his departure for St. Helena; and the "cockade of Austerlitz," a round, tricolor piece of silk that the victorious Napoleon wore on his hat at Austerlitz in December 1805.

A romantic liaison brought these gifts into the Chimay family and from them to the Bibescos. Valentine Bibesco's grandmother, the Princess de Chimay, was the daughter of Henry Leu Pellapra, a Lyons banker and his beautiful wife, Emily, née Leroy. During one of Napoleon's visits to Lyons, probably in the autumn of 1807, Madame Pellapra, who was unhappily married to her unattractive banker husband, entered upon a liaison with the Emperor, and though never as close to him as Marie Walewska, she remained within his orbit for the next seven years. It is likely, though by no means established, that as his former mistress she was also present at Malmaison in June 1815, when the defeated Emperor was about to leave France. Though not mentioned in Napoleon's St. Helena memoirs, she was remembered after his death with the gift of a fine diamond, a snuff box and a miniature. Her daughter, also named Emily, later married the Prince de Chimay.

Such was the romantic background which Valentine Bibesco embroidered with the theory that her grandmother was actually Napoleon's daughter, conceived at the time of one of his visits to Lyons—an idea that Marthe embraced with enthusiasm. "How thrilling, to be married to a descendant of the Emperor," she wrote, "and to have Napoleon's blood coursing in little Valentine's veins." And, being Marthe, she was prepared to bend the facts to fit the theory. *Une Fille de Napoléon: Mémoires d'Emilie de Pellapra, Princesse de Chimay*, edited and prefaced by Marthe, is the story of George's soi-disant "ancestress" Emily, her unhappy marriage to the banker Pellapra, and her occasional secret meetings with Napoleon. Unfortunately, the date of Emily's birth, as registered in the Municipal Archives of Lyons, checked against detailed records of the Emperor's travels, shows that Napoleon and her mother did not meet until three years after her birth. Undaunted, Marthe approached Frédéric Masson, the eminent French historian, an authority on the Napoleonic era, and asked him to write an introduction to her book. As Ghislain de Diesbach reports in his 1986 biography of Marthe Bibesco: "The historian was then very old, nearing his death. Dazzled by this young woman, so knowledgeable and beautiful, he agreed to write the introduction; never mind the slight discrepancy in the dates."

The entire episode does not reflect well on Marthe; her ambition to be "part of history" seems to have got the better of her and this was too good an occasion to miss.

Une Fille de Napoléon duly appeared in 1921 and caused many raised eyebrows in Faubourg St. Germain circles. The general public, however, liked the book, and Marthe's preface, published separately in the *Revue des Deux Mondes*, attracted a flattering commentary from Marcel Proust, who compared her writing to Chateaubriand's.

Having discharged what she considered her "filial duty" by launching the Emily Pellapra memoirs, Marthe could now concentrate on an outline for her new project—an autobiographical novel, *Le Perroquet Vert*. In the meantime *Isvor: The Land of the Willow* was published to universal acclaim.

"It is impossible not to love Romania after reading *Isvor*," wrote Paul Souday, the redoubtable critic of *Le Temps*, devoting a two-page article to the book. Already in the new year, a month before publication, rumor spread that the coveted prestigious prize of the Académie Française would—for a second time—be awarded to Marthe Bibesco. Not only was it a sign of recognition; it also meant a substantial sum of money, which would go toward the rebuilding of Mogosoëa. Critics were unanimous in extolling the virtues of the writer, who "so brilliantly understood the genius of the race and the soul of her country." It became the favorite bedside reading of the poet Rainer Maria Rilke; even the dreaded Anna de Noailles, forgetting past animosities, complimented Marthe on her descriptions of nature, which "exuded the freshness

of a newly felled woodland." An article in the *Vie Littéraire* by
F. P. Alibert, a noted critic, described the pleasure he derived from
Marthe Bibesco's "exquisite prose and the bucolic wonderland she
evoked." Even the left-wing *Ere Nouvelle* praised it and remarked
with good humor that "*un char à boeufs* (an oxcart) appeared on the
Champs-Elysées, much to everybody's enjoyment."

The Paris correspondent of *The Times* of London, reporting on
the success of *Isvor,* sparked interest in London's publishing circles. Published by Heinemann at the end of 1923, the book sold
over 20,000 copies in hardback. A U.S. and Spanish edition followed.

"Your country must be grateful to you for writing *Isvor,*" remarked the Abbé Mugnier. Marthe was not sure that it was. The
King and Queen of Romania, to whom special autographed copies
were dispatched, were certainly enthusiastic. "I like your book . . .
am reading it slowly, carefully, weighing its merits," wrote Queen
Marie. "The atmosphere is true and the descriptions genuinely
moving." The letter was complimentary, only marred by Queen
Marie's endless comments on her *own* popularity "among the *same*
simple people of Romania." "Self-centered, as ever," Marthe remarked after putting down the royal letter. It was different with
King Ferdinand—his admiration came from the heart. Marthe sent
him the book with a short little note saying, "*Et voici! —*Marthe."
He wrote to her from the Cotroceni Palace on May 7, 1923.

> *Dear Marthe:*
> *Your book is a joy! May I come over to tea at Mogosoëa and
> compliment you on it? Or would you rather come here? Your gar-
> dens are more beautiful than mine. I have a great desire to see
> you. Isvor was always with me during the recent three weeks of
> the Easter break at Scrovesti. How brilliantly you have expressed
> and understood our country people—this strange mixture of child-
> ishness and profound philosophy, resignation and ever present
> hope, the unconscious struggle between superstition and Christi-
> anity, so often ill-defined and hard for them to apprehend. . . . I
> will hope for a letter from you. With profound affection,
> Ferdinand.*

The royals obviously approved, but the Bucharest government and social circles could not understand why a book describing customs and folklore "known to all" should have such a success abroad. Marthe was criticized for writing in French and for eulogizing the peasants; it was considered disloyal to her own social class. For the Bucharest critics *Isvor* "reeked of manure and body sweat." To Marthe the criticism in her native land—much of it born out of jealousy—was not a surprise. "It is quite impossible to please my compatriots," she declared. "I will stop trying."

After the prize-giving ceremony at the Académie, elated to have been admitted to the Holy of Holies of the French literary world, Marthe left Paris with praises of *Isvor* still ringing in her ears. She returned to Romania via Venice and was in Mogosoëa in late April to tackle her autobiographical novel, *Le Perroquet Vert*. It was a period of renewed vitality in her life. Not only was she buoyed up by *Isvor*'s international success, but she had also recently met a man for whom—to her astonishment—she conceived a real physical passion. She was surprised at herself. "I am destined to love brains more than men," she once confessed to her diary. "Once they show weakness I stop admiring them, therefore loving. The physical side comes a poor second."

Henry Bertrand Léon de Jouvenel, senator of Corrèze, was certainly a strong man. Editor-in-chief of *Le Matin*, the most influential daily in France, married to the famous writer Colette, he had embarked on a flourishing political and diplomatic career. Over the next decade he was to serve as French High Commissioner in Syria and Ambassador to Italy, while writing a constant stream of books and articles. When he met Marthe in February 1923, he was forty-seven years old and had two sons—one from a previous marriage, another from a mistress—and a ten-year-old daughter with Colette called Belle-Gazou. Handsome in a square-shouldered, rustic way, with a reputation for chasing women, he had a gift for both the spoken and the written word. Jouvenel had been married to Colette for eleven years, but the marriage had come to an end, as she grew more and more involved in her career and as her lesbian affairs multiplied; they were two strong, wholly dissimilar personalities. Colette at the time was fifty-one and at the height of her popularity, having published *La Vagabonde* and *Chéri*. One day, having returned from a lecture tour, she found that Henry had left without a note. He was reputed to have told friends, "I leave my wife to her cats." They were divorced a year later.

Marthe had known and admired Colette for many years; the older woman had been kind and encouraging when Marthe, at the age of twenty-two, published *Les Huit Paradis*. In later years she attended some of the soirees at 69, Boulevard Suchet, where Colette, still as Madame de Jouvenel, entertained the leading statesmen and writers of the day. Marthe was one of the first to congratulate her when in 1920 she was named Chevalier de la Légion d'Honneur, a rare distinction for a woman in those days and one that Marthe herself coveted.

To be courted by the husband of the famous Colette was pleasing and, besides, Jouvenel laid siege at Marthe's door. Huge bouquets of exotic flowers were delivered to 71, Faubourg St. Honoré, sometimes as often as three times a day; the senator himself would arrive unexpectedly at all hours, to the open disapproval of Miss Chatfield. In between he wrote passionate letters, pledging "supreme contentment" if only she would bend herself to his will. It was a new experience for Marthe to deal with a man so overwhelmingly masculine; a "life force," as she contentedly remarked. She wrote about "compelling sensations, never before experienced." At the age of thirty-seven, for the first and last time in her life, she was in the throes of a purely physical passion for a man, who she realized was a well-known seducer and for whom she would probably be no more than a passing episode in a long line of conquests.

On the face of it, theirs was a strange liaison. Compared with Charles-Louis de Beauvau-Craon—aristocratic, supremely civilized and considerate—Jouvenel was like a volcano: explosive, driving, ambitious and selfish. He also came from a different social class than Beauvau—from a small-town provincial nobility. His views were left-wing and his private life was a mess. Yet his political gifts and single-minded pursuit of advancement propelled him toward a distinguished career and made him attractive to

Marthe. As French delegate to the League of Nations in Geneva in the latter part of 1923, he came into close association with Lord Robert Cecil, the British delegate. His letters to Marthe from that period were rated of great historical importance in France and she made use of them in her last monumental work, *La Nymphe Europe.*

Marthe and Jouvenel's friendship continued for almost three years. It was a tempestuous relationship interspersed with quarrels sparked by the senator's various infidelities—humiliating to Marthe. But Jouvenel, with all his faults, also brought about some positive changes in her. She became softer, more feminine, more pliable, losing her haughty mannerisms (her *airs d'Impératrice*), which many found irritating. Throughout 1923 and early in 1924, when their relationship was at its peak, Marthe was a woman in love, waiting for the telephone to ring, trembling with anticipation as she heard the doorbell. Jouvenel's letters to her, written during conferences and various ministerial meetings, deal mostly with politics and current affairs. They are an interesting documentary of the period. Marthe's, on the contrary, are intensely personal and almost humble: "I am ashamed to feel so inferior to you," she writes, "but I find the feeling delicious . . . I meditate on your diverse qualities and try to choose the one I like best. . . . Longing to be with you as we were in Nîmes." Here was a different Marthe—physically conquered, avid for love, vulnerable in the hands of a strong but ruthless man, who would soon find her too intense and demanding for his liking. Miss Chatfield proved to be right. The senator from Corrèze was bad news; he would only make her Princess unhappy.

It is a measure of Marthe's professionalism as a writer that the supercharged atmosphere Jouvenel's courtship created did not interfere with her work. From the moment she returned home, her stringent writing routine was resumed, and she continued to stick to it even during Jouvenel's visit to Mogosoëa and Posada. *Le Perroquet Vert* was finished in six months.

Marthe's novel is the story of her own family, disguised as émigré Russians in Biarritz before World War I, of her mother's obsession with her brother's death, of the suicide of her younger sister and her own search for elusive happiness personified by the green bird. Over all hangs the age-old family curse of incest, probably inspired by Colette's reputed attachment to her stepson. By a curious twist of fate the heroine discovers that the man she desires and plans to marry is really her half brother. She escapes to become a Carmelite nun in Madras in southern India.

It is a strange story, written with consummate technique and great charm. Its reception by the public was enthusiastic. Her new publisher, Grasset, sold 60,000 copies in three months and went into a second and third printing. The book was published in England, the United States, Germany, Switzerland, Holland and Sweden to great acclaim. Even Colette, whose relations with Marthe were now strained, magnanimously called the novel "a revelation."

Early in 1924, a few weeks before the publication of *Le Perroquet Vert*, while she was immersed in correcting the proofs and arguing with her editor about changes, Marthe received a letter from Christopher Birdwood Thomson which surprised and delighted her. Thomson had been out of her life for some time. For the last four years he had tried unsuccessfully to win a parliamentary seat and had just recently suffered another defeat in a by-election. With leisure on his hands he consoled himself by writing *Smaranda*, a memoir dedicated to Marthe, in which he tried to relive their wartime idyll, now very much in the past. His several recent attempts to meet her in Paris had been unsuccessful; he usually found her surrounded by eminent statesmen or rich society people, and though she seemed pleased enough to see him, he felt out of his element and returned depressed to his lodgings in Wales. "A poor man should avoid women like Smaranda," Thomson wrote in his book. "Such women, however human they may be, are lovely pictures and need splendid frames." And yet he would not let go of his dream. "It is entirely because of you that I continue to spend money and, what is more important, my nervous energy on politics," he wrote to her. "I would give up all this political mud if it weren't for the fact that I am determined to prove to you—before it is too late—that I am not a failure." His luck changed with the election of a Labor government in England under the premiership of Ramsay MacDonald, his close friend. Shortly thereafter Thomson was offered the post of Minister for Air with a seat in the cabinet, made a peer and elevated to the House of Lords as Lord Thomson of Cardington. It was a triumphant vindication of his efforts.

Marthe had already planned to visit London in February to go over the translation of *Isvor* with her publisher. She now sped up her departure and remained in England for a week, lunching and dining with Thomson on most days, "enjoying the feeling of being with a man who has finally attained power." She advised him on the furnishings of his ministerial office, helped him to choose an apartment within walking distance of the Houses of Parliament and promised to remain "in constant touch." Back in Paris she continued to see Jouvenel, who was now in line for a cabinet post as Minister of Education in Poincaré's government.

The sudden reinstatement of Thomson in Marthe's heart may appear somewhat abrupt, motivated as it was by the unexpected change in his political fortunes. Marthe, as she herself often said, "gravitated toward power." She had been brought up "on the steps of a throne" among men like her father who shaped history. "My destiny is to be a muse present at the theater of events," she once confided to the Abbé Mugnier. As both Thomson and Jouvenel now had front-row seats in this theater, they became even more precious to her. But there was more to it than her old friend's new importance. She genuinely liked Thomson. She trusted him, but she was not physically attracted to him, as she was to Jouvenel, who she knew could never be trusted. Still it was a pleasant situation to have two powerful men—one on each side of the Channel—competing for her affection. No wonder Marthe looked radiant when she returned to Paris in late February and was seen by her cousin Gustave Kerguézac dining with Jouvenel at La Rue in a dark red velvet dress, pearls and sables, "the very personification of glamour." On one occasion, after seeing a play and dining together rather late, Jouvenel drove Marthe to the Boulevard de la Poissonnière in the Paris newspaper district to watch *Le Matin* be "put to bed." She sat at the editor's desk, swathed in furs, cutting an incongruous figure among the harassed shirtsleeved journalists, while Jouvenel took a malicious pleasure in introducing her to the most rabidly left-wing members of his team.

In mid-April the King and Queen of Romania arrived on a state visit to Paris. Marthe, as a prominent representative of their nation and a personal friend of the sovereigns, accompanied them to the Elysée Palace banquet, a "vision in a Chanel oyster-gray satin dress and emeralds," the *Figaro* reported. She far outshone Queen Marie, who had recently put on weight and appeared "swathed in acres of mauve chiffon." After the official functions, the Queen left her husband in Paris to join her sister the Grand Duchess Kirill of Russia ("Ducky") in Nice. For two weeks Marthe acted as King Ferdinand's cicerone, escorting him around the Louvre, Versailles (of which he was "very jealous") and Malmaison, introducing him to her friends and distinguished French writers and scientists of the day. King Ferdinand was reported lunching with Marthe, Boni de Castellane, Paul Claudel and François Mauriac, visiting the laboratory of Dr. Le Bon, a scientist friend of Marthe, and of course meeting the Abbé Mugnier several times. Enchanted by the charm and breadth of knowledge of this "latter-day saint," the King called on him at the Abbé's spartan lodgings in the rue Méchain. "I am Your Majesty's *sujet de coeur*," said the Abbé, "for I have loved *Isvor*." Those were simple, relaxed days, when a visiting monarch or Prime Minister could move about a city unimpeded by the attention of the media, and Ferdinand had a good time. When malicious gossips reported to Queen Marie that the King was spending "a lot of time with the Princess Bibesco," the Queen, much to her credit, shrugged it off and replied that "it was hard to resist Marthe's charm and her knowledge of Paris and anyway King Ferdinand liked to be led."

In June, while the triumphal "flight of the green bird," as she came to call *Le Perroquet Vert*, was bringing her many praises, Marthe was told she had to have a major operation. She entered the private clinic on the Rue Bizet in Paris, where an examination by the famous gynecologist Professor Gosset revealed that a hysterectomy would have to be performed immediately. The timing could not have been more awkward. Expecting to be in Romania for the rest of the year, Marthe had let her Faubourg St. Honoré apartment to Lord Curzon, until recently Britain's Foreign Secretary. Rosita de Castries, the Abbé Mugnier's longtime friend, came to the rescue, offering Marthe her apartment on the rue de Grenelle for the period of her convalescence. Though the operation itself was successful, complications ensued, threatening pleurisy and phlebitis, and for a time Marthe's survival was at risk. At the first hint of trouble George arrived from Romania and remained a constant presence at his wife's bedside. He proudly brought with him a letter from Jon Duca, Romania's Foreign Minister, who had inherited her father's office and his desk; Marthe was moved to see the familiar stationery and to read: "*Le Perroquet* is wonderful. Bravo: how proud your father would have been."

Marthe's room overflowed with flowers; the scent of roses and peonies filled the corridors of the clinic, while a procession of celebrities from cabinet ministers to distinguished writers sent inquiries and best wishes. Lord Thomson of Cardington flew over from London for the day but was not allowed in her room, for "he might be bringing cross-Channel germs."

George's loving attention was a source of surprise to some people. "*Tiens,*" declared Anna de Noailles, looking quizzically at her cousin. "I thought you did not care for her anymore." But he did care. On the day the pulmonary infection set in and there was fear of a blood clot, George supported his wife in his arms for seven hours, forcing her to remain in an upright position to avoid the blood clot traveling to her brain.

It took Marthe a long time to come out of the labyrinth. When at last she was strong enough to read her mail, she was touched by the hundreds of letters she received, including long and affectionate ones from Queen Marie and King Ferdinand. Her daughter was in Romania at the time, but remained in constant touch with her father, who daily relayed news of her mother's progress. Only later did it become known that it was during that same summer that Valentine met the young man to whom she was to become engaged. He was the son of a former suitor of Marthe's, who, persuaded by his family that Marthe was too young to get married, went off to Africa to shoot lions, leaving the field free for George Bibesco to move in.

When at last Marthe was strong enough to travel, George accompanied her to Bagnoles-de-l'Orne, her favorite watering place in Normandy. On his return to Romania, he proceeded to break off with a mistress, who had assumed "much too soon and too publicly" that he was about to become a widower. It did not prevent him, however, from soon acquiring a new one.

George's relationship with his wife might have appeared puzzling to outsiders, but the truth was that with all his faults—selfishness, mercurial temperament and lack of discipline—George was basically a traditionalist. His version of marriage, unconventional as it may seem to us, followed a well-established Balkan pattern. He had been married to Marthe for twenty years and, though he did not always admit it, was fond of her and proud of her beauty and achievements. Seeing her in the hospital, her splendid hair spread over the pillows, huge eyes with her "harpoon eyelashes" set in a pale, emaciated face, evoked all his latent tenderness. "She looks like a child," he said to the Abbé Mugnier, who was the only other visitor allowed into Marthe's room at the hospital, his quiet presence bringing her the reassurance and peace she so much needed. To Marthe's delight the Abbé and her husband, seeing each other almost daily across her bed, became good friends; the incongruous pair could be seen pacing the corridor outside Marthe's room discussing subjects from the Orthodox religion to aviation.

"I will look after her," George promised the Abbé. He gave proof of it a few months later, when, worried about Marthe's slow return to health, her general apathy, lack of spirit and her plans to settle permanently in France, he gave her—by way of a legal deed—the entire estate of Mogosoëa, including the surrounding land. This time it was not only the house, which he had given her in 1911, when she contemplated entering a convent after breaking up with Beauvau-Craon, but the entire ancestral estate of the Brancovan princes. This reassured Marthe that the work she had undertaken with so much love and expense would always remain in her hands and rekindled her enthusiasm for life. Walking around the unfinished but magical house and the gardens, which were beginning to look overgrown in Marthe's absence, George decided that the only way to entice Marthe to return and remain was to tie her to Mogosoëa forever. He succeeded, but it was still Marthe who would have to bear the burden of his gift. She would have to work long and hard to pay for the restoration and the upkeep of what she liked to refer to as "that beloved millstone around my neck." In the course of the next two years, under the guidance of the brilliant Venetian architect Domenico Rupolo, and paid for by the money Marthe had earned from her writing, the restoration of Mogosoëa was triumphantly concluded. It became the place where statesmen from all parts of Europe liked to gather. Marthe, the devoted European, hoped that the blissful surroundings would perhaps give birth to "a plan" that would stop the impending disaster of a new war.

In July 1925 young Valentine's engagement to Dimitri Ghika-Comanesti was announced and soon afterward Marthe left for Romania to prepare for her daughter's wedding. "I have just met my future son-in-law," Marthe wrote to the Abbé Mugnier from Posada. "He arrived with his mother and his tutor and brought Valentine the famous diamond engagement ring which used to belong to Zoë Ghika, the legendary family beauty. Dimitri, or Dédé as we call him, is tall and slender with gray-blue eyes and a charming smile; he is slightly younger than Valentine, twenty-one last January, and gives the impression of being shy. I like his voice—it is agreeable and distinctive—you know how allergic I am to strident voices. Dimitri speaks French without an accent; his English is perfect and so is his German—even Romanian. . . . You will be pleased to know that he is very interested in ornithology and is preparing to write a book on the birds of the Danube delta. . . . All in all, I like him and rejoice in Valentine's happiness. They will be living in Paris for a time after the wedding, so you will soon meet him."

The wedding, a splendid event, was conducted by the Patriarch of Romania, wearing the vestments of the Patriarchs of Constantinople from the days of Justinian, and presided over by three queens—Queen Marie, Queen Sophie of Greece and Queen Mignon of Yugoslavia—as well as Crown Prince Carol, an assortment of German and Italian princes and members of the European aristocracy. The problems of etiquette were awesome and nearly drove Marthe out of her mind. "Why do queens want to come to provincial Comarnic to assist at the wedding of the little Bibesco to young Ghika?" she exclaimed in exasperation. One answer of course was that royalty in that part of the world were often bored; the prospect of a brilliant wedding in picturesque surroundings and Marthe's fame drew them in like a magnet.

Following the Orthodox custom, the ceremony took place at midnight in the family's chapel in the woods above Posada. The rustic surroundings provided a vivid contrast to the opulence of the guests—women in ball gowns, ablaze with jewels; tiaras and diadems shining in the light of hundreds of candles; men in full evening wear and medals. In Orthodox marriages it is the mother who leads her daughter to the altar. As they were driving to church through the perfect October night, on the mountain road lined with village people carrying torches, Marthe was touched to hear Valentine say, "Thank you for all the years of happiness you gave me."

After the ceremony, as Marthe and George were returning together in the car, they watched a display of fireworks—a novelty in that part of the world. The entire hillside, the river and the roads leading up to the forest were suddenly filled with dancing lights; everyone cheered. Village elders proclaimed that they had seen "nothing like it since the visit of the Emperor Franz Josef to Comarnic half a century ago."

The wedding was followed by supper and a ball, which lasted until the morning. Finally the three Queens laid aside their diadems and retired to bed, "much too late" according to Marthe. The newlyweds, accompanied by the bridegroom's Scottish butler, Hamilton, left to spend the remainder of the day at Mogosoëa, from where they were to board the Orient Express for Venice. Two days after the wedding, an exhausted but happy Marthe drove over to Mogosoëa to meet with Rupolo and discuss with him the plans for the final stage of the reconstruction of the Old Palace. They agreed that work would begin the following April.

In November the bad weather set in. Fearful of coming down with pneumonia so soon after her recent illness, Marthe decided, after consultation with George, to spend the winter in the Middle East. A telegram to Lord Lloyd, an old friend, who had recently been appointed British High Commissioner in Cairo, elicited an invitation to stay at the British Residency in Egypt over Christmas. Just before leaving, however, Marthe had the exciting experience of witnessing the advent of electricity to Mogosoëa; the cables had finally been laid and the "sleeping beauty" blazed with lights; it was a moment of great happiness.

It was snowing when Marthe boarded the Orient Express for Belgrade, accompanied by her maid, Billochon, and fourteen pieces of luggage, on a journey that was to take her through Greece, Egypt and the Holy Land and give rise to two books: *Jours d'Egypte* and *Croisade pour l'Anémone*. Queen Marie asked her, as a personal favor, to spend a day in Belgrade and visit her daughter Mignon, Queen Marie of Yugoslavia, married to Alexander I of the Karageorgevich dynasty, who was bored and homesick, forced to live in a capital which had none of the sophistication and gaiety of Bucharest. "Gray skies, heavy snow, a sad, backward-looking city" was Marthe's instant verdict on Belgrade, though she quite enjoyed the long ride from the station to the palace in a red velvet-covered royal sled, driven by four frisky horses. It reminded her of her childhood days at Balotesti.

Marthe lunched alone with the Queen, who was thrilled to see her and avid for family gossip; she particularly wanted to hear the latest about her brother Crown Prince Carol's misdemeanors. In late afternoon, gently waving aside Mignon's invitations to stay on, Marthe rejoined the train for Athens, where Ambassador Charles de Chambrun was to be her guide and host. "Attica is a delight," she recorded; "the skies are blue and the air feels springlike." On Chambrun's arm she climbed the hill to the Acropolis and visited the Parthenon for the first time in her life. She returned there again alone on Christmas Eve to see it "pure and deserted, bathed in moonlight."

The crossing between Piraeus and Alexandria was rough, but her spirits revived when Billochon spotted the approach of a white launch with a six-foot Mameluke in red-and-gold livery in the prow; she hoped he was looking for them. Indeed he was. He handed Marthe a letter from Lord Lloyd, took charge of their luggage and, waving aside the Egyptian customs, saw them off to the Alexandria railway station and onto the train for Cairo. They were now under the protection of the British Raj.

At the time of Marthe's visit Egypt was an independent country, but still a British protectorate. The British Army was stationed there, guarding Suez, the crossroads of the Empire. It was in the British interest to support a viable local regime and help with the economic development of the country; Britain's prestige in Egypt at the time was very great.

The way of life at the British Residency, with its grand building and lawns sweeping down to the Nile, surpassed in splendor any Balkan monarchy, and Lord Lloyd, handsome, learned and witty, was one of the most distinguished of the British proconsuls. Marthe was indeed fortunate to be his guest. It was a tribute to her intelligence, to her reputation as a writer and supreme communicator, as well as to her elegance and beauty, that kings and prominent statesmen considered it a privilege to have the Princess Bibesco as a guest. Admittedly in those days, before the advent of mass travel and the communication explosion, life in the outposts of the Empire was slow, well ordered and sometimes dull; no congressional or parliamentary missions disturbed them; only an occasional explorer, scientist or a writer would drop by and visitors like Marthe, all glamour and brains, must have been a pleasure to entertain. She in turn loved being driven about in Lord Lloyd's official car, flag flying, followed by an escort of motorcycles.

Marthe visited the Pyramids, gazed at the monumental Sphinx, went to Heliopolis, spent hours in the Cairo Museum and traveled to Luxor and Aswan. In the Valley of the Kings, the legendary archaeologist Howard Carter recounted his recent discovery of the tomb of Tutankhamen. She spent the last day of the year in Cairo with Jouvenel, who had come down from Syria to see her. It was a brief and friendly meeting, but Marthe was surprised at feeling "so very detached"; a change of environment, new impressions and new friends had a salutary effect on her emotions. "Perhaps I ought to be feeling sad," she wrote in her diary on that day, "but I am perfectly happy without him."

On January 1, 1926, as she was lunching in Cairo with Howard Carter, she saw in a Reuters dispatch that Crown Prince Carol had just renounced his succession to the throne in favor of his four-year-old son Michael and had left the country to live abroad with his mistress, Elena Lupescu. All her thoughts went back to Romania; she felt tremendous compassion for King Ferdinand and anger at Queen Marie, who "had brought up her son so very badly."

Marthe was well aware that the average Romanian, carefully shielded by the government and the court from hearing about the Crown Prince's irresponsible behavior, would find his sudden renunciation of the throne bewildering and might see in it some dark plot by the ruling Liberal Party and the Palace. The abdication was certainly a windfall for the enemies of the dynasty and might lead to widespread disturbances throughout the country. She considered cutting her trip short and returning "just in case," but a telegram from George reassured her. "All is quiet," he cabled, "though in the backlash of Carol's defection Bratiano is expecting to be swept out of office." He advised his wife to remain in the Middle East until spring, as the winter in Romania was unseasonably severe.

The Holy Land was a big disappointment. Describing her impressions in *Croisade pour l'Anémone*, Marthe complained of the "cheap commerciality of it all": the streets of Bethlehem reminded her of a provincial town in the Balkans on market day. The Church of the Holy Sepulchre was "ruined by the crowds of cheeky and hideous beggars" who would not leave her alone; religious shrines, no matter of what denomination, competed with each other in ugliness and pretension. "I would like to ask Samson to return to Jerusalem and bring down all these monstrosities," she scribbled furiously in her journal.

It was with relief that she returned to Cairo and to the Egypt she loved. In *Jours d'Egypte*, a "travelogue written with the eye of a painter," as one of the critics described it, she writes of the

Princess Marthe Bibesco, by Boldini

Posada, Marthe's house in the Carpathians, reconstructed after the 1916 fire

Mogosoëa

Marthe as a child in Bucharest, age five

Marthe in her thirties

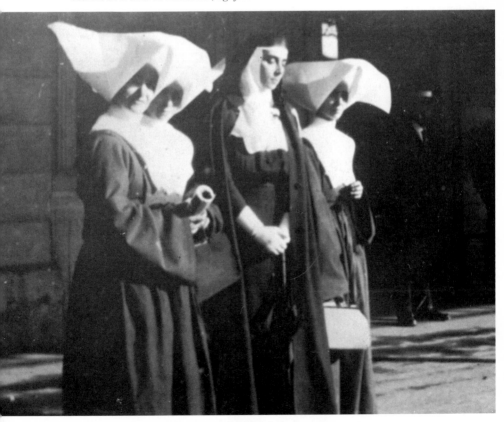

Marthe as a nurse in Hospital 118 during World War I, flanked by three Sisters of Mercy who traveled with her to Switzerland

Prince Charles-Louis de Beauvau-Craon,
Marthe's great love

Prince Emmanuel Bibesco,
Marthe's handsome and mysterious cousin;
friend of Marcel Proust

Prince Antoine Bibesco,
Emmanuel's younger brother; friend
of Marcel Proust; married to
Elizabeth Asquith, daughter of Henry Asquith,
Prime Minister of Great Britain

Anna, Countess de Noailles, poet,
Marthe's hostile cousin

*Lord Thomson
as Secretary of State for Air,
photographed at the King's Cup Air
Race, August 1924*

*Princess Bibesco
in her drawing room at Mogosoëa as painted by Vuillard*

Helen Vacaresco, Romanian hostess, jealous of Marthe's success

Marthe's husband, Prince George Bibesco

*George Bibesco at the Bucharest airport
in conversation with the president of
the International Aeronautical Federation*

*Prince and Princess Dimitri Ghika-Comanesti,
photographed in Paris shortly after their release
from prison in Romania*

*Ramsay MacDonald, Prime Minister
of Great Britain*

Marthe and her daughter, Valentine, on the day of Valentine's wedding

Marthe in her Paris apartment, photographed by Cecil Beaton two years before her death

"multicolored waters of the Nile, half pink, half blue, carrying the mysteries of the ages within them, of the feluccas anchored in midstream, resembling a forest of sugarcane," of the glory and power of Karnak with its twenty centuries behind it, which "makes the Roman emperors seem provincial."

Staying with Howard Carter in his little house, right in the middle of the desert, listening to him talk about the funeral rites in ancient Egypt, she was thrilled with the theory that the reason the ancient Egyptians, being merry and cheerful people, liked to be buried together with their household possessions was that they adored everyday life and resented its being so short. They looked forward to continuing it in the underworld of the tombs and await resurrection, "springing up each season, like the grain."

During the final week of her tour, Marthe spent a few days alone in Port Said in a house lent to her by the Suez Canal Company. She enjoyed the unaccustomed solitude, the chance to sort out her impressions, and marveled at the technical wonder of Lesseps, the canal builder, whose statue at the end of the pier dominates the horizon. On February 14 she sailed from Port Said to Marseilles on the *Moultan*, the pride of the French passenger fleet.

When she arrived in Paris at the end of February, Marthe found her desk piled high with correspondence. Lying on top of the usual stack of invitations was a copy of *Smaranda*, Lord Thomson's wartime memoir, dedicated to Marthe, "who inspired it."

Paris was awash in politics. The Briand government had just fallen; Germany had joined the League of Nations; two Communists had entered the new Poincaré government, much to the unease of Marthe's friends. George arrived from Romania, shortly followed by Valentine and her husband; they brought news of the serious illness of King Ferdinand (he had cancer) and of the general malaise caused by the defection of Crown Prince Carol, who was reported to be traveling all over Europe with Madame Lupescu. They also told of Rupolo's visit to Mogosoëa and the resumption of work on the Venetian colonnades surrounding the Spring Palace. Lord Thomson announced his arrival in May, but —much to Marthe's disappointment—was prevented from coming by the outbreak of a general strike in England.

After accompanying her husband, daughter and son-in-law on

a sentimental pilgrimage to Ménars, the birthplace of George's mother, Marthe left Paris for Romania and took up residence in Posada. She needed to be alone to complete writing *Catherine Paris*, which so far was only a title and an outline in her mind. After working on *Catherine* for most of the day it was pleasant to drive over to Mogosoëa in the evening to see how far work had progressed. The Italian workers, brought in by Rupolo to put the finishing touches on the colonnades and mosaics, were speedy and skillful; with luck the days of "camping" would soon be over.

On June 29, King Ferdinand came for a visit. He had just undergone a painful operation for cancer of the lower intestine and looked old and emaciated, but he was pathetically happy to see Marthe. "You know," he confessed to her after dinner, while they were strolling together on the grounds, "I really, really love you." Marthe was touched by this declaration. "He is like a very old Werther," she wrote in her diary, "so complex and timid and so very little appreciated as a person."

The year 1927 was a memorable one. *Catherine Paris* was published—first in France, then all over Europe and in the United States, where it became a best-seller. It was also the year of King Ferdinand's death, commemorated by Marthe in a moving article, "Une Victime Royale." And finally the rebuilding of Mogosoëa came to a triumphant conclusion and Marthe could at last take up residence in the old palace.

Catherine Paris was published in May with a first printing of 80,000 copies. The book soon acquired cult status on both sides of the Channel; French visitors traveling to London were asked by their friends to bring them a copy of *Catherine* so they could enjoy it in its original version. Marthe herself was amazed at the unexpected success of her latest work, which she considered inferior to *Le Perroquet Vert*. But the public thought otherwise. Thirty years later *Catherine Paris* was still being read and regarded as a literary classic of the interwar period.

To a large degree autobiographical, the book describes a world which came to an end with World War I. Its heroine is little Catherine Romulesco, a Romanian girl of a great family, who, having lost her parents at an early age, is brought up by her grandmother,

Princess Dragomir, who establishes herself in Paris to escape her overbearing husband and live the life of a *petite bourgeoise*, poor but free, in a modest apartment in the rue Matignon. Her granddaughter Catherine, given the middle name Paris by her mother, is educated as a French girl and becomes a devoted Parisian. At the age of eighteen, already an arresting beauty, she meets Count Adam Leopolski from one of the great feudal Polish families, owner of the Hotel Lambert, a historic house on the Ile St. Louis. At the age of thirty-eight, Adam is still unmarried and on meeting Catherine falls for her, imagining she is "a poor unknown." Agreeably surprised to learn of her background, he asks her to marry him and they leave for his feudal estates in eastern Poland, then part of the Austro-Hungarian Empire. Catherine hates her new life with all of its social splendor, the hunting parties, international intrigues among aristocratic cousins, each residing in different European countries. Adam, her husband, is unfaithful to her; she leaves him and returns to Paris, the place she loves above all. World War I comes; she meets a young Frenchman, a famous aviator named Robert Ricard, falls in love and eventually has a son by him, whom she brings up in Paris as a Frenchman.

To readers of the late 1990s, *Catherine Paris* seems dated, but there is no mistaking the beautiful writing, magical descriptions, insight into human characters and witty dialogue. The true hero of the book is France, made real by Marthe's love for the country. What she loves in France is the refinement of habit and customs and respect for intelligence. In a series of vignettes, she imparts to the reader her adoration of old Paris, its tortuous streets, the lovers on the quays, the ancient booksellers, the half-world of bohemia, the cooks on their way to market, the old-fashioned professors at the Sorbonne. "Marthe Bibesco has understood, or felt, or guessed everything about Paris," wrote Paul Claudel, "and conveyed it to us in the purest of French."

The day after *Catherine Paris*'s publication Marthe prepared to leave for Romania. "Why are you leaving?" exclaimed her publisher, Bernard Grasset. "You can't leave just as you are coming out!" But it was Marthe's long-ingrained habit "to leave it all to the critics," avoid interviewers and let the verdict of the public come to her. Judging from all indications the verdict promised to be enthusiastic.

On July 20, while Marthe was quietly dealing with her correspondence in Posada, Jean Apolzan, the old butler, appeared on the terrace looking solemn. News had come from the neighboring castle of Peleş that King Ferdinand had died that morning. She heard the ringing of bells echoing through the mountainside. Will they be ringing the bells in his beloved Sigmaringen? she wondered. She knew that Ferdinand, who for state reasons had been obliged to convert to the Orthodox faith, had asked to be buried according to Catholic rites and that all through the last phase of his life his thoughts went back to Bavaria and to the turreted castle of his childhood. The King's death created a complex constitutional situation in Romania. Since Ferdinand's son, Crown Prince Carol, had relinquished his right to the throne in order to live abroad with Madame Lupescu, his five-year-old son Michael was formally proclaimed King. Dressed in white knickers and a white silk shirt, the "Baby King" looked bewildered receiving the acclamation of the Chamber of Deputies. His mother, Princess Helen of Greece, the estranged wife of the runaway Carol, accompanied him, unsure of what would happen if her ex-husband decided to return. In the meantime the country was to be governed by a Regency Council composed of Prince Nicholas (Marie's second son), Miron Christea, the Patriarch of the Orthodox Church, and Bratiano, the Prime Minister. Queen Marie, now the Dowager Queen, was pushed into the background. They did not rule for very long; three years later, on June 6, 1930, Carol returned to Romania, deposed his son and assumed power as King Carol II.

"Crownie, all swathed in black veils, sat on my terrace in Posada among the red geraniums and the phlox," Marthe recalled. She had brought the King's gold cigarette case, studded with diamonds, Ferdinand's gift for Marthe. The two women talked about the late King, about whom Marthe was asked to write a long commemorative article for *The Saturday Evening Post* and the French *Illustration*. As Marthe recalled at the time, "the Queen contemplated the future with foreboding," torn between her love for her exiled son and the fear of his sudden return in a coup d'état.

"The Royal Victim" is a moving portrait of a man who wanted to be a scientist but whom fate willed to be King of Romania. Painfully shy, of an unprepossessing physique, he hated public occasions and was no good at small talk. In a country of dashing men, he cut a poor figure among sportsmen and could not even ride a horse during parades. His beautiful wife overshadowed him. Yet his knowledge was vast: he spoke eight languages, including ancient Greek and Hebrew; he was a learned botanist and a superb gardener; he read and wrote poetry; his knowledge of the classics was profound. Marthe recalled how a former French Ambassador to Romania, newly posted to Tokyo, was amazed when, during his leave-taking, the King talked to him about the relative merits of Japanese lyrical verse as compared with Chinese poetry. Marthe put her heart into her tribute to Ferdinand, painting a vivid picture of a man torn between his religion and his duties to the state, divided between loyalty to his native land and allegiance to the country he was serving, a man who could have been a great scientist but instead was "so little understood and so little loved."

The article, which was made into a small book, evoked wide response in the United States and in Europe. *Illustration* ran it on its front page in five columns; other papers, including *Le Temps* and *The Times* of London, printed excerpts. Paul Claudel admired it, but took issue with Marthe for depicting the King as a "near-saint." "No man who had abandoned the Catholic faith for the Orthodox Church for reasons of state could be thought of as a saint," wrote the great Catholic Claudel. "Ferdinand was a renegade, but I still admire the portrait you have painted of him. Your writing there is at its best."

The editor of *The Saturday Evening Post* joined in the chorus of praise. The magazine received "hundreds of letters from readers." He invited Marthe to write regularly for the magazine and offered substantial payment. But the tribute that truly delighted Marthe was a short message from London saying that Queen Mary read her article "and was much moved."

It was a different story in Bucharest. Queen Marie was annoyed, some said "furious," because there was hardly any mention of her in the piece; others felt it "demeaned the Orthodox Church"; still others thought it was "irreverent." But as George remarked afterward: "Surely you did not expect anything else?" The storm blew over much sooner than Marthe expected. A month later the Bibescos dined with the Queen at the Cotroceni Palace; and Marthe was surprised to be complimented by the Court Chamberlain on "the excellence of her tribute to the late King."

The day finally arrived when Mogosoëa was ready. The gigantic task of reconstruction, consuming most of Marthe's literary earnings for the last sixteen years, her stubborn dream, which at times appeared evanescent, had now become reality. Here on the flat Wallachian plain, ravaged for centuries by Tartar, Ottoman, Turkish, Bulgarian and Bosnian invaders, appeared, as if by a miracle, a genuine Byzantine-Venetian palace, an architectural gem in all the glory of its eighteenth-century past. Early in the eighteenth century a Brancovan prince sent an architect to the great University School of Architecture in Padua to study design and build him a palace which would combine Byzantine and Venetian traditions. Constantine Brancovan lived in it for only about twenty years, when he fell out of favor with the Turkish Sultan for refusing to abandon his Christian religion. The palace was destroyed and remained a ruin for two centuries until Marthe rescued it from oblivion. With the new Mogosoëa, Marthe resurrected the heritage of the Hospodars of Wallachia. Domenico Rupolo, the architect, and Fortuny, the decorator, helped her to bring it to life. Jouvenel once observed that, for Marthe, Mogosoëa was more demanding than any mistress has ever been of a man. He was right, but it was also Marthe's way of integrating Romania into Europe and giving something back to her husband, who had presented her with the "beloved ruin" years ago.

An avenue of elms, a mile long, led to the pink-colored palace, which stood facing west and south overlooking the lake. A white marble staircase led into a hall and an open-air loggia supported by Venetian columns, dug out from the ruins of the old palace. Beyond it were the lake, the wide lawns and the parterres of flowers, massed together like an Oriental carpet. On the left of the loggia, which was used as a summer sitting room, was Marthe's boudoir with a fine Louis XV fireplace, comfortable sofas and chairs. A Vuillard, a Modigliani and two Toulouse-Lautrec sketches added to the charm of the room. The so-called music room was formal, furnished with French pieces, except for a huge locally woven tapestry on one wall, portraying the exploits of the eighteenth-century reigning Prince of Wallachia. Marthe's bedroom, painted mauve with Byzantine motifs, overlooked the lake; she had a specially constructed elevated fireplace facing her bed so she could sit in bed writing and seek inspiration in the flames. Next to it was a library with an eclectic collection of books and periodicals from all over Europe. The rooms on the ground floor, the dining room and another library, opened one into another, giving an impression of airiness and space. Between the house and the lake, amidst a profusion of flowers, was the so-called Scala Veneziana, a skillfully built terrace with an Italianate garden, protected from the wind by box hedges. One particular feature of Mogosoëa in spring and summer was the fields of blue irises, which descended in terraces down to the lake. The house was grander and lacked the intimacy of Marthe's mountain retreat in Posada, but there was no denying the architectural beauty of it, the purity of the lines and the marvelously felicitous blending of Byzantium and Venice.

It was to these enchanted surroundings that guests from all over Europe and the United States came. While Marthe passed her morning at work, her visitor, occupying one of several supremely comfortable guest rooms, relaxed and enjoyed himself. There was plenty to do, from walking in the enormous park to boating on the lake or perhaps driving into Bucharest to explore the picturesque local markets. The food, carefully supervised by Marthe, was excellent, and George knew all about wines. Together they formed an unbeatable combination. But above all there was talk—excellent talk—by brilliant people, some of the best minds of the age.

Visitors, signing one of Marthe's guest books, were not encouraged to make comments, but some obviously could not resist. "Here," wrote one, "was such a high goal of perfection in food and wine, talk, books and the art of living, that to savor it exerted one's highest mental faculties." Another visitor, some years later, paid tribute to the one "who has truly become the muse of Europe."

The day after the workmen departed, Marthe celebrated with

a small dinner for George and the architect Rupolo. Soon afterward
guests started arriving. One of the first was Kit, Lord Thomson of
Cardington, happily combining a visit to Marthe with Ministry of
Air business in Bucharest. He was followed by Princess Murat and
two very old friends, Claude Anet and Louis Blériot, the famous
aviator, who had first stayed at Mogosoëa in 1909. Paul Lyautey,
the Marshal's son, came for a week; Antoine and his wife, Elizabeth, motored from Madrid, where Antoine was *en poste* at the
Legation. Letters arriving from France brought the news of *Catherine Paris*'s enormous success; sheaves of reviews, most of them
complimentary, were forwarded to Mogosoëa. The book had become the best-seller of the year in France and was on the way to
becoming one in the United States. Marthe was happy.

As the 1920s drew to a close, Marthe entered what she later
recalled as the apogee of her life. She was forty-two years old and
acknowledged to be one of the most beautiful, as well as one of
the most elegant, women of her day. A writer of international re-
pute, she was also a famous hostess with an unequaled diversity
of friends and relations. Her profound knowledge of literature, music and painting drew to her people from a wide international
spectrum.

"How can I do justice to Marthe and try to convey to you what
she was like in those days?" her cousin Princess Brancovan told
me. "She was my godmother, I knew her well and I was married
at Mogosoëa. I can still see her with her graceful figure, generous
mouth, large expressive green eyes, bordered by those famous eyelashes, a mountain of auburn hair, her long slender fingers arranging the countless flower vases on the terrace, or presiding over the
dining-room table, guiding the conversation, anxious that everyone
should be included." Unlike most women and particularly unlike
her cousin Anna de Noailles, Marthe scorned feminine gossip, although she suffered from it all her life. Gossip did not interest
her; she wanted to please and a large part of her fascination was
her gift for pleasing men. It was said of her—as it has been said
of many successful women—that she could make any man feel he
was the only one in the world. But her real passion was politics
and her ambition to promote understanding among Europeans. In
this she was well ahead of her time.

Just as George had rushed to her bedside when she was undergoing a serious operation four years before, so Marthe interrupted her work on her latest book, *Au Bal avec Marcel Proust*, and dropped all her Paris engagements to leave hurriedly for Bucharest, where her husband had again tried to shoot himself after quarreling with his latest mistress. Alerted by Jon Duca, the Foreign Minister and an old friend, she arrived in Bucharest to find George recovering, but depressed and bad-humored. "I hate the scent you are wearing" were his first words to his wife. "What is it called?" "It is called 'I hate your scent,' " Marthe replied evenly.

Gradually the "spoiled child," as Marthe was inclined to call him, regained his strength and good humor. To distract him Marthe suggested they drive to Spain to visit Antoine in Madrid. They set off in George's new Packard—"so powerful and so fast I was afraid it would kill the little birds on the way," Marthe noted in her diary. Traveling through Trieste and Milan they stopped at Hyères, near Toulon, where they called on Edith Wharton, at Ste. Claire, her château in the hills.

Marthe and Edith Wharton, who was some twenty-four years older than Marthe, had met each other in Paris fleetingly only twice, which is surprising, for they had a number of mutual friends, such as the American Walter Berry, Edith's constant companion, André Gide, Jean Cocteau and Paul Bourget. And, of course, there was the Abbé Mugnier, who often put in an appearance in Edith Wharton's salon on the rue de Varenne. After reading *Catherine Paris*, which was given to her by the Abbé, the older woman wrote a charming letter to Marthe, suggesting a visit to her château above Hyères, conveniently located on the way into Spain. Bernard Berenson and Nicky Mariano were staying with her at the time, which pleased Marthe, but George found the intellectual atmosphere pervading the house and the conversation too rarefied for his taste; they pressed on for Barcelona the next morning, departing just as Mrs. Wharton and her guests were on their way to a picnic in the hills. "It would have amused me to join them," Marthe confessed in a letter to the Abbé.

Antoine was in Barcelona to meet them; they had not seen each other for almost a year, but, as always, they picked up exactly where they had left off when they parted. They understood each other without words, and Antoine's marriage did not seem to have made any difference in their friendship. They spent a happy week together in Granada, then went on to the Holy Week ceremonies in Seville; Antoine, being an agnostic, drove back to Madrid with George after two days, leaving Marthe and Elizabeth to enjoy the pageantry and processions. After a final week in Toledo and a visit to the Prado in Madrid, the Bibescos departed for Paris by way of Biarritz, a town full of childhood memories for Marthe. When they reached Paris they heard the news of Herbert Asquith's death. Two days later Elizabeth and Antoine arrived on their way to London for the funeral. George, by now totally recovered and cheerful, having enjoyed himself in spite of his initial bad humor, returned to Romania, where Marthe was to join him in late summer. She was staying on in Paris to finish *Au Bal avec Marcel Proust* and await the birth of her first grandchild.

Jean-Nicholas Ghika was born in Paris on July 27, 1928. "This child," said one of Marthe's admirers at Grasset, "will have the youngest-looking grandmother in Europe."

A few days after Jean-Nicholas' birth Marthe's latest book, *Au Bal avec Marcel Proust*, was published. In the light of the number of biographies of Proust in later years, Marthe Bibesco's book is not an important contribution. *Au Bal avec Marcel Proust* is slight, composed mainly of Proust's letters to Antoine with the addition of Marthe's personal reminiscences of their few meetings. Proust was a part of Antoine and Emmanuel's world; he admired Marthe's looks and her *"allure de grande dame,"* and in his letters he complimented her exuberantly on her writing. But they did not have a sustained relationship. Indeed, as a very young woman, newly arrived on the Paris scene, Marthe thought him "spooky" and did her best to avoid him. In her book she describes their first meeting at the ball of the *Intransigeant* newspaper in Paris in May 1911, when Proust, "livid, bearded, with black-rimmed eyes, wearing a heavy fur coat, sat on a little gilt chair on the edge of the dance floor, pursuing her with his nocturnal eyes." "He reminded me of a fantastic figure in a Hoffmann fairy tale of my childhood: the night owl whose apparition inside the grandfather clock terrifies little Clara." She tried to "dance away from his melancholy eyes," but eventually had to meet him and they talked. "Was she writing another book?" "She was writing," she replied, "a book about happiness, *Alexandre Asiatique*, the story of Alexander the Great." Proust was appalled. "One should seek and write not about happiness but disaster." Marthe left him, but never forgot their exchange. "I sensed something supernatural about him, as if he possessed the keys to a world into which I refused to follow that evening," she wrote after his death, "but into which he has led me since." The book relates other meetings and more correspondence, and describes the last time she "almost saw him": shortly before Proust's death Antoine brought Marthe and his wife, Elizabeth, to Proust's apartment at 44, rue Hamelin one evening after the theater, and rang the doorbell twice—the old, unmistakable signal of their youth. Proust's housekeeper, the famous Céleste, opened the door and, seeing the three of them, apologized: "Monsieur has just had a terrible attack of asthma," she said. "He can hardly breathe. He is not receiving anyone, not even Prince Antoine, whose visits give him such pleasure." Eventually, after she had consulted with Proust, Antoine was allowed into the sanctum, but the ladies were asked to wait in the "outer drawing room," for, as Céleste explained, "Monsieur is very much afraid of the scent the Princesses are wearing."

In spite of its slender content, the book was well received by the critics; Cocteau liked it, and Paul Claudel, who disliked Proust, as he disliked all homosexual men, wrote to Marthe that he understood the interest one could have in his writings, "quite apart from his person."

Au Bal was only one of the four publications that appeared under Marthe's signature that year. There were also *Noblesse Oblige*, a collection of articles for French *Vogue; Quatre Portraits*, which included a description of her father, Jean Lahovary, a "portrait" of Herbert Henry Asquith, one of Anatole France, and of course the famous article on King Ferdinand. Finally there was a charming short story, "La Turquoise," later made into a film. Her literary fortunes were at their peak.

13

*Thomson
and Ramsay MacDonald*

In the general election in England on May 30, 1929, the first election in which five million women were enfranchised under the so-called Flapper Vote Act of April 1928, Labor emerged with 287 House of Commons seats against the Conservatives' 267 and the Liberals' 59. Lloyd George made clear that the support of the Liberals would be thrown behind Ramsay MacDonald and denied to Stanley Baldwin's Conservative Party. King George V invited MacDonald to form a new government and on June 8 MacDonald, accompanied by his friend Christopher Thomson and other members of the cabinet, went by train to Windsor and received their seals of office from the King. Thomson was back at the Air Ministry; that same evening he wrote to Marthe Bibesco, who was in Paris, suggesting she come to London in early July, when he would like to take her to see the tennis at Wimbledon. "I so look forward to being together again. God bless you. As ever and forever, with very best love, Kit."

He had been in love with her for fourteen years.

Being a member of the British establishment, in the House of Lords and now again in the cabinet, suited Thomson. Power enhanced his self-assurance; he now wore Savile Row clothes, and his six-foot-three figure, chiseled features and aristocratic bearing gave him a striking appearance. His influence in the cabinet was considerable; knowledgeable on an astonishingly wide range of subjects from Army matters to airships, with a perfect command of French and the literary arts, he appeared to come from a different mold than the rest of his Socialist colleagues. For Prime Minister MacDonald, a lonely man since the death of his wife, Christopher Thomson was not only a valuable member of his cabinet but a very close friend and confidant. Like the Prime Minister, Thomson too was a lonely man. He never married, for he was in pursuit of the dream that one day he might be Marthe Bibesco's husband.

As Air Minister, Christopher Thomson's most cherished project was airships. In the early twenties, inspired by the idea of a free-trade area within the Empire which would bind together its diverse territories, British technicians devised a scheme to link Sydney, New Delhi, Ottawa and Cape Town with London by means of the thrilling new medium of the air. It was to be an imperial air service, "an all-red route through the skies," which would give the imperial concept of the day a new dimension.

In 1924 Ramsay MacDonald's first government, with Christopher Thomson as Air Minister, officially adopted the Imperial Airship Scheme, intended to provide the first regular passenger service on the route to India. It was to be a beginning, and it was hoped that in years to come flotillas of those great airships would sail through the imperial skies, "saluting each other as they passed over Suez or the Atlantic."

The airship was actually a German idea. Since 1900 Graf Ferdinand von Zeppelin, the German aeronautical genius, had been developing his designs. During World War I his Zeppelins had frequently raided London; in later years several successfully crossed the Atlantic. Until 1924 all British airships had been direct copies of the Zeppelins. One of them, the R.34, had flown the Atlantic way back in 1919, but their record on the whole was not encouraging. One airship fell apart, one flew into a hill, one broke up in midair on a trial flight. But all this was to change once the Imperial Airship Scheme got underway under the energetic patronage of Christopher Thomson. From now on, the designers were to be British and over one million pounds sterling was earmarked for a research and development program. Two airships were to be built: one the R.100 (R for "rigid"), contracted to a private company, another the R.101, to be built by a government team. For the R.101 a huge shed was erected at Cardington, about sixty miles from London, where the design team was to work. So proud was Christopher Thomson of his project and so confident of its significance that when he was elevated to the peerage he took the name of the airship works for his title, and became Lord Thomson of Cardington.

Marthe arrived at the Ritz Hotel in London on July 4 and, as usual, was greeted by a gigantic bouquet of red roses from Christopher Thomson. After lunching with Lady Colefax, the famous hostess, they drove on to Wimbledon to watch Helen Wills of the United States retain the championship of the Ladies' Singles for the third time, defeating her fellow Californian Helen Jacobs. There followed a weekend at Philip Sassoon's sumptuous house in the country with King Alfonso XIII of Spain, the Marquess and Marchioness of Salisbury and other distinguished guests. Sassoon and Thomson, though on opposite sides in politics, shared a common interest in aviation and were working together on the preparation of the Schneider Trophy (international aeronautical prize founded by a German industrialist) that summer.

It had been an exciting week for Marthe. London was at its best in perfect weather; she stayed at Taplow, home of the Desboroughs, with Lady Diana Cooper and Winston Churchill; dined at Clarence House, the residence of the Duke and Duchess of Connaught, Queen Victoria's youngest son, whom she had once entertained at Posada; spent some time with her close friend Lady Leslie, Winston Churchill's aunt; and attended a number of concerts and exhibitions. But the highlight of the stay was her meeting with the Prime Minister. One afternoon, as Marthe was having tea with Lord Thomson on the terrace of the House of Lords overlooking the Thames, reminiscing about another river—the

Danube—she saw a tall "strikingly handsome white-haired man" coming toward them. It was Ramsay MacDonald, the Prime Minister. Being an intimate friend of Lord Thomson, MacDonald knew of his affection for Marthe, but curiously he had been reluctant to meet her. "Why make her come out of the pages of *Smaranda?*" he chided Thomson. "She might turn out to be a disappointment when I see her." But, like his friend, MacDonald soon fell under Marthe's charm. It was the beginning of a close friendship, which was to last for the next nine years until his death.

During the same week, Lord Thomson confided to Marthe that he was being considered as the next British Viceroy in India. Lord Irwin, the present Viceroy, was due to complete his tour of office in early 1931; there seemed to be no one in the party suitable for that high office and MacDonald had apparently asked Lord Thomson to "think it over." "You don't have to accept yet," he told him. "You would be a great loss to me here, but there is no more vital post than India—especially at this time." For Christopher Thomson, who had been born in India, it would mean the return to the land of his birth in the highest office of the state.

According to Marthe's diaries and to Christopher Thomson's biographer Sir Peter Masefield, Lord Thomson hoped that one day Marthe would become free and join him there. Although there is no doubt that Thomson's appointment to India had been considered by MacDonald, he was only one among a number of candidates lining up for the succession. What is highly unlikely, however, is that either he or Marthe would have seriously thought that she might have ever become his Vicereine. No divorced woman, let alone a foreigner, would have been allowed to represent the Empire in that high post. In the circumstances it is easy to understand Christopher Thomson's hesitation and his melancholy remark: "The appointment is for five years—what would the future hold for us then?" Sadly the future was soon to provide its own tragic solution.

After her annual cure at Bagnoles-de-l'Orne, Marthe returned to Romania in late summer. She went to Posada, as the heat and drought of that year had been stifling and there was a shortage of water at Mogosoëa. She loved her retreat in the mountains. "The dahlias under my window are a riot of color," she noted in her diary. "Baba Outza, who knows everything, warns me that there will be frost in the night and that they will be turning black. . . . I laughed at her, but it happened—not only the dahlias but the daisies, geraniums and the buddleia—only the roses survived, but the day's sun is hot under a bright blue sky and there is no wind; nothing moves. . . . I can hear the distant flute of the shepherd on the mountain slope . . . and the laughter of girls on the banks of the river; they are busy immersing yards of newly woven cloth in the stream; soaking it in the crystal-clear water and laying it out on the bank to be dried in the sun; they are preparing their trousseaus."

The routine of writing was the same, whether Marthe resided at Posada or at Mogosoëa: she remained in her room working every day until lunchtime, protected by the famous Miss Chatfield (Chatty) and Baba Outza. That autumn Marthe was drawing up an outline for a gigantic historical work, *La Nymphe Europe*, which she hoped would be published by Grasset. Based on her family's history, it was to run to thirty volumes and mirror the ebb and flow of the fortunes and the genealogical connections of the great families of Eastern Europe; she died before it was completed.

Closer in time, in a profile of Marshal Lyautey, the distinguished French proconsul and Resident-General in Morocco in the early twenties, she described her recent trip to Morocco, which she visited earlier that year with George. (George, in order to get over his complicated love affairs, had been shooting lions in Africa; Marthe went to meet him in Oran and they traveled together by car through Morocco to Paris.) They were both enchanted with Morocco—the people, the food, the splendid gardens and most of all the prevailing order. "Everything there speaks of Lyautey— it's his domain," Marthe wrote in an enthusiastic letter to Antoine, urging him to go there for a holiday. She sent a copy of *Catherine Paris* to the Marshal, now retired and living in France; she dedicated the book to "the royalist, who had given an Empire to the Republic."

It had been a busy autumn at Mogosoëa, overshadowed by the

political uncertainty hanging over Crown Prince Carol's attempted return and Queen Marie's unhappiness at being, as she complained to Marthe, "shunted aside" by the Prime Minister and the Regency Council. It was with a feeling of relief that Marthe, this time accompanied by her husband, stepped onto the Orient Express for Paris, where they arrived in the first week of December. As her lease at 71, Faubourg St. Honoré was expiring, she had moved to 51, rue de l'Université, where she occupied an entire floor in a beautiful old building, which once belonged to the Pozzo di Borgo family. "What a pleasure to live on the Left Bank," she exclaimed. "I am back in the heart of the Faubourg."

The year 1930 was the year during which Marthe could truly say, "I have been intimately connected with the sources of power in Europe." Early in January, as she was settling down in her new Paris apartment, she received a telephone call from King Alfonso of Spain, insisting they meet in Barcelona, where he was to open the great 1930 Exhibition. Marthe always found it difficult to resist the passionate urging of a king, and Alfonso XIII was one of the most charming and cultivated men of his day. She went to Barcelona, spent three days feted, admired and escorted by the man "whose face appears on all the coins."

Soon after, it was time to fulfill her engagements in England. There a delightful surprise awaited her—an invitation from the Prime Minister to spend a weekend with him and Lord Thomson at Chequers, his country residence, in July. If this wasn't enough, Sir Philip Sassoon, at whose house she was staying, presented her with an unexpected gift: an emerald-and-sapphire brooch which Napoleon gave to Marie Walewska when he learned she was expecting his child. It was Philip Sassoon's "thank you" to Marthe for the introduction she wrote to his book *The Third Way*, describing his recent air exploits.

In the meantime Christopher Thomson's great project was nearing completion. It appeared that nothing had been spared to make the R.101 a supreme example of British technology. It looked magnificent with gilded pillars in the "smoking room," a huge dining room with potted palms, "positively an aerial hotel," as one observer reported. In reality, however, it was a rather amateurish and makeshift construction. The R.101 made her trial flight in September 1929, just before the next Imperial Conference in London, to be attended by the representatives of all self-governing dominions and of India. How grand, thought Lord Thomson; the biggest airship on earth would take the Air Minister from London to Delhi and bring him back to Westminster for the conference.

It was with immense satisfaction that Lord Thomson informed Marthe of these plans when she arrived in London on July 18. She had spent the preceding three months in Romania and was at Mo-gosoëa on the evening of June 6, quietly working on her latest book, *Croisade pour l'Anémone*, when her cousin Simky Lahovary, Queen Marie's former lady-in-waiting, telephoned with the news that the former Crown Prince had returned. Bucharest was plunged into turmoil.

The coup that brought Carol home, as Marthe later recounted to Lord Thomson, was accomplished with the help of Prime Minister Iuliu Maniu and the Army, where the former Crown Prince had always been popular, in spite of his wartime desertion. The coup was executed without the knowledge of his mother, Queen Marie. Prime Minister Maniu laid three conditions before the "prodigal son": first, that he return only as Regent, leaving his son on the throne; second, that he would leave Madame Lupescu behind; and third, that he would reconcile himself with his wife, Princess Helen. Carol agreed to everything but had no intention of abiding by his promises. On arrival in Bucharest he went straight to his old Army barracks, where he was cheered by the soldiers. He then drove to the Cotroceni Palace, where his brother Nicholas, member of the Regency Council, was waiting. Nicholas hated being Regent; he hoped to leave Romania and rejoin the British Navy. The two brothers embraced, and Carol announced that he planned to occupy the throne at once. In spite of the Prime Minister's objections, both the cabinet and the Regency Council voted to accept him as King, and the next day Parliament took the crown away from young Michael and proclaimed his father as King Carol II. When Queen Marie returned from abroad, she found that her prerogatives as Queen Mother were being drastically curtailed. A few days later Madame Lupescu arrived and took possession of a luxurious four-story villa near the palace. Carol's wife, Helen, was treated as an unwelcome stranger; the education of former King Michael was taken over by his father. It was a tragedy not only for Queen Helen but also for the Dowager Queen, who found that most of her entourage, whom she had known and trusted for years, were now being forced to leave Romania or retire. In pursuing a one-man rule, the new King proceeded to relegate his Prime Minister and cabinet to positions of errand boys, filling important posts with adventurers and ill-mannered acolytes collected during his years of exile. Stirbey, Bratiano and others familiar to the Romanian public for years were no longer allowed near the palace.

In the midst of these goings-on Marthe received a visit from Michael, the former boy king, now lumbered with the exotic title of "Voivode of Alba Julia." He was brought over by his English governess to "provide him with a change from the gloom of his father's palace" and let him see the black swans on the lake at Mogosoëa. Much amused, Marthe watched him empty his pockets of their contents, which included bits of string, pocketknives and an assortment of tiny models of locomotives, for he wanted to be "an engine driver or a mechanic when he grew up."

Marthe, of course, disapproved of the "farcical and burlesque" proceedings at the court of Carol II, and it was with immense relief that she left to accompany George at the International Aeronautical Congress in Copenhagen. From there she traveled to London and to the Ritz, where she was greeted by the usual gigantic bouquet of red roses from her "knight-errant."

On Saturday, July 19, Marthe and Lord Thomson drove together to Chequers in his Air Ministry car. "It was a happy, intimate weekend," she wrote to the Abbé Mugnier. "We walked in the park, which contains some of the oldest trees in the kingdom—I particularly loved the gigantic tulip tree on the terrace, which greets the guests on arrival; it happened to be in full flower." There were no other guests; the three spent most of the time talking, and Marthe marveled at MacDonald and Thomson's close rapport. "They understand each other without words," she noted; "no wonder the Prime Minister refers to them as 'David and Jonathan.' "

On their return to London, Lord Thomson was caught up in a series of meetings and official engagements, while Marthe visited old friends such as Lady Leslie and the widowed Margot Asquith, attended a garden party at Buckingham Palace, spent a day with Lady Ottoline Morrell and Lytton Strachey and a weekend with Enid Bagnold. She saw Thomson once more before leaving. They had tea on the terrace of the House of Lords and later walked together in St. James's Park. "It was a beautiful evening," Marthe recalled. "We sat on a bench in the park for a long time, talking about his possible nomination as Viceroy—'I think I can have it, if I want to,' he said—and about the R.101 maiden flight to Karachi. He told me the airship was making good progress and would surely be ready on time. We parted at the door of the Ritz. It was the last time I saw him."

On the evening of October 4 the distinguished passengers arrived at the Royal Airship Works at Cardington for the great flight. It was a gray, cold night, but as they stepped from their limousines, they saw the vast silver shape of the R.101 shining magnificently above their heads. A big crowd had gathered at the airfield and the lights of hundreds of cars illuminated the scene, "giving it an air of fantasy and nightmare," as one of the witnesses recalled. The crew had been working frantically at last-minute improvements, but there was a feeling of uncertainty among them: "We are just not ready," the airship captain Flight Lieutenant Carmichael Irwin confided to a journalist; "they are rushing us."

Fifty-four people boarded the R.101 that evening, all men: twelve officials and forty-two crew. Slowly the engines spluttered, the airship moved clear of the tower and began to gain height, making its way heavily to the south. After dinner some of the passengers sat in the huge lounge, while others went to the smoking room and gazed through the rain-smeared windows. The weather forecast was ominous. Over France the drizzle developed into gusty squalls and the winds strengthened. Flying over the Channel, the R.101 was blown almost sideways by their force:

sometimes it might even have been moving backward. Shortly after two in the morning the radio operator exchanged messages with the airport at Le Bourget in Paris and confirmed that the airship was near Beauvais, a market city some eighty miles north of the capital. She was flying slowly, shaken by winds. Suddenly one of the crew, looking out of the window, saw a few yards away from the airship the roof of a building "stuck about with pinnacles." It was the roof of the Beauvais Cathedral. He had hardly had time to alert his companions when they heard a tremendous breaking roar, a frenzied ringing of bells, a clatter of feet and the shout of an officer somewhere: "We're down, lads! We're down!" Almost at once there was a deafening explosion and a vast column of fire rose into the sky.

All but eight men on the R.101 died in the accident; two more died later of their burns. Lord Thomson, Sir Sefton Brancker, chief of the project, the pilot Irwin, representatives of the Indian and Australian governments, the designers and chief constructors of the great airship all died. Nothing was left of their work but a colossal pile of metal on the edge of a wood near Beauvais. So catastrophic was the tragedy, so humiliating to British pride, that the Imperial Airship Scheme was abandoned; the other ship, the R.100, was broken up and no more British airships were built. The field was left to the Germans with their *Graf Spee* and *Hindenburg*, until tragedy overcame them too and the whole breed of intercontinental airships passed into legend and conjecture.

It was dawn in Mogosoëa, a thousand miles away from Beauvais, when Marthe awoke from a deep sleep with an overwhelming feeling of malaise. "I knew something dreadful was happening," she later said. "I experienced a frightening tightness in my chest; afraid I might be having a heart attack, I woke up the servants. George appeared and tried to calm me." They led her to an armchair, where she sat watching the sun rise over the lake. The following morning George drove into Bucharest, planning to return in late evening. But he was back before lunch with the tragic news.

Afterward came the details: appalling descriptions of bodies burned alive in the wreckage, cries for help which no one answered in the stormy night, agonizing photographs and days of dramatic coverage in French and British newspapers.

Marthe was at first too stunned to take it all in. For a day and a night she cried, unable to stop; she mourned Kit, her "knight-errant," the man who had loved her for fifteen years without ever getting much in return. She remembered Bucharest during the war, how he had risked his life to protect her, and his unflinching devotion in the twenties, when she—busy with her social life—often could not find time to see him.

A telegram arrived from the Prime Minister: "In profound sympathy. Bodies lie in state Westminster Hall; Memorial Service St. Paul's Cathedral Monday noon. Funeral Saturday. Ramsay MacDonald."

They brought them home on the destroyer HMS *Tempest*; Marthe did not go to England for the funeral, but asked that one red rose be dropped for her into Thomson's grave; the Prime Minister saw that it was done. Later Ramsay MacDonald wrote to her: "I was glad to have your letter. You and I know what each other feels; life will be more weary without him, but we must go on. This is the day of the memorial service and tomorrow is the funeral. I go to both and shall take you with me. He would like that. I met him at Victoria at 2 o'clock on Tuesday morning; I could not let him come back without being there to greet him. Ever yours, Ramsay MacDonald."

In December, Marthe and the Abbé Mugnier traveled to Beauvais. She brought with her fifteen red roses—one for each year of their friendship. The sky was cloudy, a weak wintry sun shone over the forest of Allonne. They walked about in the newly plowed field, looking for the exact spot. A workman, his beret in hand, led them to an opening in the wood, where a huge pile of metal was being broken up and dismantled. "We collected their watches, cameras, cuff links—*they* survived—but the bodies were burned." The Abbé pronounced words of peace and an absolution. They then slowly made their way back to the car.

On Christmas Eve of that memorable year a basket filled with red roses arrived at Marthe's rue de l'Université apartment, accompanied by an envelope addressed in Lord Thomson's familiar hand. The card inside read: "for delivery on Christmas Eve 1930"; the date, August 28, 1930, a day he happened to be in Paris. The note said:

> *If not September, not even October, then for Christmas and for always. Here with all my love now and forever, some more of our roses for yesterday and for tomorrow. They come for one who has brightened fifteen long years since 1915—so long ago and now so far away. They come from one who cheerfully then began to suffer that incurable malady, which some call love; and I call Marthe.*
> *A very Happy Christmas, dearest,*
> *From my heart and mind, with my devotion eternally:*
> *Ever yours—*
> *KIT*

To Marthe, as to most people of her generation, the thirties were a deeply troubling time, when events that could not be controlled seemed to be leading to the same catastrophe that had engulfed the world some twenty-odd years before. To the Abbé Mugnier and others who had lived through the 1870 Franco-Prussian War, the prospect of a "third time around" was a nightmare. "Events have faces for me," Marthe often said. "I always link them with the personalities I have known." From early childhood, Marthe had heard about the "balance of power" and had watched statesmen hopelessly striving to realize this elusive goal. While she was still grieving over the death of Lord Thomson, one particular statesman became interlinked with her life: Ramsay MacDonald, the Prime Minister of Great Britain. The loss they shared brought them close together. It was as if Kit had bequeathed Marthe to his dearest friend. For the next five years, while in office and later as a private person, Ramsay MacDonald wrote to Marthe at least once a week, sometimes more—poetic, humorous or simply factual letters in which comments on current events intermingled with philosophical musings and growing affection.

"I was so glad to have you at Chequers and to beat you at

croquet!—the only accomplishment at which I can beat you," he wrote in his first letter on July 27, 1930, shortly after Marthe and Lord Thomson first stayed with him for the weekend. "I have to lunch with King Feisal on Wednesday, but if you could join me in my room at the House of Commons at 3 pm we might walk over together to Downing Street and you could have a glimpse of my pictures." Two days later, on July 29, he wrote again to thank her for sending him *Jours d'Egypte*: "Its pages were like those choicely planted nooks hidden in gardens upon which the stranger stumbles and is dumb with the beauty thereof. But when I master the beauty I begin to quarrel with you for saying that, from the beginning of Time, no-one has believed in death. That is not so; men have always known death and have been afraid to make Fate a belief. That is just my challenge to show you that I have read with care as well as with joy."

After Thomson's death Marthe visited Ramsay MacDonald regularly in Downing Street, at Chequers and at Lossiemouth, his Scottish home. In contrast to Edith Londonderry, the famous "Circe" often said to have been MacDonald's Egeria in earlier years, Marthe extended her friendship to MacDonald's children, establishing close links with his three daughters and son Malcolm, the future Minister of the Colonies.

Early in the New Year, Marthe received a letter from the Prime Minister inviting her to spend the coming weekend at Chequers. She crossed to England on January 16, was met at Victoria Station by Lord Lloyd and conveyed to Chequers in the Prime Minister's "well-known, comfortable blue car." Alone for most of the time —Ishbel, the Prime Minister's daughter, did not arrive until Sunday—they walked, read, sat by the fire and talked. He told her about his childhood in Scotland as the illegitimate son of a workman and Annie, a domestic servant; how, having left school at fifteen with a few shillings in his pocket, he set off for London to make his life in the big city. Strikingly handsome, he won the affection of Margaret Gladstone, daughter of a rich Socialist businessman, one of the founders of the YMCA, who provided him with the means to educate himself further and to travel; she also made him extremely happy. After her death in 1911, he wrote a touching book of reminiscences, which Thomson gave Marthe to read before their first visit to Chequers.

The Prime Minister, with a glass of whiskey in his hand, and Marthe, bent over a piece of embroidery, discussed the vicissitudes of the Treaty of Versailles, about which he had always shared Christopher Thomson's misgivings. He told her about his meeting with Lenin in the early twenties and his encounter with Mussolini, for whom he harbored "an amused sympathy." After dinner, while he worked on his speech for the forthcoming debate on India, Marthe "helped him to sort out letters." "It was a quiet, serene evening, in the depths of the Buckinghamshire countryside, at the side of this handsome and silent Scot, who happened to be Prime Minister of a great Empire."

That same week, while in England, Marthe made a pilgrimage to Devon to meet Christopher Thomson's mother, with whom he had been very close. She wanted to retrace the journey Kit must have taken so many times in his life. She found a remarkable woman of eighty-six "with a fresh, alert face and a halo of silvery hair," who received her as if she had known her all her life. Marthe knew that Kit had told his mother about his "Romanian princess" and that she had read *Smaranda*; she must have realized long ago why her son never married. Yet no trace of resentment surfaced during the long afternoon the two women spent together in the charming cottage by the sea. "I had ten children in thirteen years of my married life," she told Marthe, "but Christopher was very different from the others. . . . He was the brightest of them and the most ambitious. . . . He always reached for the stars." They parted like very close friends.

In the spring of 1931 George was elected president of the International Aeronautical Federation. A brand-new airplane was shipped from the United States in parts and reassembled in London. He flew it over to Paris and prepared for his first presidential flight—Rome, Ismailia in Egypt, Baghdad, Allahabad and Benares—a long and dangerous journey. George was a brilliant pilot, but even he must have felt some anxiety, for he accompanied Marthe to church in Paris on Easter Sunday. "He stood by me, arms crossed, seemingly unaware of the service, but I knew that he prayed—and so did I." It was agreed that they would meet in Marseilles in two weeks' time.

The airport at Le Bourget, where Marthe bade farewell to her husband, was bitterly cold, and the next day she came down with a violent attack of bronchitis. She was in bed when she heard of King Alfonso XIII's abdication and his exit from Madrid in an automobile accompanied solely by his driver, "the same one who had driven us all around Barcelona last year." The Spanish Republic was proclaimed on April 17. The King telephoned her the next morning: "I left to avoid a civil war. Am in Paris on my way to the Quai d'Orsay to get a residence permit." But next morning all thoughts of the dethroned King were pushed into the background by a telegram from India: "Prince Bibesco's plane crashed in flames near Allahabad. He recovered consciousness, but is seriously wounded; the others still unconscious." Frantic, Marthe tried to obtain more details; when attempts to contact the air attaché at the British Embassy in Paris came to nothing, she telephoned Enid Bagnold in London, whose husband, Sir Roderick Jones, was head of the Reuters News Agency. A signal was sent to a Reuters agent in Benares to proceed to the scene of the accident and telephone Princess Bibesco in Paris with a report. "After what seemed an eternity the telephone finally rang and I heard a reassuring English voice: 'The Prince is seriously wounded in the legs, but his general condition is satisfactory. He and his three companions are being transported to the Edward VII Hospital in Benares, a military hospital well equipped to look after them. The cause of the accident was a collision with a particularly large vulture.' "

There followed an agonizing series of days during which Marthe realized how much she cared for her errant husband. Her first thought was to fly to his bedside, but this turned out to be impossible, as regular air communication did not exist in those days. Thanks to daily reports forwarded by Reuters from Benares, Marthe could follow George's recovery step by step. He was lucky; both his copilot and the navigator died of wounds in the hospital. But it would still be at least a month before he could be transported by ship to Marseilles. In the meantime, advised by the

Abbé Mugnier, who worried about the strain imposed on her by the constant stream of visitors and sympathetic inquirers, Marthe decided to take up MacDonald's invitation to visit him at his Scotland home over the parliamentary recess in May. Sir Roderick Jones promised that the Reuters reports would be forwarded to her there.

Marthe arrived in England on the day when the *Daily Express* was publishing excerpts from *Smaranda*, accompanied by photographs of Lord Thomson and her. The photographs, taken a few years before, were flattering: "She looks more like a flower than an ordinary human," ran a headline. She lunched with Sir Roderick Jones and Harold Nicolson, the diarist, and visited the Chelsea Flower Show with Lord Lloyd. Then it was off to Downing Street to dine with the Prime Minister, who was leaving for Scotland by plane the next day. Marthe and MacDonald's daughter Ishbel traveled to Lossiemouth together by train.

"Hillocks is a very ordinary Scottish house—a spacious stone cottage with a garden, in a fishermen's village by the sea," Marthe noted in her diary for May 23, 1931. "It is sparsely furnished; there is a small sitting room with a stone fireplace, a few bedrooms, rather spartan. . . . The PM's bedroom has a narrow, uncomfortable-looking bed; there is a reproduction of Raphael's 'Madonna della Sedia' over his bed, strange for a Presbyterian, but he says he has always liked it. He pointed to the curtains (rather ugly red and green linen) made from cloth woven by his grandmother Ishbel Allen. 'The color has not changed for fifty years!' Villagers here are used to the Prime Minister's presence—he is one of them and they pay no attention to his comings and goings.

"The night after my arrival the PM was scheduled to broadcast to the nation on the occasion of the closing of the Dominions Conference. The little house was suddenly full of wires and technicians; they installed the microphone in his bedroom. Silence fell, then his famous baritone Scottish voice, with its dramatic risings and fallings, its emotional richness and its expressive cadences, which could hold a crowd spellbound at political meetings, rose in the air. It was a historic occasion. What was I doing there? I asked myself. What strange caprice of fate has deposited me, an international aristocrat, a Romanian, in the midst of a village in northern Scotland, to listen to a speech made by this apostle of Socialism? How strange is my destiny and how odd that I should feel so perfectly at home here in this land of witches and fairies."

As the ship on which George was returning sailed into Marseilles, Marthe saw her husband leaning against the railing, looking cheerful, as if nothing had happened. She saw him wave aside a nurse who tried to bring him crutches. It was only when he disembarked and was comfortably installed in the Paris Express, that she noticed the outsize trousers, hiding thick bandages over his wounds; he was obviously in acute pain, but determined not to show it. Marthe telegraphed to Paris for an ambulance to take them to the Clinic on the rue Bizet.

Their return to Romania was a triumphant occasion. Military planes escorted the train from the frontier all the way to the Bucharest station, where a huge crowd had gathered to welcome their "air hero." Two very tall men—aviators and friends of George— carried him to the car, carefully propping him with cushions on the seat. They drove to the royal palace, where the King himself, aware of George's condition, came to the car and pinned a medal for bravery on his chest. The crowds continued to cheer. As everywhere else in Europe in those days, the conquest of the air captured the popular imagination.

The next ten days were taken up with the International Aeronautical Federation Congress, meeting for the first time on Romanian soil at Sinaia and later at Mogosöea. As president, George delivered the opening speech; Marthe, of course, wrote it for him, as she did many of the subsequent talks, including the much acclaimed closing address, which the delegates found "inspiring and delivered in poetic language." "I recognize your hand in the text," Queen Marie said to Marthe as they sat together on the podium during the closing ceremony. Marthe smiled and shook her head in denial.

Marthe shuttled between Mogosoëa and Posada until the end of July, entertaining George's international crowd of aviation guests and writing. As usual, she spent every morning in her room working—this time putting finishing touches to a collection of articles about her trip to the Holy Land, later published under the title *Croisade pour l'Anémone*. A project close to her heart was a biography, *The Destiny of Lord Thomson of Cardington*, to which Ramsay MacDonald promised to write a foreword.

After assisting at the marriage of Ileana, Queen Marie's youngest daughter, to Anton Hapsburg, "a marriage between two moribund dynasties," as she called it, Marthe boarded the faithful Orient Express for Vienna and Paris, where she arrived in early August. At the rue de l'Université apartment she found a letter from Ishbel, Prime Minister MacDonald's daughter, telling her that shortly after her departure in May her father ordered twenty willow trees to be planted in front of their house at Lossiemouth to screen the house from onlookers and "to remind him of *Isvor*"! Ishbel wrote that her father was "absolutely exhausted."

And no wonder. The summer of 1931 was a period fraught with disasters for the Labor government and for England, as indeed it was for most of Europe. The miseries of the Great Depression plunged countries everywhere into utter confusion. Unemployment in England increased from 1.5 million to 2.75 million. In Germany, where the French refused to cancel war reparations, it went over 5 million; hyperinflation set in, producing a climate in which the rise of Hitler became inevitable. After nearly fifty years, unemployment had again become a nightmare. In Great Britain "the slump" struck an economy that had already begun to decline. The Labor government, strangled by increasingly stagnating business production, a vacillating currency and mounting unemployment, tried desperately to balance the budget by cutting the pay of civil servants and reducing the Army, public services and, finally, unemployment benefits. As the reserves of the Bank of England became almost exhausted, the government had to abandon convertibility; sterling sank. MacDonald's cabinet was deeply split, as the majority of its members refused to go along with the proposed budget cuts.

The Prime Minister now realized that a Labor government could no longer remain in office and submitted his resignation to King George V. On the morning of August 23 he went to see the King, to inform him formally of the situation. But the King liked

MacDonald and believed that "he was the only person who could carry the country through." He urged him to remain in office. After a series of consultations with Conservative and Liberal leaders, and in view of the threatening economic situation, a National Government was formed with Ramsay MacDonald as Prime Minister. Most of his Socialist colleagues resigned, but MacDonald remained Prime Minister and continued in office after the national election later that year.

Needless to say, Marthe followed the news from England with avid interest. "I am giving Sonia Cahen d'Anvers, who is going to London tomorrow, a bouquet of assorted heathers to deposit in Downing Street for the Prime Minister; I hope it brings him luck; he needs it," she noted in her diary.

She was touched to receive a brief note from MacDonald written on the very evening the National Government was being formed. "That he should have found the time to write to me gives me the most acute pleasure." He wrote again on August 29 telling her that Lord Londonderry had become Minister for Air, the post that was once held by "their friend." "He would have been a great comfort to me now," he ended wistfully.

The general election in England on October 27, 1931, was a sweeping victory for the National Government and MacDonald; they won 558 seats against 56 for the Opposition. A delighted King George V declared, "Please God, shall now have a little peace and less worries." Marthe's contribution was a telegram in Gaelic to her friend: *"Lang may yer lum reek"* ("Long may your fires burn").

Winter came early to Mogosoëa that year; snow covered the manicured lawns; the lake froze; the swans, out of their element, promenaded in front of Marthe's bedroom windows, flapping their wings, looking like angels suddenly metamorphosed into swans; the sun shone, lighting up the icicles on the trees; everything was white and blue, "like the Prince's family colors," remarked Jean Apolzan, the old butler.

At the risk of becoming marooned in the snow, Marthe went up to Posada, which looked more than ever like a winter wonderland, to make the usual round of pre-Christmas visits in the village, taking gifts and dispensing money where needed. Dressed in a knee-length beaver coat, fur bonnet and soft felt boots, she first called on old Ion Vlad, the blind man, whom she found sitting on a wooden stool in front of the fire, playing the flute for his seven children. Next was Marie, the widow, who shared a house with a cow, two dogs and several children, who all rushed for cover when the Princess came in, then carefully trooped out one by one from behind the big bed, where they all slept. Urged by their mother, they greeted Marthe timidly, half hiding their faces. The sweets and the money she brought were padlocked by the widow in a large painted trunk, to be opened the day before Christmas.

Baba Outza suggested that Marthe visit her cousin "Mother Safta—old as Time," who had nothing, "not even a dog to guard her." "There was no answer when I knocked," Marthe recalled. "I came in and found the old woman sleeping on a shelf by the stove, rolled up in a ball, like an old serpent. She woke up with a moan as I came in, and said she had dreamt that she was dead and wished it had been so. She will take the money I gave her to the Orthodox priest in the village, who promised to 'arrange for her to die very soon.' She believes him and kisses the coins one by one; they are her assurance of a speedy deliverance from this life."

Further down the road, as she walked, she heard uproarious laughter. Young Ion Fussoï and Nicholas, the kitchen boy, had picked a goose for dinner and were about to bring it to the cook on a sled normally used for transporting firewood. But the top of the sled was slippery and the goose, unable to move or take off, kept flapping its wings, half demented, emitting piercing cries. A crowd of children gathered around, enjoying the spectacle; they all stopped laughing as Marthe came by—probably afraid she might disapprove.

Marthe recalled how she ran into Anika on her way home. Anika told her that last week, on the night of St. Andrew's, she and her friends Kiva, Stanca and Anicoutza had consulted an oracle about their future. They started by each melting a spoonful of lead over the fire, holding it until it became liquid, then throwing it into a bucketful of cold water. Strange figures and landscapes appeared, from which Maria-Soloméa, an experienced fortune-teller, could foretell the events of the coming year; if she saw a shape like a church, a wedding was guaranteed; ditto if she spotted a table or a bed; but sometimes she could only distinguish a cross or something resembling a boat stranded onshore—that meant illness or even death.

To make sure, the girls then went to consult the pigs, for "everyone knows pigs are great prophets." Late in the evening, one after another tiptoed to the enclosure where the pigs were asleep: "Hatza, will it be this year?" A grunt signifies that a wedding is near; silence means "no." "Hatza, answer me! Will it be *next* year?" With her ear to the fence, the girl listens intently; there are times when the pigs remain ominously silent. "Hatza—for the third time—will it be the year *after* next?" Each girl is allowed only three questions. Generally, however, the pigs answer at once, much to everybody's relief.

To reassure themselves, the girls sometimes go into a sheepfold at night and pick up a beast at random in the dark. If it turns out to be a ram, all will be well and the longed-for husband will soon materialize in the village. If, however, she has got hold of a ewe, she will probably remain an old maid.

Isvor and its world of magic and superstitions were what kept Marthe's sense of wonder alive and lent depth and originality to her writing. It is why she felt as at home in Baba Outza's cottage as she did when dining with a king or a Prime Minister. For her roots were in Isvor, no matter how many layers of international life came between them.

Deep snow was piled on both sides of the road to Bucharest when Marthe boarded the new train—the Simplon Express—for Venice; from there she was going to Rome to meet her husband and officiate at the giving of prizes in a new air race, the Bibesco Cup, inaugurated and funded by George. Afterward it was to be Paris and Christmas with Valentine, her husband and the little Jean-Nicholas Ghika, now three and a half years old. While Valentine's husband was completing his studies in Paris, the young family divided their time among an apartment in the rue de l'Université, close to Marthe, Mogosoëa and the Ghika family estates of Comanesti in Moldavia.

In March 1932, Aristide Briand, the great statesman and three times the Prime Minister of France, died in Paris. Briand was Marthe's friend and her mentor. He taught her to believe that, after the horrors of war, the time had come "to speak European." At the newly formed League of Nations he proposed a European Union with common institutions, security and guarantees and coined the term "Common Market," later revived by Jean Monnet. But his project was premature and soon got buried in dust in the chancelleries of Europe. At his funeral, attended by all the European chiefs of state, Marthe noticed a multitude of large placards proclaiming immediate disarmament and heard the crowds chanting, "Down with the cannons" and "Long live peace." It reflected the mood of the time, not only in France but also in England.

Prime Minister Briand's sudden death delayed for a long time one of Marthe's cherished ambitions: the award of the French Légion d'Honneur for "services to literature." Briand had promised he would support her nomination, first suggested by Paul Claudel and subscribed to by at least thirty prominent writers, among them Daniel Halévy, Emile Henriot, Maurice Donnay and others, including the Minister of Education, Maurice Roustan. The nomination was on its way to the Elysée when Briand died. And there it remained. For they had not counted on the jealousy of Helen Vacaresco and Anna de Noailles. The moment the two women heard about it, they set to work and a vicious campaign was started to prevent her from receiving the prestigious award. A fake photograph of Marthe surrounded by German officers in Bucharest during the 1914 war was printed in the Paris weekly *Carrefour*. "Why does she need the Légion d'Honneur?" said the caption. "She already has the Iron Cross." Without her friend at the Elysée to defend her, the project was abandoned for the time being. "What a shame," declared Paul Claudel, "that feminine jealousy should have prevented one of France's most brilliant writers from being given this well-deserved recognition." It took another thirty years for Marthe to finally obtain it.

In early 1932, Marthe had just finished her book *The Destiny of Lord Thomson of Cardington* when she heard from Ramsay Mac-

Donald's secretary that the Prime Minister had just undergone a
painful eye operation and was spending a week in a private hospital in London; he would much welcome a visit.

She found him looking handsome in an aubergine-colored
dressing gown, his abundant silver hair shiny and newly trimmed.
Ishbel was with him, fending off telephone calls and requests for
press interviews. Presently Lady Londonderry arrived, the woman
whom popular gossip in England had long associated with the
Prime Minister. Edith Londonderry was then in her mid-fifties,
about ten years older than Marthe; born Edith Chaplin, cousin of
the Duke of Sutherland and brought up in the Scottish Highlands,
she was married to the Marquess of Londonderry, one of the
richest and most handsome men in the country. Her position in
the highest circles of court and society endowed her with great
influence. She knew everybody, and her receptions at Londonderry House in Park Lane, attended by royalty and the entire political world, were noted for their brilliance. She was a handsome
woman with beautiful skin, a youthful figure and great physical
toughness. (She wore a tattoo—a snake climbing up her left leg,
which was supposed to denote a free spirit but turned out to be a
nuisance during the prevailing fashion of short skirts.) A notable
sportswoman, she rode horses and sailed like a man.

Lady Londonderry met MacDonald shortly after he was first
elected Prime Minister in 1924; they became friends and corresponded regularly. Being close to the everyday political developments in the kingdom, she often acted as a conduit of information
for the Prime Minister and he was known to ask her advice. Like
Marthe, Edith enjoyed being close to the center of power, and
having a Prime Minister at her feet brought pleasure. Though very
fond of MacDonald, as her letters to him indicate, she was nevertheless deeply in love with her "Charley," the seventh Marquess, her splendid-looking and notoriously unfaithful husband,
who had a particular weakness for beautiful American women married into the British aristocracy.*

Much to the annoyance of his Socialist friends, such as Beatrice

---

* Consuelo Vanderbilt, later Madame Balsan, and Eloise Ancaster.

Webb, Ramsay MacDonald never felt any inhibitions about asso-
ciating with the Tories or Tory hostesses. He had always liked
grandeur, ease of manner and pageantry, which to him was tied
up with tradition. As a Highlander, he thought of himself as not
belonging to any particular class. Bernard Shaw said of him that
"he was not really a Socialist in the true sense of the word; he was
a seventeenth-century Highlander, quite at home in feudal society
and out of it among English trade unionists." He also much enjoyed
meeting writers and prominent artists; he once had Charlie Chaplin
and Marthe Bibesco staying with him at Chequers together—a
weekend which turned out to be singularly successful. But with all
this the Prime Minister was a lonely man; his best friend died in the
R.101 crash, his children were grown up and, with the exception of
Ishbel, who helped occasionally as a hostess, busy with their own
lives. He liked the company of women to a degree rare among his
compatriots; they brought out in him a romanticism based on
myths and legends of the Scottish history he adored.

When Marthe Bibesco came into MacDonald's life after the
death of Lord Thomson, he was still deeply attached to Edith
Londonderry and remained so for most of the years of his premiership, but gradually, as the focus of the Londonderrys' life
shifted to Mount Stewart, their palatial house in Northern Ireland,
the links loosened, while his correspondence with Marthe grew
more and more intimate. Considering the crushing burden of office, of which he often complained, it is amazing that he could find
the time to write so frequently and at such length. Now and then
he asked Marthe to, please, destroy his letters, lest they fall into
unauthorized hands. But she could never bring herself to do it.

One can observe the progression of the friendship from the
opening paragraphs of their letters. In 1930 and until Marthe's first
weekend alone at Chequers it was "My dear Princess" and "My
dear Prime Minister." Their correspondence at that time was
mainly concerned with details relating to Lord Thomson. In the
closing months of 1931 they were addressing each other as "My
dear Friend"; later still it became "Dearest Friend" on Marthe's
part and "You of the fairy swanland, who lives in my dreams . . ."
from the romantic and increasingly besotted Prime Minister.

He wrote to her from Cornwall, where he was taking a short holiday:

> *My dear, dear Friend,*
>
> *Your news and comments on life come to me here in a hotel perched high with Atlantic rollers beating on both sides and a wild north-easter blowing a gale over me. I am better and went to Land's End today by car. It is cold, sunny and bracing. . . . I think I told you that when we went into the possibility of a journey to Morocco [she wanted to meet him there] we found it quite impossible. But how tempting the photographs and the descriptions you sent me! I am keeping them and one day, if Fate be kind . . . perhaps . . .*
>
> *Aren't these gossips monkeys? [There had been some gossip about their friendship.] One can do nothing without it being sent wandering through the whispering galleries of London. We seem to be imitating the delightful, but terrible ways of French politics, when Richelieu courted Marie de Rohan & Mazarin showed great kindness to Anne . . . I look forward to the English translation of your book on our friend with great expectation. I feel better; my friends who prescribe "fun" for me are probably right, but how is it to be had whilst I remain faithful to the most fickle jade of all —the destiny of this world??*
>
> > *As ever,*
> >
> > *JRM*

The Destiny of Lord Thomson of Cardington met with a mixed reception. It is quite different from Marthe's other books and somehow fails to convince; it is egocentric; there is too much of Marthe in it and not enough of Christopher Thomson. The French public reacted with indifference; in Britain, where MacDonald's foreword lent it weight, the translation achieved a moderate success; but it did become quite popular in Sweden and Norway, where Lord Thomson had long had the status of a Nordic hero.

Marthe returned to Romania in June, finding the country in a state of chaos. The economic crisis, bad in the rest of Europe, was acute in Romania, aggravated by King Carol's wild expenditures, dynastic quarrels and widespread corruption. In a country "swimming in oil," smothered with grain and timber, there was no money to pay civil servants or the Army. King Carol's Greek wife, Queen Helen, constantly humiliated by her husband, who flaunted Madame Lupescu everywhere, finally left the country for exile in Florence. Nicholas, Carol's younger brother, who had supported him during the coup, was exiled because the King did not approve of his marriage to a commoner. Marie, the Dowager Queen, was allowed home only from time to time, and was forced to spend most of the year with her daughter Mignon in Belgrade or in Vienna. Her allowance had been drastically curtailed by her son and for the first time in her life she suffered from a lack of money. Stirbey, long since exiled and living in Switzerland, was helping her. With the treasury almost empty, draconian currency controls were about to be introduced. "Thank God for my international job," George told Marthe as she met him at Bucharest's Baneasa Airport on his return from a conference with his friend Air Marshal Italo Balbo in Rome. "At least the new law, if it passes, will not concern me. But prudence demands that I remain on friendly terms with King Carol, no matter how much I disapprove of his conduct."

That same year, after her annual cure at Bagnoles-de-l'Orne in Normandy, Marthe accompanied her husband to an International Aeronautical Federation Congress, this time in The Hague. They flew in George's private plane and she delighted in the flight, though she wished "they would make these little planes less noisy."

A message was waiting for her at the London Ritz when she arrived there from Holland: "Hearty welcome! Ring up and say if you can join me and the girls for supper at 7 tonight." The signature was a picture of three swans.

The Prime Minister's eldest daughter, Joan, was getting married to a Dr. Joseph MacKinnon later that month in a family ceremony in Downing Street. The Bibescos were among only a handful of couples asked to the wedding. George reluctantly consented to be present, for he hated ceremonies and social occasions when he thought no attention would be paid to him, and left immediately afterward for Romania.

Marthe stayed on in England for a while to go over the English translation of her book on Lord Thomson, to be published by Jonathan Cape later that year. Going over the proofs with the Prime Minister revived their joint memories of the friend who had brought them together. "We were sitting side by side on a bench in the Downing Street rose garden with the proofs of the book spread on the grass around us, when he looked at me wistfully and said, 'He is gone, but the need of him is not gone.' He took my hand and held it for a while. We went in, but he asked me to stay on while he dictated letters by telephone to his ministers. I am so touched and honored by the absolute confidence he has in my discretion," Marthe confided to her diary. That night they dined on grouse, sent over from Balmoral with an accompanying note from King George V: "I shot them myself." They remained talking until late, and as it was a beautiful evening, the Prime Minister accompanied Marthe back to the Ritz, walking across the Horse Guards Parade and St. James's Park, while the inevitable detective trailed discreetly behind.

Marthe had committed herself to a great opus, *La Nymphe Europe*, which was to be her life's work but which she would never complete. It required extensive research. Constantinople, being the cradle of the Mavrocordato family, was where she started. As luck would have it, a good friend had just been posted there. Charles de Chambrun, her host in Athens of a few years before, was now French Ambassador in Turkey. His appointment considerably smoothed the path of her research in the local archives.

MacDonald's communications followed her there: "I have read with greatest pleasure your wonderful letters from Constantinople," he wrote on October 13, 1931. "You write lusciously, like in the *Eight Paradises*, which I still keep by my bed. What would I give to be with you visiting Saint Sophia, walking on the battlements . . . but it is not to be, or at least not immediately. . . . I am overwhelmed with work and worry at the moment. Herriot [the French Prime Minister] is coming here in about ten minutes, so I must end. As soon as I can, I shall send you a longer and fuller gossip. I kiss your hand for each swan."

A week later came a rather forlorn little message, forwarded back to Mogosoëa by the French Embassy in Constantinople: "Where on earth are you? I have written to every capital in heaven and earth and my letters have been returned. With whom have you run away?"

It must indeed have been hard to keep track of Marthe in between her endless moves. Left to herself, she would have prolonged her stay in Constantinople, which was an enchantment to her, then remained at Mogosoëa until Christmas, quietly working, entertaining visitors and hoping that MacDonald might perhaps be among them. But her husband's new position as president of the International Aeronautical Federation imposed duties. In early November we find her visiting with George in Bohemia, at Hermannmestec, the enormous château of Count Kinsky, head of the Austrian branch of the Aeronautical Federation, and assisting at a gigantic pheasant shoot to which all the best guns in Europe were invited. "It was a weekend straight out of *Catherine Paris*," Marthe noted in a letter to the Abbé Mugnier. "Most of Europe's *Almanach de Gotha* were present and the bag was over two thousand pheasants and assorted other small creatures. I hated it!"

The year 1933 was filled with fateful events: on January 30, Hitler became Chancellor of Germany; the Japanese attack on Manchuria was condemned by the League of Nations, prompting Japan to walk out; then, in October, Hitler took Germany out of the League and denounced the World Disarmament Conference. The threat of Germany's growing power was perceived by only a handful of politicians, Churchill among them, but the majority of people did not want to hear his message; pacifism was growing both as a mood and as a policy; the main preoccupation of the time was unemployment. It was not until the spring of 1935 that MacDonald realized how dangerous Germany was becoming and took a strong line against Hitler.

Like MacDonald, Marthe was slow to realize the dangers of pacifism. She was an ardent proponent of European unity and too close to the memories of World War I to even consider the possibility of another conflict. As time went on, however, it became clear to her that the prophecies of Lord Thomson had been right.

Curiously it was George who saw it all coming. As president of the International Aeronautical Federation, he regularly visited Germany, where he watched the buildup of the German Air Force and talked to his friends among the flyers. "You had better start building air defenses along the Channel," he told Philip Sassoon in the course of a leisurely weekend at Port Lympne. "It won't be long now before the German Air Force is the equal of that of Britain."

The spring of 1933 was a season of international conferences, which provided an opportunity for MacDonald to visit Paris frequently and see Marthe. She was now regularly included on the British Embassy's guest list and the Prime Minister's schedule was adjusted so he would have time to take tea at her new apartment on the Quay Bourbon, on the Ile St. Louis. An entry in her diary for March 9, 1933, describes one of their meetings: "This morning a letter from JRM, signed 'Three Swans.' He is in Paris. Happiness! Dinner with JRM in 'Pauline's Nest' [the British Embassy in Paris is the former house of Pauline Borghese, Napoleon's sister]. All Paris would like to be in my place. What is this place? How did I get to it? Lovely intimate dinner in the small dining room of the Embassy. He, Ishbel, the MacKinnons, Sir John Simon [the Foreign Minister], the Campbells—all English. JRM looks well, good-humored, leaving for Geneva for the Disarmament Conference tomorrow morning. Whom did I represent? Not Romania, not even France—I suppose I represented the Continent of Europe. . . . Or just myself. . . . I was sitting at JRM's right; afterward, in the yellow salon he came and sat next to me on a little sofa by the fire, but kept his distance, as others were watching . . . the dear Puritan! We laughed a lot."

Marthe liked to think that she inspired some of MacDonald's speeches, such as the one during the Disarmament Conference when he said, "We have acted as true Europeans—I could even say as Catholics in the universal sense of the word." That day she noted in her diary, "It gave me divine pleasure to read it—those were *my* words."

Marthe returned to Mogosoëa that spring by air, in a small

plane piloted by her husband. The flight between Le Bourget and Baneasa Airport took ten hours, with four refueling stops; in spite of the 4 a.m. takeoff from Le Bourget, Marthe adored it; she was becoming an air travel addict.

At Mogosoëa there was the usual succession of guests: French cabinet ministers, including Prime Minister Joseph Paul-Boncour, journalists and a flow of visiting aviators, friends of George. Marthe's favorite visitor was Antoine de Saint-Exupéry, who enchanted her by his descriptions of the poetry of air travel. Years later, after his untimely death in 1944, Marthe recalled those long June evenings at Mogosoëa, when they rowed together in her little boat on the lake, talking about Tennyson, who had predicted powered flight way back in 1842, and H. G. Wells's *The War in the Air*, which appeared in 1908, the year Blériot flew across the Channel. Saint-Exupéry became a frequent visitor and one of Marthe and George's closest friends.

In early July, Antoine arrived unexpectedly from Madrid, bringing with him a letter from Ramsay MacDonald, posted in Washington, where he was paying an official visit to President Roosevelt. The letter had landed at the Barcelona Ritz and was given to Antoine while he was passing through. "So much for security," he laughed, handing it over to Marthe. The letter contained a description of the Prime Minister's visit to the White House and ended with a quote, which pleased Marthe, and would have amused Antoine: "Sweet constancy, with eyes of hope. Though miles apart, yet as one."

London was in the throes of a heat wave when Marthe arrived at the Ritz during the last week of July 1933. As usual, her schedule was full: she attended a garden party at Buckingham Palace, during which Queen Mary spoke to her about "the lack of manners" of Nicholas of Romania, Carol's exiled brother, now living in London; she dined with the Prince of Wales at Sir Philip Sassoon's house, saw Leonie Lady Leslie and lunched with Sybil Colefax. On her last evening in London she dined alone with the Prime Minister at Downing Street.

Tension had been building between them: the letters, the visits, the frequent telephone calls, which had become more and more urgent of late, were slowly leading to a climax. Conversations had become intimate. It was well past midnight when Marthe rose to say goodbye. "Before I knew what was happening I was in his arms," she recalled. "I will never forget his kiss, so young, so strangely chaste, insistent, searching my lips and sealing them with his . . . a moment we both felt had been coming. . . . I remained in his arms for a long time. . . . I feel happy and immensely spoiled." On the way back to Paris in Philip Sassoon's plane, Marthe relived the events of the night before, touching her arm "now and then" to make sure it had "really happened".

Bagnoles-de-l'Orne, the watering spa where she usually spent the first two weeks of August every year, was a welcome release from the emotional atmosphere of London; it also enabled Marthe to complete a series of articles for *The Saturday Evening Post*, a source of precious foreign currency in those days. Antoine, who was being transferred from Madrid, much to his fury, stayed with her in Bagnoles for a week, providing comic distraction with his caustic stories about the goings-on at the court of Carol II in Bucharest, and the "dumb ignorance" of the Romanian Foreign Service, who failed to recognize what an asset he was to them and to the country.

Marthe was now forty-seven. She was no longer the "woman flower" of the days of Beauvau-Craon, or even Jouvenel, or the romantic, ethereal "Smaranda" of the war years, but she was still an arresting and beautiful woman of great elegance, who made an immediate impression. "One knew it was *somebody*, the moment she entered a room," wrote Alfred Fabre-Luce, one of her admirers, in a contemporary profile. Though her figure had gradually suffered from the aftereffects of the hysterectomy operation she had undergone nine years before, her eyes—always her greatest asset—remained extraordinarily expressive. Her voice, with its attractive foreign accent in English, was persuasive and soft; she excelled at the art of conversation. Dressed mostly by Chanel, who often designed clothes specially for her, with splendid jewels and furs, she was one of the most photographed and talked-about women of the period. Many found it hard to believe that this "glorious creature," as Fabre-Luce described her, spent long hours of each day, isolated from life, writing. As she embarked on what she referred to as "the project of a lifetime," *La Nymphe Europe*, she had no doubt that her creative ability was at its peak. Flattered to be the object of a romantic infatuation on the part of the Prime Minister of England, while resigned to the emotional escapades of her ever philandering husband, to whom she remained deeply attached, and happy with her daughter's growing family, Marthe found life agreeable and secure. Much of that feeling was also derived from Mogosoëa, which continued to be her great joy. Not only was it an aesthetic delight but it served its function as a center for unifying European thought. "I am the needle through which pass the filaments and the strands of our disjointed Europe to be threaded together in a necklace," she liked to remark to her friends, when they complimented her on a particularly successful international gathering at Mogosoëa.

Marthe spent the autumn in Posada, busy restructuring and replanting the flower terraces around the house with the help of her English gardener. She was also working on *Le Rire de la Naïade* (*The Laughter of a Water Nymph*), a collection of short stories to be published in the Paris *Illustration* early the next year. MacDonald's letters followed her there. He was at Balmoral in Scotland for the Prime Minister's yearly visit with the King. The envelope with the crown and red seals created a sensation at the tiny Comarnic post office and was respectfully delivered by hand by the local postman on a bicycle. In four tightly spaced pages on heavy royal writing paper, the Prime Minister gave full rein to his romantic musings: he imagined her flying into his room at Balmoral "on a moonbeam in a magic chariot driven by four swans from Posada." He went on: "The magic of the world has indeed been active and potent around you and me. . . . You strolled into my room in the most commanding way with the swans and the pussy-cat and made a sensation. . . . On leaving, you squeezed through my key and have left behind in the key-hole a strand of swansdown, which I shall keep as a memento of your visit. I do up the slipper of swansdown in tissue paper and say 'good night' with devotion."

The poetic mood persisted when he returned to Downing Street later that autumn. In his letter of October 20, 1933: "Oh,

you of the Swan magic, you make me tremble. You behold wonderful things not dreamt of in John Knox's philosophy. You command the highways of dream and nothing is closed against you.
What a World! You make me imagine that there is no Germany
in it and that all is felicity and golden enjoyment."

Three imaginary characters make an appearance in the Prime
Minister's fantasy world: a Mrs. Worry and a Mademoiselle Drudg-
ery, who seem to control his daily life, and a Mr. Care, who is
particularly susceptible to Marthe's charm. "Mr. C. will know at
once whether the drawing you·sent me [some of Marthe's letters
were accompanied by sketches] is the child of magic—if it is not
he will not stand up in front of it and do homage. . . . He loves
the upright demeanour you give him in your pictures. . . . Have
you any idea how much he loves these pictures and their appeal?"

After expressing his longing to be with her and anger against
circumstances that prevent it, he tells how the letter she sent describing her "moon-bathing all naked" affected him; he imagines
himself at her side, then: "I should put a flower on Mr. C.'s head,
like a nightcap, and you would laugh at his absurd appearance!"

Were they lovers? The question will never be answered, but it
is certain they were so in their dreams. "Mr. C. was in fine, upright
form, as I awoke at cock-crow this morning; I was sad that the day
was not as the night had been and that no ring was on Mr. C." At
the time of his most ardent letters the Prime Minister was nearing
seventy, twenty-five years older than Marthe; he was in poor
health and worn down by the demands of his office. Given time
away from Downing Street, in relaxed circumstances, had he been
able to come to Posada—a place he would have adored—or a rest
on neutral territory, it would perhaps have been different; High-
landers do not age like other men. But there is no question of the
attraction his Romanian princess held for him and of his genuine
affection for her. That was why he found Marthe's constant traveling upsetting. "You bewilder me with your fickleness as regards
your dwelling places. I thought you were at Mogosoëa; there I flew
the swans and there I sent my dongs. When my letters arrived
they found your front door closed, no-one ruling in drawing-rooms
or reclining on State beds. . . . I would have hoped that you would

have seen to it that a blissful couch had been prepared for me with hot waters and soothing scents. . . . I could then forget how mad the German rulers are. . . . They bother me with their whims and their antics and they give me a bad return for all I have done for them by keeping me from Mogosoëa." MacDonald's desire to be with her was genuine. A lonely man, at the pinnacle of power and accustomed to lead, he was forced to present an immaculate public front at all times. It must have been a pleasure and a welcome relief to spend time in the company of an outstandingly intelligent, well-informed and beautiful woman whom he trusted. In her absence he tried to sublimate his feelings in the misty fantasy world of Celtic imagination. The sheer bulk of his letters to her—one or two every week for seven years—testifies to his devotion.

And Marthe? To her, he was above all the Prime Minister of a great Empire, whose adoration flattered her and confirmed once again her belief in her role as "the Egeria of Europe." But the man himself fascinated her. Unlike most of her "grand" English friends, MacDonald came from a humble background—he was self-made with everyday simple tastes. Yet he was delightful company, a scholar and an outstanding orator. He also was wonderful-looking. But, above all, he was the Prime Minister in whose hands rested the levers of power, and for Marthe power was the greatest aphrodisiac.

14

The Drift to War

As the 1930s went by and the world moved inexorably toward war, flying became a great passion in Marthe's life. For some time now, Sir Philip Sassoon had been putting his private aircraft at her disposal for visits between Paris and London; now, with George occupying the prestigious presidency of the International Aeronautical Federation, there came opportunities for longer flights to places she had never visited. "In all of our married life we never spent as much time together as we do now," she noted in a letter to Antoine, "yet sadly it does not bring us any closer. George in fact has recently acquired a new mistress."

Marthe's diaries of the period describe their various air journeys. In the spring of 1934 they were in Libya for the Aviation Gold Cup, as guests of Air Marshal Italo Balbo, hero of the Italian Air Force and Mussolini's close friend. While George was busy with the conferences, Marthe visited Leptis Magna, which was being excavated by Italian archaeologists. She found it "a haunting place" with its echoes of the Phoenician Empire, the grandeur of the Roman ruins and the Septimius Severus arches. Before that it was Egypt; then Athens and again Rome, where the Bibescos were received in private audience by Pope Pius XI. Marthe later called on former King Alfonso XIII of Spain, now living as an exile in Rome—"unchanged, uncomplaining, only a little bit wistful at times."

Throughout her air journeys Marthe carefully noted her impressions in the green exercise book she carried at all times. They are interesting to read, as they reveal an aspect of her talent not immediately apparent in her books. As many of the flights were made at comparatively low altitudes, she had the opportunity to describe the progression of landscapes below, noting the play of light on the clouds and the variety of the ever changing horizons. In one of the notes in her diary dated September 27, 1933, she observes how very lucky she is to be living at the time when flying is still in its infancy and one is able to experience the "blessed sense of wonder—the fresh virgin sensations, as if in a state of grace," which she compares with being in love for the first time. "I feel as if air travel had been invented for me," she adds with a certain lack of modesty of which her contemporaries sometimes accused her.

Meanwhile events of doom and portent followed fast one after another. While in Cairo in the first week of 1934, Marthe and George received news of the assassination of Jon Duca— Marthe's oldest friend—by members of Corneliu Codreanu's Iron Guard. One of the few incorruptible politicians left in Romania, a Western-style liberal and newly appointed Prime Minister by King Carol II, Jon Duca worried about the growing power of Codreanu's Iron Guard, a pro-German, anti-Semitic organization which believed in overt violence (Codreanu had recently shot the mayor of Jassy, whom he accused of being pro-Semite). Their objective was to transfer Romania's traditional allegiance from France to Hitlerite Germany. Upon receiving the premiership, Duca asked for the King's permission to outlaw the Iron Guard. "I cannot govern Romania with the Legionnaires out of hand and anarchy rampant," he told King Carol, and issued orders for the arrest of Codreanu and his followers. Within two weeks Jon Duca was shot down by

a member of the Iron Guard on a platform of the Sinaia railway
station. At the subsequent trial the murderer calmly declared that
he had no regret in killing "the friend of the Jews." His punish-
ment was light, and King Carol, displaying a total lack of moral
fiber, continued to pay subsidies to the Iron Guard. Eight years
later they brought his downfall.

Marthe, deeply shaken, cut short her stay in Egypt to rush
home for Duca's funeral.

In Paris, where she arrived in early March, there was rioting in
the streets, sparked by the left-wing Front Populaire; the government of Camille Chautemps had fallen and—in the constant game
of musical chairs—Paul-Boncour was appointed War Minister.
MacDonald, writing to Marthe to thank her for sending him Duff
Cooper's *Talleyrand*, remarked, "The French situation is most trying to the whole of Europe; why do they go on this way? The
French, the Americans and the Germans doom us to distress and
unsettlement. Goodwill and consideration could so easily bring
peace."

On June 30, 1934, during the "Night of the Long Knives,"
Major Ernst Röhm, head of the SS, the man who contributed more
than anyone else to Hitler's ascent to power, was arrested near
Munich together with his homosexual companions, handed a re-
volver and ordered to shoot himself. He refused and was shot the
next morning on Hitler's orders. The Führer now stood unchal-
lenged. Three weeks later the Austrian Chancellor, Dolfuss, was
assassinated in Vienna, followed by a Nazi coup in Austria, the
foretaste of the Anschluss four years later. To add to the dismal
list of events that fateful year, King Alexander of Yugoslavia, Mignon's husband, who was on a state visit to France, was gunned
down in Marseilles by a Croatian terrorist while riding in an open
car with French Foreign Minister Louis Barthou. Finally, in December, Sergei Kirov, member of the Politburo and Leningrad
Party secretary, was found dead in a corridor in the Smolny Palace
in Leningrad. His death heralded the beginning of the Stalinist
terror in Russia. It had been a very bleak year.

Marthe visited England again in the late spring, spending a
long weekend at Chequers with the Prime Minister. "I have come

to know Chequers like the back of my hand," she proudly noted in her diary. She was getting used to being woken up at 8 a.m. by MacDonald's voice, wishing her "good morning" and arranging plans for the day. They drove back to London on Sunday night "alone in the Prime Minister's blue car." The next Tuesday at Question Time she spent the afternoon in the House of Commons listening to government ministers answering questions and "admiring young Anthony Eden's profile on the front bench." After lunching with Duff Cooper and going to the theater with Philip Sassoon to see the play *Constant Nymph*, she returned to Paris in his private plane, "filled with roses, tulips and freesias."

That same spring Marthe launched herself on a new enterprise. Realizing that her autobiographical opus *La Nymphe Europe* might take years to complete, and in need of additional funds to sustain her own and George's style of living (currency restrictions in Romania made transfers of money difficult), she decided to write a series of popular romances destined for a mass-market circulation (the "midinette world"). The idea came to her at a literary lunch in Paris, when someone quoted Flaubert's dictum: "A true writer is one who is capable of writing a popular romance understood by the greatest possible number of readers." She decided to try it. Reluctant to "debase" her own name, she chose the pseudonym of Lucile Decaux; to her surprise, the venture turned out to be immensely successful. From Lucile Decaux's pen came several historical romances: *Katia*, the story of Alexander II's morganatic wife, Catherine Dolgoruky, later made into a film; *Maximilian and Charlotte of Mexico*; *Loulou*, a fictional account of the life of Napoleon III's son, who was killed fighting the Zulus in Africa; and *The Sad Story of Napoleon and Marie Walewska*, a romantic fantasy tale of one of Napoleon's loves. The books sold widely, but were never reviewed, and Marthe was always reluctant to admit to their authorship. One day at a charity sale in the late thirties, she amused herself by displaying side by side books by Bibesco and Lucile Decaux; she noticed that the latter sold very briskly, while Bibesco languished on the table. It was not her kind of a public.

To earn precious American dollars she continued with her articles for *The Saturday Evening Post*, commenting on current events, and published regularly in the Paris *Illustration*, where a serial en-titled *Egalité* brought her 25,000 francs—the equivalent of about $10,000 in our day.

As usual, she spent most of the summer in Posada, with occa-sional visits by friends, discussing the dismal political news. Her old friend Marshal Lyautey died in July, the same week as Hin-denburg. "The giants are leaving the scene," she noted on July 31. "Who is going to stand up to Hitler?"

Marthe, who had never been an attentive mother—she was too young when Valentine was born—now found particular pleasure in being with her six-year-old grandson, Jean-Nicholas Ghika. She read him books, taught him how to ride and to play croquet. Rid-ing was a sport in which Marthe had always excelled; she looked wonderful on a horse, riding sidesaddle through the forest paths around Posada. Life was still peaceful in that faraway corner of Europe; the serenity of her summer days would have remained undisturbed had the old, recurring problem in her marriage not returned to haunt her.

George's new mistress, Elena Leonte, whom Marthe had nick-named "La Toboso," after a character from Cervantes' *Don Qui-xote*, was a far more formidable opponent than any of her predecessors. Intelligent, well educated, wife of a Bucharest doctor—herself a medical student—she was determined to marry George and become the Princess Bibesco. In the meantime, her extravagant financial demands were ruining him. It was hard to fight her. "She seems to have some sort of a sinister hold over him," Marthe wrote to the Abbé Mugnier, to whom she always turned at difficult moments of her life. "He is becoming more and more irritable—even cruel. Please pray for me."

What Marthe failed to admit to herself was that the pattern she established long ago for their marriage had ceased to be satisfactory to George, who was now in his mid-fifties and in the initial stage of an illness from which he would die in six years. He needed a steady companion and one who knew how to cope with his recur-ring attacks of depression. Marthe, whom the world found so ad-mirable, had for years been only a sporadic presence by his side; in the past he had preferred it that way, but recently he began to wish for something more. La Toboso was clever enough to sense this. And yet—how could any woman replace Marthe? And who would write his speeches for the aeronautical conferences?

The truth became evident that autumn, when an invitation arrived for a meeting of the International Aeronautical Federation in Washington. George Bibesco, in his role as president, and Louis Blériot, as a representative of France, and their wives, were expected to attend.

On September 27, 1934, the Bibescos and the Blériots embarked on the *Paris* for New York. Marthe's cabin suite was full of flowers from assorted well-wishers. She noted that on the third day at sea they would be crossing paths with the *Nova Scotia*, on which MacDonald and Ishbel were returning to England from Canada. That morning—to her delight—she was handed a ship's cable: "The Swans of Nova Scotia wish you a happy journey." "How faithful he is—and how dear," she confided to her diary.

The *Paris* tied up at the West Fifty-third Street pier on a warm, sunny afternoon in October. Before them spread the glittering panorama of New York, which the four visitors were viewing for the first time. As the representatives of the press came on board to interview George, one of them asked whether Marthe was the author of *Catherine Paris*, the literary success of the season. "It would be better for your book if you had come here alone and not in the role of a wife," said the representative of the *New York Herald Tribune*. "Why don't you divorce right away?" As flashbulbs popped, Marthe replied with a smile, "Well, you see, my husband and I married young and have been together now for a long time, so we are used to each other"—a quick answer, which nevertheless accurately summed up their situation. Staying at the Waldorf-Astoria, where the luxury of the bathrooms particularly impressed her, inundated with invitations from the U.S. representatives of the Aeronautical Federation and New York's society matrons, Marthe had barely any time to visit the Metropolitan Museum, which she had been longing to see. New York enchanted her with its "Gothic splendor." "It is Chartres, Amiens, Bourges, combined in a new Babylon," she wrote in her diary. They dined with the Vanderbilts and the Otto Kahns, stayed with the Cabots in Boston and had tea with the President and Mrs. Roosevelt at the White House. But the three people who left an indelible impression on her—whom she described in *Images d'Epinal,* her collection of profiles—were Alice Longworth, Theodore Roosevelt's daughter, and Charles and Anne Lindbergh.

At the time of Marthe's visit to the United States, Alice Longworth had just published her book of memoirs, *Crowded Hours,* and was one of the best-known and most admired women in America. Daughter of an immensely popular President, she had, as she explained to Marthe, a genuine curiosity about people, which gave her good public standing as her father's hostess. Still politically active, though a staunch Republican—she disapproved of the politics of the "other branch of the family at the White House"—she had, as Marthe later remarked, the rare gift of overshadowing every other person in the room by the sheer force of her personality. "She certainly does not care about clothes," Marthe recalled. "She wore the same gray print dress every time I saw her and her hair drawn in an old-fashioned chignon does nothing to compliment her features. Yet she was always surrounded by people hanging on her every word. I asked her why she did not run for the Senate. The blue eyes, clear like a child's, fixed me with a penetrating glance. 'I can talk, but I cannot speak,' she answered. 'I haven't got that particular gift.' "

They saw each other several times during Marthe's stay in the United States. Alice Longworth took her on a trip up the Hudson to show her the family seat, and they spent a long weekend together at Oyster Bay on Long Island. "She made me understand America," Marthe wrote in her profile of Alice Longworth. "It might have been a one-sided understanding—Alice, after all, is a patrician—but I shall always be grateful to her for those insights."

On their last day before leaving New York the Bibescos lunched with Mrs. Harry Guggenheim in her Fifth Avenue apartment overlooking Central Park. Anne and Charles Lindbergh were there, just back from a 40,000-mile-long air voyage across four continents to study the development of future air routes. Only a few months before, the police had finally arrested Bruno Hauptmann and identified him as the murderer of the Lindberghs' little boy.

When they first arrived in New York, George told Marthe how anxious he was to meet the heroic aviator, but she prevailed upon him not to try, to leave their privacy undisturbed. But suddenly here they were at a small private luncheon party. "He is tall, blond, his blue eyes have a distant look," Marthe observed. She recalled his arrival at Le Bourget on May 21, 1927 (he had covered three thousand miles in thirty-three and a half hours); his strikingly modest demeanor in the face of the frantically applauding crowds. "I am Charles Lindbergh," he said, and offered the French officials his letter of identification. She did not think he had changed much from the photographs she had seen at the time; he had looked to her then like a young Scandinavian god, irritated by the press. "He is still rather shy," she noted, "but his eyes light up when he looks at his wife. But she—how can I describe her? She is tiny, graceful and absolutely intrepid. Her courage defies imagination. She has followed him in his career, learned his craft, embraced his vocation and now shares his religion—the air. Other women in the face of a tragedy such as theirs would have broken down or become neurotic; Anne Lindbergh rose above it, finding consolation in her writing, but above all in being with him. She accompanies him on all his travels. They are the perfect universal couple."

In the course of their table conversation, Lindbergh expounded on the future development of air routes. When George mentioned the difficulties fog often caused in the Azores, Lindbergh predicted that soon fog would cease to be a problem, for "we will be flying on instruments and later still in the stratosphere, through unlimited space the color of deep sapphire, where weather will not affect us. We will be able to fly from Paris to New York and back in one day," he announced to his incredulous audience. This—as recorded by Marthe—was said in November 1934, thirty-six years before the first Concorde took to the air.

Before leaving North America, Marthe traveled to Toronto to deliver a lecture at the local women's club on the subject of French literature in the postwar period. It was a success; Marthe, who had never lectured before, found it a stimulating experience and an excellent way to earn money.

On November 11 the Bibescos embarked on the *Ile de France*

for the journey home. The weather was rough and she spent most of the time in her cabin, sorting out her notes and her impressions of the New World. Waking up on the first morning at sea, she smiled happily as she was handed a cable from Ramsay MacDonald in London: "The Swans wish you a happy voyage."

A mountain of correspondence awaited her at the Ile St. Louis apartment, among them a pile of letters from MacDonald; he had just been to the wedding of the Duke of Kent and Princess Marina of Greece, "wearing my gold braid and stiff gold collar." He saw all the existing kings and queens assembled in their finery, "but you, Queen of the Swanland, were absent." He longed to see her—not only to hear her impressions of the New Deal but also to know what new clothes she had bought and "what kind of new gadgets the Americans have invented. His old friend the fictional character Mrs. Worry "had been bothering him a lot of late," he wrote, but now that Marthe was back "she was going to recede into the background."

For a week after their return the Bibescos resumed the Parisian social round. Then, urged by Ramsay MacDonald's impatient telephone calls, Marthe flew to London in mid-December to spend a weekend at Chequers with the Prime Minister and Ishbel. London was piercingly cold; a dense fog enveloped the city. Not for the first time Marthe was grateful for her wonderful coat of Russian sables, presented by George a few years before in a fit of remorse after one of his romantic escapades. She arrived in London at a propitious moment. Enid Bagnold's masterly translation of *Alexandre Asiatique*, written twenty-odd years before, was just being published under the title *Alexander of Asia*. The reviews were enthusiastic and, once again, Marthe was reminded that the only way for her to find fulfillment was through writing. Never mind if *La Nymphe Europe* was to take the rest of her life; she believed that through her painstaking unraveling of her complex family tree, with its roots deep in the Byzantine Empire, she would find the ultimate answer to the question "Who am I?" and contribute to the welding together of the disparate people of Eastern Europe.

But in the meantime the British Prime Minister needed her presence and solace. She found him looking tired and depressed.

Ishbel told her that he longed to lay down the burden of office, but could not make up his mind to do so, for he was becoming convinced that the world was drifting toward war. Many people in London's political circles speculated on when MacDonald would go, but Marthe was taken aback when Margot Asquith—now Lady Oxford—took her aside at a lunch party and suggested that she discuss resignation with the Prime Minister. "He loves you and he will listen to you," she told her. To her credit Marthe would have none of it. "You know very well, Margot, that I never discuss politics with the Prime Minister," she answered, which was not strictly true, but the only possible reply given the situation.

In January 1935 a plebiscite was held in the Valley of the Saar, a rich coal and metallurgical basin of great strategic importance, the ownership of which was disputed by Germany and France. Under the terms of the Treaty of Versailles it was being administered by a committee of the League of Nations. The result of the vote favored Germany by a 90 percent margin, and soon afterward Hitler reoccupied it. "It is sad," the Abbé Mugnier remarked to Lord Lloyd, who was visiting Marthe in Paris that week, "that we should have remained in the Saar for fifteen years and did not succeed in being liked." "Look at us, Monsieur l'Abbé," replied the ever courteous Lord Lloyd, "we have now been in Ireland for five hundred years and they still hate us there."

Following the occupation of the Saar, Hitler reintroduced compulsory military service—forbidden under the terms of the Versailles Treaty—and in the absence of a protest from London or Paris, began a massive reconstruction of the German military forces. Germany's growing power began to cast a shadow over the continent of Europe.

In her Paris apartment on the Ile St. Louis, Marthe continued to entertain a variety of statesmen and was conscious, more than most people, of the disarray caused by their lack of agreement on how to confront Germany. In France, where the Pierre Laval government was now in power, there was little appetite to rearm; in England, only Churchill saw the situation clearly, and Hitler had many admirers, among them people of great influence, such as the Londonderrys, the Astors, Geoffrey Dawson, the editor of *The*

Times, and of course the Prince of Wales, the future Edward VIII. England headed by the Prince of Wales is pro-German, French journalists were telling Marthe.

By then MacDonald had realized the danger that Hitler posed, and suggested a meeting in Stresa in the Italian Alps between the heads of Britain and France and Mussolini, whom he hoped to wean away from Hitler. The purpose was to condemn German rearmament and reaffirm the principles of the League of Nations. He telegraphed Marthe before leaving London in early April to suggest that they have tea together at the British Embassy on his way over through Paris. As it happened, the Prime Minister's plane was delayed by fog at the airport and there was only time for a short drink. "I urged him to visit the gardens of the Isola Bella in Stresa," Marthe recalled. "But, of course, he said that there would be no time—the poor man." On his return, however, a week later, after what appeared to have been a very successful conference, MacDonald arrived at the Ile St. Louis apartment at 7 a.m. for breakfast. Fitzroy Maclean, the writer, then twenty-two, working as a third secretary at the British Embassy in Paris, recalls his surprise when, after being dispatched to meet the Prime Minister's train at the Gare de Lyon in the early morning, he was ordered to drive to the Quay Bourbon instead of to the British Embassy, where he was expected for breakfast.

Marthe gave an account of this visit in a letter to the Abbé Mugnier. "I went to great trouble to put together a breakfast similar to the one he is used to at Chequers: grapefruit (hard to get at this time of year), Earl Grey tea, brown bread, honey and soft-boiled eggs. We sat down at the table by the window as the chimes of the church of St. Gervais rang eight o'clock. He seemed very relaxed and obviously pleased with the results of the conference. He regretted there had been no time to visit the famous gardens and admire the white peacocks I told him about. 'It is a life of forced labor I lead,' he remarked. He loved the view from my windows and the Boucher paintings on the walls; then he asked how long it would take to walk to the British Embassy. I said it would take half an hour. 'Let's go,' he said. 'It will be nice to see Paris as a tourist—for once!' I rushed upstairs to get my hat and we set off along the Pont Louis Philippe, the quays, then crossed over to the Louvre, where I made him admire the Cour Carrée. We were followed at a discreet distance by three detectives—two French and one from Scotland Yard. On across the Tuileries, to the Place de la Concorde, where he stopped to rejoice in the view, then on to the Faubourg St. Honoré. I left him at the door of the Embassy."

The next morning Marthe's maid, Blanche Caniot, picking up the morning paper, was surprised to read that the British Prime Minister had breakfasted at the British Embassy with Sir George Clarke. "The papers don't really tell one the truth—ever" was her comment.

The Abbé Mugnier's progressive blindness was a great sadness for Marthe that spring of 1935. The saintly, erudite old cleric, her best friend, adviser and confessor, "the only person who had never let her down," was nearing eighty; he had a cataract operation, but now there was trouble with his optic nerve and he was told by his doctors they could not help him. It was a cruel blow for a profoundly independent man, used to being at the center of things, who devoted all his available free time to reading and writing letters to his "spiritual wards." On hearing the dismal news, Marthe redoubled her efforts to keep the Abbé "in the picture" and to relay all the political gossip he so enjoyed. She arranged for him to be read to and, when she was in Paris, she visited him every day. "You possess a rare gift of friendship," the Abbé said to her, an opinion shared by her friends.

It was just as well that Marthe had good friends to confide in, for back at Mogosoëa that summer her horizon again was clouded by George's increasing hostility and his constant bad humor. "It is nearly two months since he has slept at home," she notes in her diary. "He comes here only if I invite La Toboso with him. He spends all his time with her at our Bucharest house in spite of the heat." She took comfort in making notes for *La Nymphe Europe* and planning a trip to Constantinople in the autumn. MacDonald, who was now close to resigning, wrote to say that when at last he became free he would join her in Constantinople to "assist with research." It remained a dream, like the swans, but his need of her was ever present.

In London it was the time of King George V's jubilee and the

capital was in a festive mood. The Prime Minister had to appear
at various functions wearing his court dress. "I have been living
in Swansdown with its robes and tiaras, its trains and its laces,
processions and feasts," he wrote to Marthe on May 15, 1935, from
Chequers. "Last night I had endless trouble dressing . . . there
were the hooks and eyes, which I could not get to behave properly.
When one went in the other went out and I was inclined to let
the magnificent garments fall to the floor. And when they were all
done up they were too tight, but though uncomfortable, showed
a figure passably handsome with not too many protuberances—
just enough to give interest. . . . When I next clothe myself in that
garb you must, but you must, be around to show me how to fix
things—particularly the stockings—so they do not separate from
the knee-breeches. Oh, why have you gone to Romania and I have
to put up with London alone!"

On June 7, 1935, Ramsay MacDonald resigned and Stanley
Baldwin succeeded him as Prime Minister. The entry in his diary
for that day reads a doleful "I die today." He cheered up, however,
after his audience with the King. "You have been the Prime Minister I liked best," George V told him. "You have kept up the
dignity of the office without using it." He asked MacDonald to
remain in the cabinet as Lord President of the Council. Laying
down the burden of office was traumatic, but it also had its compensations. MacDonald was freer, and from his house in Hampstead he now could write to Marthe without fear of his
correspondence being opened by "Downing Street moles."

"Of course I was sorry to go, before the work was finished, but
it will never be finished, and I may well claim that a fairly well-
marked piece of it is done. . . . When I received your letter the
clouds lifted. Now I am no longer solitary in a dreary world. Oh,
my dear, all the Swan magic is now here. . . . I cannot put in
writing what a tonic your letter was. . . . Do send me more tonics.
You are quite safe now, for there is no other eye than 'Mr. C.' to
see and no other heart than mine to love you."

If Marthe's letters were a tonic for MacDonald, his letters,
which she impatiently awaited, were a help during her difficult
summer with George. More and more he mentioned divorce,

though just as often, in what Marthe called his "spoiled child manner," he wished it were possible to have two wives. "What's wrong with bigamy?" he asked, turning to Antoine at a Bucharest Jockey Club lunch. "It seems like an eminently sensible idea." "You have been practicing it all your life," Antoine told him, "so what's new?"

"My strange life with George," Marthe sighed to her diary, noting that he asked her to accompany him to an International Aeronautical Federation meeting at Dubrovnik in September and that she agreed to come and write his speeches. Dubrovnik, or, as it was then called, Ragusa, held many happy memories for her; she had been there with Emmanuel and later with Beauvau-Craon, now nearly a quarter of a century ago. While George exchanged views with aviators from thirty-three countries, she revisited the beautiful city, walked on the ramparts and dreamed.

When they returned home they were greeted at the airport with news that Italy had invaded Abyssinia. So much for Mussolini's promises to MacDonald in Stresa. But this event, which was to have serious international consequences, was overshadowed for Marthe by the news of Henry de Jouvenel's death. He was found lying on a pavement in Paris, apparently having suffered a heart attack on his way home after a late dinner with friends. It had been months since Marthe thought about him, but the news depressed her deeply. She mourned him as a witty, stimulating companion and because he was part of her youth. "I suffered when he was unfaithful to me," she told Antoine, who was the first to tell her about Jouvenel's death, "but he always made me feel intensely alive." It was an odd coincidence, she thought, that her friend should have been found dead at the corner of the avenues Gabriel and Matignon, the very spot he had once suggested for a scene in *Catherine Paris*.

With Antoine and his wife, Elizabeth, Marthe and George listened to the news on their recently acquired radio, still a novelty in Eastern Europe and called "the devil's box" by their servants. On that October day when the weather was—as Marthe described it—"as sweet as honey," the "box" transmitted frenetic scenes from the Palazzo di Venezia in Rome of crowds shouting "Duce,

Duce," acclaiming the invasion of Abyssinia. "A shudder ran
through me," Marthe recalled. "I left the room and went out onto
the terrace to seek comfort in the view I so loved."

That week MacDonald wrote to her, "Your gloom-clouded letters have found me in the same mood. The folly of Italy fills me
with disappointment and despair."

※

As the winter set in and the swans of Mogosoëa departed, Marthe
boarded the Orient Express for her annual stay in Paris, leaving
George to La Toboso. It was not for the first time that she wondered whether it was a wise move, but, as she noted in her diary,
"the time has not yet come for a showdown—I will see."

The romance between Wallis Simpson and the Prince of Wales
was a major subject of conversation in Paris that winter. The
French press and magazines were full of it, unlike in Britain, where
the situation was known only to a relatively small part of society.
When on January 21, 1936, King George V died at Sandringham
and the Prince of Wales was proclaimed King as Edward VIII,
speculation as to whether he would marry Mrs. Simpson reached
fever pitch. *Illustration*, the popular French magazine, asked Marthe to travel to London as their correspondent for the funeral of
the late King.

Bad weather had grounded all flights and she had to return
from Le Bourget to take the cross-Channel ferry in "atrocious conditions." But when it came to work Marthe was an intrepid professional of long standing. Her English contacts were useful to her,
for she obtained permission to enter Westminster Hall on the night
when the new King and his three brothers joined the officers of
the Household Brigade to guard the catafalque. It was a moving
experience. The next day she was present in St. George's Chapel
in Windsor for the funeral service, making her way there through
dense crowds, which scorned a raw winter morning to bid farewell
to their beloved monarch. She witnessed the arrival of foreign sovereigns, including her own King Carol of Roumania. She marveled
at the dignity and the fortitude of the widowed Queen and observed the new King, who in his forty-second year still seemed to
her to "hold the promise of youth."

Her article, entitled "The King's Four Sons," was well received by the public and later formed part of a collection of profiles entitled *Feuilles du Calendrier* (*Leaves from a Calendar*).

A few months later, when in London, Marthe dined at Philip Sassoon's house with King Edward VIII and Mrs. Wallis Simpson. With her novelist's instinct she formed an absolute conviction that the King would marry Wallis. "He would rather abdicate than be separated from her," she told her host. Most people in England did not share her opinion at the time.

According to the notes in her diary and her letters to the Abbé Mugnier, Marthe's spring and summer of 1936 were busy entertaining and traveling between assorted European capitals and Mogosoëa. On May 14, while in Rome, she heard through her friend the French Ambassador that the Duce had expressed a desire to see her. Why? she wondered. It was—as an Italian official explained to her—due to her reputation as a writer, a proponent of European unity and, last but not least, a beautiful woman. She described the interview in her journal of May 15, 1936:

"Seen at close distance he looked like Napoleon—or at least like his brother Jérôme; his skin is pale, alabaster. He sizes one up from the corner of the eye, while throwing his head backward all the time. He is small, very small—I felt tall when standing next to him—and quite square, but the head is magnificent, animal-like with a huge mouth and a prominent upper lip. The hand he tendered me was small, soft and warm; he kept mine in his for a moment and kissed it twice. There is something magnetic about his presence, but I think it is because one sees his face all the time on the posters. My interview was short and I never discovered why he had wanted to see me. 'Tell your friends that you found me calm, logical, and that I desire peace, no matter what they may think of my actions.' "

Marthe relayed her impressions of the Duce to her political friends in both London and Paris, but the interview did nothing to relieve her ever present sense of foreboding.

In June she was at Mogosoëa, again entertaining for the International Aeronautical Federation. "My life here is too busy for my liking," she wrote to the Abbé. "But it will soon calm down after the present round of festivities; the aviation school, thank God, is coming to an end. I had to give a ball at Mogosoëa, arrange for fireworks, a Venetian fete on the lake and dinner for two hundred people seated in our lovely cool subterranean caves that Fortuny compared to the Baths of Diocletian. It all went very well, and now, as the torches die out and guests depart, I can look forward to my solitude, listen to the croaking of frogs and admire the water lilies on the pond—such wise creatures: they close their petals at sundown and reappear on the surface of the water with the first rays of the sun in the morning."

In the autumn, after their return from yet another Aeronautical Congress, this time in Athens, the Bibescos entertained Lord and Lady Londonderry at Mogosoëa.

The Marquess of Londonderry, who had succeeded Lord Thomson as Minister for Air in MacDonald's government, was known as a sympathizer of Hitler and Nazi Germany. It may be said in his defense that at the time Britain had neither the will nor the resources to build a powerful Air Force; the only answer therefore—as he saw it—was to be friends with Hitler, whom for some reason he trusted, and he let himself be persuaded of the Führer's peaceful intentions.

The Londonderrys visited Göring, at his invitation, soon after the funeral of King George V. They were treated like royalty— taken to look at airfields, schools, lecture halls, to watch a flyby of the famous Richthofen Squadron, to assist at all the festivities of the third anniversary of Hitler's accession to power, to listen to stirring speeches by the Führer, to dine with Göring and senior Nazi officials. They were fed Nazi propaganda and listened to a lot of Wagner. They also visited and "admired" Karinhall, Göring's lavish hunting lodge on his country estate near Berlin, where the host, dressed up as an intrepid hunter, cut a comical figure, striding through the forest in lederhosen and a huge hunter's hat, and where the talk was full of hostility against Jews. One wonders how a couple as civilized as the Londonderrys, with a centuries-old tradition of refinement and a good sense of humor, could have enjoyed the vulgarity of Karinhall and Göring's antics, and been taken in by his Nazi friends, their compliments and their assurances of German friendship toward England. It is even more surprising to read the subsequent exchange of correspondence with their host, in which Edith addressed Hermann Göring as "My dear Siegfried, for you are my conception of the heroic Siegfried in modern times." She even managed to insert in her "bread and butter" letter to the Marshal a disparaging reference to Jews, who—as she wrote—"unfortunately control a large segment of the English press, causing it to be hostile to Germany."

It was quite a shock to the Londonderrys when on March 7— soon after their return to England—Hitler's troops marched into the Rhineland and Germany unilaterally revoked the Locarno Peace Treaty. Nevertheless, they continued to correspond with Göring and other members of the Nazi hierarchy, even inviting the boorish Ribbentrop, Nazi Ambassador to England, to their home in London and entertaining him at Mount Stewart, their lovely country estate in Ireland.

Marthe very much disapproved of the Londonderrys' friendship with Göring, and during her visits to London had many arguments with "Charley" about it; nevertheless, the descendant of the great Castlereagh and his wife were a very important couple and their arrival at Mogosoëa in early October created a stir. King Carol, who had met them in London at George V's funeral, expressed the desire to arrange a shoot in their honor in the ancient royal preserve of Archduke Rudolf Hapsburg (of Mayerling fame) and to entertain them on his yacht on the Danube. To Marthe's relief George decided to temporarily reenter the family circle and be on hand for the festivities. "He was perfectly charming to me all that week," she remembered.

As was to be expected, the "semi-royals" were enchanted with Mogosoëa, adored Posada ("a bit of England in faraway Ruritania," Edith wrote to a friend), were taken on sightseeing tours and down the Danube on the royal yacht. In glorious weather they stalked red deer in the Carpathians and shot duck and migrating wild geese on the mountain lakes. They left delighted with their visit. Marthe, after bidding them goodbye at the airport, retired to bed to recover.

That evening in a friendly conversation with George on the terrace at Mogosoëa, she tried to point out to her husband how unsuitable Elena Leonte was to be his companion. "Even if I were ill and had only six months to live I would beg you not to marry her," she told him. "And even if I agreed to a divorce it would take years to come through, as I am a Catholic. Tell her to hang on to her doctor husband." George looked reflective and decided that he now had a good argument with which to stop the recriminations of his mistress and perhaps live in peace.

Marthe was at Mogosoëa when news came of Edward VIII's abdication. "The little man finally did it," she wrote in her diary. "I knew he would rather abdicate than be separated from her." At a concert that night at the Cotroceni Palace, Dowager Queen Marie, now visibly aged and much upset by the news of her cousin's behavior, said to Marthe, "I should like to smack him." Much as she disagreed with the Duke of Windsor's decision to abandon his country, Marthe felt that Marie had little right to criticize him, as her own son King Carol did exactly the same eight years before. "I suppose Romania is, like most places," Ramsay MacDonald wrote to Marthe on December 10, 1936, "full of our court news. Personally I am pleased that there is a second Monarch of loving, heroic tenderness on our throne. But it has been a dreadful week!" But when she saw him in London ten days later, MacDonald was in a much happier mood. "The new King is a pet," he declared. "Yesterday he arranged for a meeting of the Privy Council to be held one hour earlier, so as to allow me to catch my train to Glasgow for Christmas. Wasn't it kind?"

An event which for Marthe far overshadowed the drama of the abdication was the birth of her new grandson in a Paris clinic. She left London on December 19 after Valentine telephoned that she was about to enter the hospital. The pregnancy had been difficult, and Marthe was worried. She rushed straight from the airport to the clinic to find that her second grandson, a bouncing and healthy baby, had arrived. Valentine, still somewhat pale, her black hair falling in waves around her face, smiled happily at her mother.

The arrival of this particular boy infant meant something special to the Bibesco family, for he was destined to perpetuate the dynasty of the Hospodars of Wallachia. Since her operation in Paris twelve years before, Marthe had known that she could not have another child; it was a source of regret that she had been unable to provide George with a male heir. On the day of her marriage to Dimitri Ghika, Valentine promised her parents that if she had two sons she would "present" them with the second one, to be called by the family name of George Bibesco and brought up as a Bibesco heir. This strange custom was prevalent in the Balkans, where so many ancient bloodlines tended to become extinct in constant warfare. Twice already, the Bibesco name had passed to cousins like the Brancovans or the Stirbeys; this time a young Ghika (of whom there were many about) would take up George Bibesco's succession. All were happy until, three days after the birth of little George, Valentine developed a high fever; soon she was at death's door. It was the exact repetition of the illness that had struck Marthe at Posada after Valentine's birth years ago. "Come at once; our daughter's condition critical," Marthe telegraphed to George in Romania. She felt guilty that she had encouraged the fragile young Valentine to become pregnant again. "It is all my fault," she wrote to the Abbé Mugnier. "Sheer vanity on my part, because I myself was not able to give birth. And for this my only daughter, the child of my innocence, who has never given me any worries, is to die. What is a name after all? An echo, lost amidst peaks in a mountain valley in Romania—an illusion—certainly not worth the sacrifice of a life."

The uncertainty and the torment lasted for nearly a month. Finally, at the end of January, Valentine slowly recovered, and Marthe, whom her daughter's illness had left emotionally drained, was able to resume normal life, which meant writing.

Katia, the story of Catherine Dolgoruky and Tsar Alexander II of Russia, published under the pseudonym of Lucile Decaux two years before, was being made into a film, starring Danielle Darrieux and John Loder. Marthe was paid 100,000 francs in cash, which went a long way to solve her currency problems. Her "two-tier career"—as she called it—was working well. While continuing with the first draft of *La Nymphe Europe*, she was at the same time dictating to her secretary the story of the Mexican adventure of

Archduke Maximilian and Carlotta under the title of *Les Amants Chimériques* (*Carlota* in the English translation), a historical fantasy officially authored by Lucile Decaux, which also turned out to be financially rewarding.

In a different league was the literary success of Marthe's *Images d'Epinal*, a series of portraits: Empress Eugénie, Alice Longworth, Marshal Lyautey, Charles Lindbergh and Charlie Chaplin, among others, published in the spring of 1937. Paul Claudel, who had become a close friend, was enchanted with it. He ended a long, complimentary letter by saying, "After I am dead I wish to come back to earth and look over your shoulder, hoping you will be writing not my obituary but my profile. . . . Your writing gives me a deep and delicate pleasure."

In January of that year Marthe celebrated her fifty-first birthday. It did not worry her. "Don't be afraid of getting old," she told Ishbel MacDonald. "I am much happier now than I was in the days when I wrote *Alexandre Asiatique*." Marthe discovered the joys of being a grandmother by assisting with Jean-Nicholas' education. Now there was another grandson, a Bibesco heir, whom she could bring up in her image as the son she never had; and she still felt young enough to do it. Indeed, with her wonderful hair and flowing walk she gave the impression of youth. Now and then, when in Paris or Rome, she would find herself being followed by some unknown admirer, who would want to know her identity and pay homage. "The only thing I regret, when I look in the mirror and see the lines around my eyes," she confided to a friend, "is that I can't anymore give the same aesthetic pleasure to strangers who look at me, in a train or an airplane, as I used to—without really trying."

But there were compensations. Even if her beauty was passing, she now had fame and serenity and she was fully in charge of her own life. She had also become an important unofficial channel of communication between her country and British and French political circles. In the spring of 1937, when in London, she found a way to suggest to the British Foreign Office and the court that an invitation should be issued to King Carol II to come to England on an official visit. This was done, much to the satisfaction of the Romanian court circles, for it strengthened the King's stand against the Iron Guard, whose goal was to ally Romania with Hitler.

After Easter, which she spent at Mogosoëa with her daughter and her two grandsons, Marthe traveled to London with nine-year-old Jean-Nicholas, now a student at Ampleforth School in Yorkshire. Invited to stay with the Londonderrys for George VI's coronation, she arranged for her little grandson to spend a few days with her to witness the historic occasion.

Coronation week in London was festive, filled with excitement and social occasions. Ramsay MacDonald, who was now Lord Privy Seal, but about to go back into private life, presided over the Coronation Committee. He and Marthe saw each other often, though fleetingly, for he was busy with official functions. It was only after the coronation was over, and she was dining with him alone at his house in Hampstead in London one evening, that she realized how much he had changed during the past three months. He looked depressed, very much older, and complained that his head had "almost refused to work." Gone were his former enthusiasm and teasing wit; all he wanted was to retire to Lossiemouth and search for "that most elusive of all forms of happiness—rest." A sea voyage and a holiday in South America were vaguely planned for November. "I shall be a new man when I return from my sea voyage," he told her. "I may even come to Mogosoëa next spring, now that I am at last a private person."

After her annual cure at Bagnoles-de-l'Orne ("where I renew myself every year"), Marthe spent the rest of the summer at Mogosoëa and Posada working on *La Nymphe Europe* and another of Lucile Decaux's "romances," *Louison: Le Bel Amour du Dernier Roi de France*, a fantasy tale of a love affair between the Comte d'Artois and a Madame de Polastron. An obscure subject, lost in the mists of history, it was the least successful of the Decaux series.

One afternoon, as she was walking around her lake at Mogosoëa discussing the autumn planting with her English gardener, Marthe saw the elegant silhouette of Sir Reginald Hoare, the British Minister in Bucharest, coming toward her. "I brought you a present," he announced. "I think you ought to read it." It was the English translation of Hitler's *Mein Kampf.* "He certainly makes his intentions quite obvious," Marthe wrote to the Abbé Mugnier a few days later. "He wants to obliterate France, Belgium and Holland by blitz warfare, but he hopes to negotiate an alliance with England—no chance of it—in spite of what Ribbentrop may be telling him." And she added sadly, "We are not drifting toward war, we are rushing into it at great speed."

The same feeling of an approaching catastrophe pervaded the distinguished assembly of guests who gathered at Marthe's mountain retreat of Posada that late summer. It was a predominantly English crowd: Violet Trefusis, Lady Oxford and her granddaughter Priscilla, Sir Reginald and Lady Hoare, the Leland Harrisons (he was U.S. Minister in Bucharest) and assorted young upperclass Englishmen, "splendid specimens of the race." Madame Blériot, now a widow, came from Paris, bringing with her Antoine de Saint-Exupéry, "who charmed us all." There was also a German visitor: Prince Frederick von Hohenzollern, cousin of the Kronprinz, who arrived in Romania to "prospect" the possibilities of marrying his daughter to young Prince Michael. When asked by Marthe what the Kronprinz, her old friend, was doing these days, Hohenzollern replied, laughing, "He does nothing—he flirts—that's all."

On Wednesday, November 10, 1937, as Marthe was about to lunch with Prince Bertil of Sweden and others at Mogosoëa, Antoine arrived from Bucharest, looking grave. "I have news that will make you very sad," he said to Marthe, putting his arm around her. She excused herself from her guests and led him onto the terrace. There he told her that Ramsay MacDonald died the night before on board the *Reina del Pacífico* from heart failure; his daughter Sheila was with him at the time. "I felt I was drowning," Marthe wrote in her diary that night. She reread MacDonald's last letter—written while waiting for the ship to cast anchor—and wept. "My dearest Friend, my very dear Friend. I bring out the sherry, the tokay and the champagne. . . . You will have arrived travelling by a privileged ticket in Cabin 7 of the *Reina del Pacífico.*

The first stop will be at Kingston, Jamaica, and I shall walk out with you to the Myrtle Beach Hotel, where we shall have a feast. The King [King George VI] has just broken into my reverie with a message of good will, but I refuse to be disturbed. My cabin is hung with green so you cannot miss it. . . . We shall dine at 7.30 and have coffee afterwards every evening. Mr. C. will sit up and we will have a happy time. . . . I am sure that the Swans will not miss the boat and bring the beautiful granny (sic!) to me. . . . I am going to bed early this evening, so I may rise first in the morning, as after Stresa."

She had grown accustomed to receiving these letters—one or more every week for the last seven years—the "Three Swans" were part of her life. How was she going to live without them? Marthe put on a coat and a hat and went out; it was foggy; the long alley of elms looked ghostlike, full of autumnal dead leaves; somewhere in the distance the gardener boys had started a wood fire—the blue smoke mixing with fog, like a funeral pyre.

The papers were full of praise for MacDonald; there were long, splendid obituaries from London, Paris, Geneva and Bucharest, extolling his virtues as a statesman and his political courage. "Why, oh, why could they not have said some of it while he was alive?" thought Marthe. "It would have made all the difference to his days."

On the writing table in her father's cabin Sheila found a half-finished letter to Marthe, written when the ship was approaching Bermuda, the last day of his life. She sent it to Mogosoëa "unread."

The *Reina del Pacifico* docked in Hamilton, Bermuda, and MacDonald's body was taken back to England on the cruiser HMS *Apollo* and then by train to London for a public funeral service at Westminster Abbey. Marthe's bouquet of anemones was included in the family wreath, which remained on the coffin until the very end.

Never in Marthe's crowded and peripatetic life had there been a year when so many historic events occurred in such rapid succession. For Europe it was the last full year of peace and—as invariably happens when disaster is near—the weather was unusually beautiful, making the contrast with outside developments even more poignant.

In the first week of January 1938, Marthe took her grandson with her to Vienna. She wanted to pay a last visit to this city "before something happened." In the geographical sequence of *La Nymphe Europe*, Austria—as Marthe had known it—was to form a separate volume. They stayed at the British Legation with her friends Michael and Mary Palairet; opposite, on the other side of the Metternichgasse, loomed the huge German Embassy, where Franz von Papen resided in splendor.

The first people she saw were Karl-Emil Fürstenberg and his wife. Prince Fürstenberg, a very old friend, had been Austrian Minister to Romania during World War I and had once ordered the Austrian frontier to be opened to allow little Valentine and her nanny to pass into the safety of Switzerland. A charming, witty aristocrat, married to a half-English, half-Hungarian wife, who was pretty (and loved pleasure "for pleasure's sake," as she liked to say), Karl-Emil was an outspoken opponent of the Nazis and faced an uncertain future if the Anschluss took place. And indeed, two months later, as the German troops marched into Vienna, Karl-Emil was arrested and sent to a concentration camp, where he died. She saw other friends and acquaintances; some of whom later managed to escape or went underground, others of whom tried to collaborate with the Nazis, hoping to survive the occupation. Vienna was tense and subdued and "disturbingly quiet." There was hardly any traffic because of the gasoline shortage; people wore haunted expressions while bands of exuberant Hitler Jugend filled the Opera Platz every evening. Marthe and young Ghika visited the familiar landmarks—the Schatzkammer, where the imperial jewels were kept, the crypt of the Capuchin friars, where the Hapsburgs lay buried—and drove out to Schönbrunn to revisit the old palace of Francis II.

Returning to Paris on the Orient Express with its blue ornamental seats and pink-shaded lamps, Marthe found much work awaiting her, for *Katia*—the film based on her Lucile Decaux book—was in full production at the Joinville Studios near Paris, and Raymond Bernard, the director, was clamoring for her assistance. As usual, numerous friends made their way to the "lantern," as she named her apartment on the Quay Bourbon. There were fittings for clothes at Chanel and at the newly opened Lanvin, and George was having his portrait painted to be hung in the offices of the International Aeronautical Federation; he much resented the long hours of sitting and kept on summoning Marthe to "keep him abreast of current Parisian gossip." Running out of time and ideas, Marthe called on Elsie de Wolfe, the well-known Paris decorator and hostess, to help. "Rumor has it that the Duchess of Windsor is pregnant—just a little," Elsie reported to George. "They are both furious with the royal family." "Why?" asked Marthe. "After all, he had the magic wand and let it go."

An event that gave Marthe much pleasure that spring was Claudel's reading of his masterpiece, *Joan of Arc*, which took place in the drawing room of her apartment, before the most distinguished literary assembly in Paris. It was the great man's tribute to his friendship with Marthe and to her eminence as a writer.

On March 13, Germany occupied Austria. Two days later, surrounded by his black-uniformed SS troops, Hitler made a triumphal entry into the capital of the Hapsburgs, which he had left twenty-five years before to escape military duty. There was no place in Hitler's empire for intellectuals, who had given luster to Vienna in the preceding fifty years; those who were not arrested went into exile, never to return; a savage persecution of Jews began almost at once. Sigmund Freud was imprisoned, but managed to escape and find refuge in England; thousands of others perished in concentration camps.

In Marthe's "lantern," politicians and intellectuals talked for hours, but no one could offer much hope; they all knew their various governments' motto was "No confrontation." Marthe wrote in her diary: "The British and the French who cry over the fate that has befallen Austria remind me of myself as a child, when I tore out the petals of a daisy one by one and then wept because the stem looked so ugly."

Sheila MacDonald was the youngest of Ramsay MacDonald's children and the one most affected by her father's death. Marthe, on a flying visit to London in early April, suggested that she spend some weeks with her, as her guest, traveling. After a tour of northern Italy, they came to Rome two days before Hitler's historic visit to Mussolini. The Duce decreed that to greet "the Tedesco," the Eternal City must put on its most impressive show, "reminiscent of the time of the Caesars." There were illuminations, flaming torches; all facades were floodlit; red-and-black German flags fluttered from every building. At the Hotel de Russie, where they stayed, there was a message for Marthe from an old admirer, former King Alfonso of Spain, suggesting that they meet and view the "grand entry" together. Marthe described the event: "Night had fallen; the lurid illuminations had transformed the city into a Wagnerian stage set; in the middle of the ocean of lights only the Vatican stood out as a darkened black hole. Pope Pius XI had left town and gone to Castel Gandolfo. Standing next to Alfonso XIII, we watched the unfolding spectacle from the balcony of the Palazzo Michatelli, the former residence of Napoleon's mother, Madame Laetitia Bonaparte. The Führer came into view seated next to King Victor Emmanuel in an open red Mercedes car with wheels painted red and black. He was dressed in a khaki uniform—a small man with a little mustache and a black lock of hair, exactly as portrayed by Charlie Chaplin. Behind him came a procession of military vehicles, filled with German officers in field uniforms, fully armed. The crowds fell silent and King Alfonso turned to me in amazement: '*Invasione!*' Yes, it looked like an invasion, a prelude to one anyway. A strange way to visit an ally."

Two days later, while sightseeing with Sheila, they saw Hitler again, this time escorted by Mussolini, reviewing 50,000 of the Duce's Elite Corps, who paraded to the sound of the march from *Lohengrin*. Marthe decided that "the Tedesco" looked "like a bottle of mustard with a black label," while Goebbels reminded her of an unpleasant insect. The next day, heaving a sigh of relief, she and Sheila left for Greece.

Two months later Marthe again found herself in Hitler's realm, accompanying George to the Third Congress of the International Aeronautical Federation in Berlin. It was a sentimental journey for her, for she was revisiting Berlin for the first time since June 1909, when the Kronprinz—then at the zenith of power—had fallen in love with her. That romantic interlude, now twenty-nine years ago, had remained one of the cherished memories of her youth. The man who would have been Wilhelm III if Germany had won the last war was now living in uneasy retirement at Potsdam, spied on and barely tolerated by the Nazis. Marthe wondered whether she would be able to see this "phantom of the past." No sooner did they arrive than the telephone at the Kaiser Hof Hotel was ringing. "Is it you, Marthe?" His voice had not changed. He hoped that the Bibescos would be able to dine with him and his wife at the Palace of Cecilienhof in Potsdam the next night, seven-thirty, black tie; he would send his car to bring them. "What do you look like these days?" the Kronprinz asked. "I look like *eine grosse Mutter*," Marthe replied, laughing. What to wear? She decided on a long white Chanel lace dress "in which I still look pretty good" and her emeralds. The drive through the lovely wooded countryside, the lakes and the pervading scent of the lime trees brought back the memories of the first visit, when she was twenty-three years old and beautiful.

He had aged; instead of being all blond, he was all white; his small head stood on a long, long neck, his blue eyes were now faded, his face lined, but he still had the same smile—slightly crooked—and the nose of the Great Frederick. He kissed her hand, while she plunged into a deep curtsy. "I wish the Nazis could see how it's done," he said, smiling. "They have forbidden our people to curtsy to us—we are the living dead, not supposed to exist." Soon the Kronprinzessin arrived, dressed in brown chiffon and pearls—"much fatter, but otherwise unchanged." They discussed politics. "I soon saw," Marthe wrote in her diary, "that they are full of resentment, badly treated and humiliated by the Nazis. They dream of peace, admire England and watch current developments with mounting horror."

The Kronprinz kept them talking until late and was reluctant to let them go. The visit, full of reminiscences, was a melancholic echo of the past, like closing a circle with the "living dead" left bereft inside.

Next day the Bibescos were in a different world and the contrast could not have been more startling. At the official Aeronautical Federation banquet Marthe was seated on the right of Marshal Göring and George on Frau Göring's right. "Göring bears a striking resemblance to our Zufall [the Bibescos' former Swiss butler]—very fat with heavy circles under bulging blue eyes; he has large hands with short fingers and insisted on showing me his rings one by one; he talked nonstop, mainly about himself, and whistled tunes after we got up from the table." The Air Marshal invited the Bibescos and the Londonderrys to dine at Karinhall, his country residence, the next day. Curiosity getting the better of her, Marthe prodded George to accept.

Göring's powerful Mercedes roared ahead. Marthe was amazed to note that the Air Marshal used the same first three notes from *Siegfried* on his horn which had once been reserved for the imperial family. Marthe and George rode in the first car, with the Londonderrys following behind. "Strange is my destiny," Marthe mused, not without satisfaction; "after twenty-nine years and under a different regime I am still riding ahead of everyone else!" She was wistful, remembering the sadness of their last evening at Potsdam, but not entirely displeased to be visiting "Caligula—the beast in his den."

Marthe cast a critical eye over Karinhall's garishly painted ceilings, the heavy, overgilded furniture, the family photographs sent by "fellow dictators," the paintings taken from various museums and overpolished "like cavalry boots." She recalled what the Kronprinz had said: "My family, the Kings of Prussia, bought art to give to museums—*they* take it out of museums to hang on their walls."

Soon Göring came into the room. "He obviously does not mind looking ridiculous," Marthe whispered to Lady Londonderry. The Marshal was wearing a voluminous white linen shirt, finely pleated, a green waistcoat fastened with animal teeth, very tight green lederhosen, revealing his enormous buttocks and fat legs, beige silk stockings and brown antelope boots; attached to his belt was a golden dagger heavily encrusted with jewels; he smelled of verveine and citronella. To Marthe he was the personification of bad taste. "Do you think Napoleon's marshals could have been like him in their day?" she asked George. "They did like to dress up," said her husband. "But at least they had charm."

While taking her annual cure at Bagnoles-de-l'Orne in July, Marthe learned of the death of Queen Marie at the royal castle of Pelès in Sinaia. The dying Queen had traveled back to Romania on a slow train from a clinic in Dresden, where she was being treated for a rare liver disease, resulting in frequent hemorrhages. Although the doctors advised transporting Marie by plane, King Carol objected to the cost. Ever jealous of his mother's popularity with the Romanian people, he ordered that she travel by train. It was a nightmarish journey through the mountains in appalling heat with the summer sun blazing mercilessly on the steel coaches. When the train came onto Romanian soil, stationmasters doffed their hats and clumps of people waited at railway crossings to catch a glimpse of their Queen. "The Regina is dying," they whispered among themselves. Marie died two days later; she was sixty-two years old. Perhaps the timing of her death was lucky, for she died before the outbreak of World War II, which heralded the collapse of the Balkan dynasties and the Communist takeover of her country.

Marthe's reaction to her former friend's death was a mixture of sorrow and indifference. She had been close to the Queen when they were both young, during Marie's days as Crown Princess and for many years afterward. In her youth Marthe had been an uncritical admirer of the dazzling blond English princess, ten years older than she, who had come to a distant Balkan country, married a dull, unprepossessing heir to the throne and lived in an uncomfortable Bucharest palace under the stern eye of "der Onkel," the old King. It was in Marthe's house that Marie met Barbo Stirbey, who became the love of her life, and it was while she was spending a night in Posada that the Crown Princess first learned that she had become Queen. Marthe was the first of her subjects to congratulate her. They remained close throughout most of the first decade of Queen Marie's reign, but Marthe was deeply hurt when in the aftermath of World War I the Queen sided with malicious gossip, accusing her friend of having collaborated with the Germans while working in Hospital 101. It was only when the prisoners of war returned home, full of praise for Marthe's heroism, that Bucharest opinion shifted in her favor and the Queen regretted her stand. But by then the harm had been done and the former

intimacy between the two women had vanished. Nevertheless, the
Queen continued to ask Marthe's advice and visited her at Posada
and Mogosoëa. During King Ferdinand's extended battle with cancer, Marthe paid him regular visits at his request, for the King had
always admired her and enjoyed her company, and as time went
on he became romantically attached to her. Queen Marie resented
their friendship, though—as she admitted herself—she spent a
minimum of time at her husband's bedside.

But all this was now in the past, and on hearing the news of
her death Marthe—as she admitted to her diary—felt "immensely
sad" for the Dowager Queen, who in the last years of her life had
suffered cruelly from the abominable conduct of her son, King
Carol II, who had cut her off from her revenues and her friends
(Stirbey was exiled to Switzerland). The spectacular state funeral
that the King stage-managed for his mother and the burial in the
royal crypt at Alba Julia did little to compensate for her sufferings,
"but she would have been very pleased," noted Marthe, "by the
genuine expressions of sympathy and regret from the public which
came flooding to the palace after her death."

"Posada, my beloved mountain retreat. . . . Oh, the joy of waking up in my flower-filled room, the willow trees glistening in the
morning dew, the little robin singing outside my window from its
nest in the old tree trunk, the peace and the beauty of it." Marthe
arrived home the night before on the Orient Express from Paris
with Jean-Nicholas. Valentine and her husband met the train at
the Sinaia railway station; George drove up soon after and gave a
vivid description of Queen Marie's funeral, at which he had represented the local landowners.

Summer days went by peacefully in glorious weather—croquet
parties on the lawn, forest walks, riding with Jean-Nicholas on
mountain trails. Guests came and went: John Reed, the young
expert on Proust; Geoffrey Keane of the International Commission
on the Danube; Priscilla Bibesco and a friend, William Bell; Barbo
Catargi from Bucharest; Colonel Gano, a Polish intelligence expert,
predicting Hitler's annexation of Czechoslovakia; various Mavrocordato and Cantacuzène cousins and others. Every morning
Marthe remained in her room working on her great opus, *La*

Nymphe Europe—its first volume was beginning to take shape. But far away from Posada the political horizon was clouding. "I always love a talk with you about all things of the heart and mind we both care about," wrote Anne Chamberlain to Marthe from 10 Downing Street in early September. "I hardly see Neville these days, as he works all the time; the situation is not good. . . . We spent last weekend at Chequers, where the red roses in the garden below the house you know so well are all you can imagine, but I could not even get my husband to look at them."

On September 15, Neville Chamberlain flew out to Berchtesgaden, met Hitler and, without consulting the Czechoslovak government, promised him the Sudetenland as a token of peace. As the Sudetenland was being annexed to the Reich, France started to mobilize and Czechoslovakia declared a general call to arms. Chamberlain flew out again to see Hitler ten days later; he returned from Munich with the promise of "Peace in Our Time."

In Posada, Marthe and her guests remained glued to the radio; even the young abandoned a mushroom-picking expedition to hear Chamberlain's broadcast. "I know it will start again," Marthe recalled Lord Thomson's words after Versailles and her last conversation with Ramsay MacDonald, when he turned to her, while walking in the garden at Chequers, and said, "We are drifting, drifting toward disaster." From her days with MacDonald she had come to know Downing Street very well. She could see it all now: the comings and goings in the red-carpeted corridor, the cabinet room, the street outside full of people, the brilliantly polished brass numeral 10 on the door, the airport at Croydon, where Chamberlain landed. She knew that the respite was only temporary— yet, like most Europeans, she was thankful for it. It also enabled little Jean-Nicholas to go back to his school the next day. George arrived from Bucharest in excellent humor. "You must write to Chamberlain," he told Marthe. "Write and thank him. He bought much valuable time."

The film *Katia* was to have its premiere at the Marivaux Theater in Paris in mid-October. Marthe left Posada—its "luminous skies and golden leaves"—with reluctance, but her spirits revived when she arrived at the Gare de Lyon and saw dozens of posters advertising *Katia*. Its first night was to be the social event of the season, attended by *"tout Paris,"* including the Duke and Duchess of Windsor. At a time of general unease, a romantic, beautifully acted love story starring the famous Danielle Darrieux was welcomed by the public. Marthe, dressed in a white Chanel dress bordered with white fox fur, the Bibesco emeralds in her ears, received a multitude of congratulations. Later that year there was to be an English showing in London; the Romanian version, alas, fell victim to King Carol's censorship; he feared that the scene describing the assassination of the Tsar might "give ideas" to his Iron Guard enemies. His fears were probably justified, for ever since the assassination of Jon Duca the influence of the Iron Guard—the Greenshirts—had continued to grow, threatening the existence of the monarchy. The movement, which in later years proved unfit for government, even criminal, appeared to many Romanians at the time as a youthful, invigorating force and their good-looking leader, Corneliu Codreanu, as a charismatic proconsul, more attractive than King Carol. The King fought back and under the pretext of a plot against the state had Codreanu arrested. But not for long. After Munich, King Carol was summoned to Berchtesgaden by Hitler and ordered to release his Gauleiter. The Greenshirts were on the way to becoming the ascendant force in the country.

Marthe hurriedly returned to Mogosoëa after her Paris and London triumphs to welcome the director of the Louvre Museum, George Huismans, who was to open an exhibition of drawings from the Louvre at the Bucharest State Museum. She also wanted to be present at the official unveiling of a statue of Ion Bratiano, her old friend.

One day in late November, while she was quietly lunching at Mogosoëa with her friends Michael Palairet, the British Minister in Romania, and his wife, Jean Apolzan, the old butler, came in and whispered the news that the newly freed Codreanu and fourteen of his Legionnaires had been assassinated on orders from King Carol. "He obviously wants to secure his position," said Palairet, "but it will make Hitler mad. The King has panicked—there will now be a dictatorship; you had better be careful what you write in your diaries."

After her friends left for Bucharest, Marthe went down to the little harbor on the lake, got into her canoe and paddled quietly toward a large clump of reeds. "I shall talk only to you from now on," she murmured; "you will hold all my secrets." She was to repeat this ritual many times in the course of the coming troubled years.

15

❧

From the German Hammer to the Red Menace

ow does it feel?" Marthe asked her maid, Blanche Caniot, as she awoke in her sun-filled bedroom at Posada on the last day of August 1939. "Does it feel like war or like peace?" Blanche carefully opened the curtains and placed milk for Ben, the cat, on the terrace. "It feels like peace," she gravely informed her mistress. It was indeed a perfect morning—the outline of the mountains crystal clear for miles on end. No war yet, not today. Yet Marthe wondered how many perfect days were left. She set to work on the outline of a speech George was to deliver at a conference of the International Aeronautical Federation in Athens. But when he arrived for lunch from Bucharest, he told her that the Greeks had canceled the meeting. "It's never happened before—it must mean that the balloon is about to go up."

The next morning, Friday, September 1, Marthe woke up with the news that German tanks were rolling across Poland; two days later France and Great Britain entered the war; meanwhile Poland was being annihilated in the now familiar blitzkrieg. Suddenly the

Russian troops were on the march, occupying eastern Poland, as agreed under the Ribbentrop-Molotov pact. They stood poised on the frontier of Romania.

"What will Romania do?" was the question all Europe was asking. "You are the guests of a neutral kingdom," Romanian frontier officials told the remnants of the Polish Army and the thousands of civilians fleeing from the Russian occupation. Many of Marthe's social friends were among the prominent Polish refugees who made their way to Bucharest and received hospitality at Mogosoëa, an oasis of peace in the midst of a Europe in turmoil.

As soon as the war started, Marthe's primary concern was to get young Jean-Nicholas out of the country and back to school in England. On September 20 they departed in George's private airplane for Athens. As the plane rose in the air, they could see beneath them—lined wing to wing at Baneasa Airport—hundreds of Polish Air Force planes that had managed to escape from German and Russian invaders. In Athens, Michael Palairet, who was now British Minister in Greece, arranged a seat for Jean-Nicholas on an Imperial Airways flight to London. It had been a traumatic day for the boy. That morning, as he and his grandmother were leaving Posada, Jean-Nicholas cast a last glance at the house he loved; he was close to tears. "I shall never see Posada again," he said sadly. He was wrong, but fifty-six years would pass before he would be allowed to come back for a visit.

Marthe returned to a troubled country. At the start of World War II, Romania was in an impossible situation, poised between the German hammer and the Russian anvil. "We are in a trap," Marthe complained. "Mice cohabiting with two hungry cats."

Bucharest was nervous. On Calea Victoriei, the main shopping street, crowds out for their evening promenade cast anxious glances at the neon-lit window of the German Information Office, displaying a map of Poland partitioned between Germany and Russia. A black swastika obliterated Warsaw. The "rival establishment"—the modest British Information Office opposite—was full of jolly travel posters, advertising the beauties of the English countryside. Crowds looked at it skeptically. Britain had guaranteed the independence of Romania that spring, but it also had promised to come to the assistance of Poland. Where were they now?

Near the end of the main thoroughfare, at the crossroads, where the statue of turbaned boyar Cantacuzène pointed the way to the open-air market, peasants were selling great baskets of melons, eggplants, artichokes, young coral carrots, mushrooms, mountain raspberries, apricots, peaches, apples and grapes. The men were still in their tight frieze trousers, short jackets and peaked caps, a style of dress dating back to Roman times. The women wore embroidered blouses and fan-pleated skirts of red, yellow, black and blue, colors richer than those of the faded outfits of the ubiquitous gypsies. As soon as they could afford it, these women would throw off their country costumes and drape themselves in black city dresses and wide shoulder-padded jackets. But for now the young girls in cotton skirts of sugar pinks, plum reds and greens of old bottle glass were running around selling ices. On the other side of the street, prominently displayed in a shopwindow, were assorted French cheeses, caviar, gray river fish, lobsters and crayfish from the mountain streams. The country was bursting with food; it was plentiful and cheap; there seemed to be enough for everyone to last forever. Why worry?

A month later the popular mood darkened. Marthe was at Mogosoëa when news came of the Prime Minister's assassination. Armand Calinescu, gunned down by German agents of the Iron Guard, was the last pro-Allied Prime Minister. As German successes multiplied, Romania abandoned its neutrality and joined the fighting on the German side. By the end of the war they found themselves under Soviet occupation.

But this was still in the future. In the meantime, Romania's situation was made worse by King Carol's lack of political acumen. The King's instant reaction to the murder of his second Prime Minister was to execute without trial ten members of the Iron Guard and order that their bodies be displayed in Bucharest's open market for five days, as the Sultans used to do in centuries past. He misjudged the mood of the country. Romanians were certainly not pro-German—their traditional enemies were the Russians—

but they were tired of corruption and longed for a just government. The Greenshirts, with their idealistic slogans, appealed to many. The death penalty was already in force in Romania, and Calinescu's assassins could have had a summary trial and been executed. But letting their bodies rot in a public place offended the religious feelings of most Romanians, brought discredit on the King and of course provoked the implacable hatred of the Legionnaires. It gave the Germans a wonderful opportunity to exploit the Iron Guard as an instrument of their own.

Marthe was surprised when, shortly after her return from Greece, a call came from the palace summoning her to lunch with the King. She had known Carol ever since he was a little boy—undisciplined, ill-mannered, desperately spoiled by his mother, but by no means unintelligent. He was now a man of forty-six, rather portly, but still handsome with the Hohenzollerns' slightly bulging blue eyes and an attractive smile. She had always thought of him as vain, stubborn, willful and sadly devoid of humor. Since his return after the notorious coup of June 1930, he had been living in relative contentment with his mistress, Elena Lupescu, the half-Jewish daughter of an apothecary in Jassy, who had changed his name from Wolff. She met Carol in 1923, when he was still the Crown Prince and she the wife of an Army officer, whom she quietly divorced after meeting Carol. Three years younger than Carol, Elena Lupescu, with her flaming red hair, dazzlingly white skin, high intelligence and ambition, was a mistress in the tradition of a Du Barry or a Pompadour; her charms were such that the Crown Prince abdicated his succession to be with her. She returned with him to Romania in 1930 and now had "contacts" in all the key positions of the realm. It was even rumored that she had her own secret police. As the King, in his unwedded state, could not have a regular court, he and Lupescu surrounded themselves with a tight camarilla, composed mainly of sycophantic old cronies. Romanian society, who would not have minded if the King had twenty mistresses, disliked Lupescu because of her Jewishness and her influence on the King. She, however, longed to be "received in society." One day the autumn before, as Marthe was entertaining guests at Mogosoëa, she was disagreeably surprised when Jean Apolzan informed her, "with an embarrassed look on his face," that Madame Lupescu had just telephoned to say she would like to stop off for tea on her way to Sinaia. "Who is there with the Princess?" she inquired. Apolzan listed the guests, who were mainly foreign diplomats. "It's all right, I will be with you in an hour," she announced.

Marthe had met the "favorite" only once before and pronounced her "vulgar," which was not particularly surprising; there was little likelihood the two women would ever become friends. But, taken unexpectedly off guard, there was little Marthe could do, except to beg her friends to remain and lend support; she was thankful that George happened to be away from home. The visit passed without mishap.

While on her way to lunch with King Carol, Marthe wondered whether pressure would be put upon her to "ease Elena Lupescu's way into Bucharest society." With a monarch who was a virtual dictator, the situation might easily become awkward. Luckily, Carol only mentioned Lupescu in passing; what he really wanted was Marthe's opinion: whether at this early stage in the war England was likely to conclude a separate peace with Germany, as his cousin the Duke of Windsor was hoping. The King was well aware of Marthe's international contacts and valued her intelligence. "What are they saying in Athens? And in Constantinople?" he asked. "What are Palairet's views? What does he think is going to happen here, and how about his French and Italian colleagues?" She thought the King looked depressed and "rather helpless" and worried about the approaching storm. She told him that England would "certainly fight" and quoted a recently received letter from a high British official, Robert Vansittart: "No hope for settlement with a beast determined to reduce the earth to slavery."

Instinct told Marthe that this was going to be a long war, worse than the one she had lived through as a young woman. "I feel strong, but curiously detached," she wrote to the Abbé Mugnier from Mogosoëa on October 24, 1939. "I have my two houses and the two gardens I created—the one on the plain and the one in the mountains—and the fields and forests of Balotesti I inherited from my father, who loved them. But even if I were to lose everything, I now know that my security lies within me. I have written *Isvor*—it will always be mine and so will the image of the mountains around Posada and the sleeping waters of Mogosoëa." But she worried about "little George," her three-year-old grandson, who was to perpetuate the Bibesco family name, and was much relieved when her friend Rosita de Castries offered to look after him on her Biarritz estate "if things got really bad in Romania."

As refugees from Poland and the frightened inhabitants of the border towns of Bessarabia continued to flock into Bucharest, Marthe's mountain retreat of Posada (which in Spanish means inn) was fully living up to its name. "This morning Mr. Henry Martin, the Swiss Minister in Warsaw, turned up on my doorstep, unable to find a hotel room in the town or at his own Swiss Legation," Marthe noted in her ever present visitors' book. "He told me of his dramatic escape from Warsaw, strafed all the way by low-flying German Stukas with little respect for Swiss neutrality. Count Roman Potocki and Charles Radziwill arrived at lunchtime in a Lancia car peppered with shots, which Radziwill drove for three days under continual bombardment. . . . Yesterday I had to provide shelter for the old Princess Andrew Lubomirska, aged seventy-four, who had walked on foot from her palatial home across the frontier, hiding in forests from the Russians." The descriptions of the refugees' flight from both the Russians and the Germans were horrifying. "It's them today—it may be us tomorrow," Marthe remarked to herself. With the efficient help of Lady Hoare, wife of the British Minister in Bucharest, she was indefatigable in organizing food, clothing and shelter for the refugees and helping Polish soldiers and airmen make their way over to France to continue the fight. George was busy prospecting for places to house an Office of Information for Air Prisoners; he was also presiding over a meeting of the International Aeronautical Federation in Berne, which because of the war was attended by only a small number of representatives from neutral countries.

As winter came, attention was concentrated on the Russian invasion of Finland and the Finns' heroic fight against their powerful neighbor. Feeling against the Russians ran high. At a dinner

Marthe gave for the Finnish Minister before Christmas, all the ladies wore white to show sympathy for the Finns who fought their aggressors in deep snow.

Christmas that year, which at first Marthe had dreaded—it was the first time in many years she was spending it at Mogosoëa— turned out to be unexpectedly jolly, enlivened by the arrival of Louise de Vilmorin and her Hungarian husband, Count Paul Palffy. Louise de Vilmorin was beautiful, witty and talented. Called "Loulou" by Cocteau, who adored her, she combined an inexhaustible zest for life with feminine charm and great looks. She wrote books, poetry, played music and sang to perfection. Men found her irresistible and she in turn found it difficult to resist them. At the age of twenty she became engaged to Antoine de Saint-Exupéry; she left him, but remained, according to him, the only woman he had ever loved. At twenty-two she married Henry Leigh-Hunt, an American friend of her brothers, sixteen years older than she; the marriage was as eccentric as it was unexpected. Henry Leigh-Hunt was an "entrepreneur" in the grand tradition of the Vanderbilts and the Rockefellers; he swept her off to Las Vegas, Nevada, then a small village, which was supposed to offer "glittering development prospects." After five years of solitary life in Las Vegas (Leigh-Hunt was always away "prospecting"), Louise returned to France in 1931 with her American husband and their two children. Delighted to be back in her own Paris milieu, she plunged headlong into the frantic social life of *les années folles*. She was seen everywhere and admired by everyone, including André Malraux, with whom she had a long love affair, the publisher Gallimard and many others. It was the Abbé Mugnier, the *"conseiller* of the Faubourg,"* who channeled her vitality and creative talents into writing novels and poetry. Poor Leigh-Hunt, who remained a bewildered and often angry spectator of his wife's triumphs, agreed to divorce in 1936. Soon after, in October 1937, Louise met Count Palffy, a Hungarian aristocrat with vast estates in what is today Slovakia. Palffy, nicknamed "Pali" by his friends, was a giant of a man, immensely good-looking, with blue eyes, dark hair and an outdoor complexion; he spoke at least six languages fluently and was at home in every European capital; his charm was legendary; adored by women, he had already been married four times.

Louise was swept off her feet, married him in the spring of 1938, just as Austria was being annexed into the German Reich, and—impervious to her brothers' warnings—departed with him for Hungary to become the mistress of the feudal castle of Pudmerice, nestled among snow-covered forests and miles from the nearest town or railway station. At first she was enchanted—everything was immense—the castle, the oak forests, the great snowy plains, the limitless horizons. Swathed in furs, she and Pali went for endless sleigh rides in the moonlight; he taught her how to shoot lynx and stalk stags; she learned to speak Hungarian and became adept at tzigane songs; Louise was living the romance of a lifetime.

With the outbreak of war, as neutral Hungary leaned more and more toward Germany, Pali was often with Hungarian or Austrian cronies shooting and attending race meetings, while Louise, the bride, was left alone in the huge castle, which due to wartime restrictions was becoming impossible to heat. Just as she was beginning to feel desperate, a visit to Marthe in Romania was suggested. The two women had met in Paris earlier in the thirties; as an older woman, Marthe admired Louise's exuberance and her wit, although she did not think much of her writing. But, as Antoine sardonically remarked, "she was a life enhancer—if nothing else —and that's what was needed at the moment."

So Christmas, the first of the war, passed in a haze of champagne, tokay and singing of gypsy and Hungarian ballads; they shot boar in the mountains above Posada, pheasants on the plains in Wallachia and wild duck on the lakes at Mogosoëa. A Russian friend, an accomplished pianist, played beautiful Chopin and Liszt; the house vibrated with poems and songs; Valentine and her husband were enchanted and so was little George. Village children performed the traditional ritual of bringing the Christmas star to the house; carrying their little lanterns, they went from door to door through the snow singing carols and were given stockings filled with apples, nuts and money. "My thoughts were with Jean-Nicholas and the Abbé Mugnier," noted Marthe, "the two people I would have loved to have with me at this time." She was happy that George was with them—"even if only for a few days," for he still spent most of his time in Bucharest with La Toboso.

The weather was beautiful—snow and brilliant sun reflected

in the waters of the lakes. "You live inside a blue sapphire," Louise told Marthe. They went by sleigh to Bucharest to dine with Foreign Minister Gafencu. At this decisive moment in its history Romania did not lack gifted men. Gafencu, Titulescu and Tilea, the current Romanian Minister in London, were all exceedingly able, well educated, multilingual statesmen, highly respected in the League of Nations; throughout the thirties they had made their mark in the councils of the Little Entente (which included Czechoslovakia, Yugoslavia and Romania). But there was not much they could accomplish in the face of the unfortunate geographical position of their country. "Romania is a little place full of wise, useless statesmen," Gafencu remarked to Marthe bitterly over an excellent dish of white truffles.

"The year that lost its spring" was how Marthe recalled 1940. As snows began to melt at Mogosoëa, the war drew closer and closer. "Like the sword of Damocles, waiting for the other shoe to drop over the body of a sleeping man," people were saying. In spite of a general dislike of the Germans, the Norwegian campaign undermined faith in the Allies. Crowds gathered in front of the German Information Office in Bucharest, to look at pictures of British battleships being sunk in Norwegian waters. Arrows cut out of red cardboard pointed in the direction of the German attack. A week after the German invasion of Denmark and Norway, the Allied retreat was announced; the menacing red arrows mesmerized the crowds; some papers, usually pro-British, predicted a counterattack, but soon news came that four thousand Norwegians had surrendered and that their government had fled to England. The Allies took to the sea. It was another victory for the Germans.

Marthe was determined to return to France while it was still possible. She wanted to spend a few days with the Abbé Mugnier, probably for the last time, and to visit Jean-Nicholas at his school in England. There was also an official reason for her visit: to establish in a neutral country an office like the Red Cross that would relay information on air prisoners to their families. It was a project conceived and developed by George; they at first thought of Switzerland, but after consulting Leland Harrison, the U.S. Minister in Berne and an old friend, it was decided to locate the office in Rome or possibly Lisbon.

In late February, Marthe boarded the Orient Express to Paris. The familiar old train, whose free run across frontiers would soon be interrupted by Italy's entry into the war, was taking her back to France. It had been a part of her life ever since her childhood; the blue seats with pink lights, the comfortable berths, the smiling, uniformed attendants, most of whom were known to her by name—forty-eight hours of motion, unhindered by politics or the strife of war. The train was steeped in history; one wondered how many friendships and romances it had spawned.

At the Budapest station only German papers were sold. Trieste was full of flowers and the people were smiling. When Marthe got out of the train under the huge dome of the station in Milan to buy a *Corrière della Sera*, an unknown Italian gallant, casting an admiring glance at her face, paid for it and walked off. It lifted her spirits.

Paris was bitterly cold; gasoline restrictions were in force and most taxis had vanished from the streets. Instead of going back to the windy and inaccessible Quay Bourbon, Marthe decided to stay at the Elysée Hotel, in the center. "You ask what is happening in Paris?" Marthe wrote in a letter to George. "It is waiting—waiting for something to happen. The only good news at the moment is that the ice on the Danube is still solid and our oil is not reaching the Germans."

The "phony war" still had two months to run, and in the meantime the Paris social round continued. The Abbé had not yet arrived; he was staying with Rosita de Castries on her estate near Biarritz, but most of the other friends were still there. She saw Paul Claudel almost daily and accompanied the entire family to the showing of his play *Joan of Arc*; dined with the Castellane, anxious for news of their Polish relatives, who had escaped to Romania; and visited the Chambrun and Misia Sert. She also ordered a quantity of clothes and a fur-lined coat at Lanvin, as the war might be long and very cold. In England, Marthe spent most of her time with Jean-Nicholas at his school in Ampleforth; she found him "rosy-cheeked and well adjusted to school life." With the help of the principal she planned where he would spend his school holidays, as he would probably be cut off from his home by the war.

Leonie Lady Leslie, Winston Churchill's aunt, traveled from Ireland to see her; she lunched with her friend Lady Cholmondeley, Philip Sassoon's sister—"elegant and attractive in her new Red Cross uniform with a tricornered hat perched over her silver hair." On her last day in London, Marthe dined with the Neville Chamberlains at Downing Street. There was just enough time to catch the night ferry to Dunkirk on the way back to Paris.

As the Abbé Mugnier had been ill, it was not until early April that he rejoined Marthe in Paris. From then on they saw each other daily. They both knew that, after thirty years of friendship, this would be the last time they would meet. More than ever, Marthe needed his spiritual guidance and wise counsel to fortify her for what fate would bring in the years to come. Marthe left France in late May as the German panzers were racing toward Paris. Her last social engagement was a lunch at the house of Sir Charles and Lady Mendl in Versailles. "Like the Duchess of Richmond's ball before Waterloo," she noted in her diary that evening. "One could hear the booming of the distant cannon. . . . Around us people were packing and burning papers."

Rome was unchanged, bathed in golden sunlight, serene, untouched by war fever. At the Grand Hotel, Marthe made her first call on the former King Alfonso of Spain, who occupied a large suite on the same floor. Her old admirer had aged and was growing deaf, but there was still the old charm and grandeur. He was delighted to see her. "Always so beautifully dressed," he exclaimed as she came into the room wearing her new black-and-white Lanvin suit. Moved by old memories, King Alphonso confessed that he had loved her "for a very long time"—ever since 1914, he said.

She saw him frequently. "Come and lunch at number thirty-two," he would often say over the telephone in the mornings. King Alfonso, being a Bourbon, loved France. The unrelenting push of the German armies, threatening the *patrie* of his ancestors, distressed him. On the table in his sunny sitting room, overlooking the Baths of Caracalla, within sound of the bells of Santa Maria dei Angeli, he had spread out a large military map of France and marked the positions of the armies with little colored flags. But the news grew worse and worse every day. After the collapse of Belgium only the successful British Army evacuation from Dunkirk provided a small satisfaction. He knew that the battle for France was about to begin and he dreaded the outcome. "I shall always remember," Marthe wrote years later, "his splendid patrician head, the product of centuries of fine breeding, bent over the military map, hoping for a miracle to happen. He had had everything in his life—Goyas, El Grecos, Velázquezes and priceless jewels—but there was nothing left of all that. He had a bad heart condition and knew he did not have long to live."

George Bibesco had hoped that Italy would remain neutral and that he would be able to locate his office in Rome. It was what his friend Air Marshal Italo Balbo had promised him, but the pro-Allied Balbo had been relegated by Mussolini to the Italian possession of Tripolitania on the North African coast. He no longer had power and all he could do was order a gigantic bouquet of red roses to be sent to Marthe from the best florist in Rome.

It did not take Marthe long to realize, after she had made contact with a few people "in the know," that Italy was about to enter the war on Hitler's side. "Will you remain neutral?" she asked Count Galeazzo Ciano, the Italian Foreign Minister, when she met him at a large dinner party in the Quirinale. He evaded the question, gallantly kissing her hand instead and telling her how beautiful she looked. She now knew that it would not be possible to site the Office of Information for Air Prisoners in Rome, or, for that matter, in Lisbon. Her duty was to return home as soon as possible; she could not risk being cut off from George, whose health, she knew, was beginning to deteriorate.

Marthe would always remember two occasions from her last stay in Rome: the first was her meeting with Pope Pius XII. The Pontiff received her in a private audience and blessed her while they prayed. "I saw great suffering on his face," she recalled. "Unhappy Father of the Christians, whose children are killing each other in a fratricidal war." The other was the visit she paid to her old friend François Poncet, recently French Ambassador in Berlin, now posted to Rome and residing in one of the most beautiful houses in Europe—the Palais Farnèse. She called on him on the day when the British Army was evacuating from Dunkirk, abandoning the coastline of France to the enemy. They were packing suitcases at the residence and burning papers. After dinner, when other guests had left, Poncet accompanied her to the door along the red-carpeted passages, hung with priceless eighteenth-century prints. "I sent tons of reports from Berlin, but no one in Paris read them; I told them what the German Air Force was like, so did your husband, and so did General Milch of the German Army staff, when he visited Paris, but *they* wouldn't listen." He spoke with great bitterness.

Marthe left Rome on May 30, taking the Simplon Express to Venice; her carriage was full of roses, sent by the former King Alfonso; in her bag was a rosary, given and blessed by the Pope. It was raining in Venice; the Piazza San Marco was deserted; chairs on the terrace of Florian's Café were stacked up; no tourists were expected that summer. In the evening she dined with Fortuny; in a desultory way they discussed various items of decoration for Mogosoëa, but their heart was not really in it. Their world was crumbling.

George looked ill when he met her at the Bucharest railway station. He had lost weight, his complexion was yellow and he complained of pain in the joints. The military defeat of France depressed him. "There is a pronounced anti-French feeling about," he told Marthe. "Romanian Army officers are refusing all invitations from the French; they think the Germans are invincible and it is better to stick to the winning side." Antoine, who came to dinner that evening, declared that Romania was behaving like a Circassian slave, "adjusting her makeup in the mirror while potential buyers [Germany and the Soviet Union] are haggling about the price of her body."

Marthe spent the first week of June, the week of the battle for France, glued to the radio. The names of the places mentioned in the war bulletins distressed her. "They are at Fécamp in Flaubert's country," she noted on June 7. "They have occupied

Amiens; they are entering Rheims." On June 10, Italy declared war on the German side; at his farewell audience before leaving Rome, Ambassador Poncet said to Ciano, "Remember that the Germans are very hard masters." Ciano was gloomy; his heart wasn't in it and he knew that many Italians shared his feeling.

June 14 was a day of immense sadness. The Germans entered Paris and Hitler announced, "I will pass under the Arc de Triomphe." Four days later, in a desperate last-minute effort to avoid French capitulation, Churchill flew to Bordeaux to offer union with Britain. "A marriage in extremis," said George. Marthe recalled the words of Balzac's Paquita on her deathbed: "Too late, *ma bien aimée*, too late."

As they drove along Bucharest's Calea Victoriei on their way to the British Legation that evening, Marthe averted her eyes from the window of the German Information Office, which was blazing with lights. A black swastika covered Paris; crowds looked at it in shocked disbelief. "We are alone now," Sir Reginald Hoare said to George. Imperturbable, as always, the diplomat had spent the afternoon playing croquet.

It did not take long for the Russian and German allies to profit from the changed international order. Acting under the secret terms of the Nazi-Soviet pact, Russia dispatched an ultimatum to King Carol demanding the immediate secession of Romania's eastern province of Bessarabia as well as northern Bukovina. Two months later, Hitler, who needed Romania's oil supplies and planned to reduce the country to the status of a protectorate, "awarded" Transylvania—the much cherished province—to his allies the Hungarians. Bulgaria took the opportunity to grab southern Dobrudja. The days of "greater Romania," so successfully negotiated by Queen Marie at Versailles, were over. Facing mounting public outcry, the government of the bon vivant Gafencu resigned. In its place came a military strongman, General Ion Antonescu, a German protégé, who formed a new government with members of the Fascist Iron Guard. The Greenshirts now reigned supreme, parading in the streets of the capital, shouting slogans, carrying banners with pictures of their former leader Codreanu and demanding the King's abdication. The word *abdica* was heard all over town. The Plaza-Athénée, Bucharest's most fashionable hotel, famous for its superb cuisine, was now full of Wehrmacht officers; the Horst Wessel song resounded from the crowded bar; British and French visitors were unwelcome.

In early September, King Carol was told by the German Ambassador to abdicate and leave the country. He left by train, under Army guard, for Switzerland, taking with him Madame Lupescu and much of Romania's gold. Few people missed him. For the second time in fifteen years his son, the eighteen-year-old Michael, succeeded to the now almost powerless position of King of Romania. Marthe, who came into Bucharest every day to work in the Office for Air Prisoners, saw him standing on a balcony of the palace, "looking tearful, like a child, and raising his hands in salute." He had wanted to follow his father into exile, but was prevented from doing so by Antonescu. Carol's discarded wife, Queen Helen, Michael's mother, now returned from Florence to take up the duties of Queen Mother.

Three weeks later, Antonescu, now promoted to marshal, took Romania into the war on the side of the Axis powers. From then on, only the formalities of kingship were upheld. The King continued to live in the royal palace, where he had a small personal staff; he was allowed to perform ceremonial functions, but his every move was watched by Antonescu's spies and there was nothing he could do to arrest the creeping Nazification of his country.

Marthe was disappointed when Queen Helen telephoned her to explain that she would not be allowed to see either Marthe or any of her old friends. "Forbidden by orders of Marshal Antonescu," as a subsequent visit of the Queen's lady-in-waiting made clear.

Marthe herself was put in an embarrassing situation when the Marshal's office telephoned and suggested she should receive Madame Fabricius, wife of the newly arrived German Ambassador, who was of Irish extraction and apparently was eager to meet "the famous writer." There was nothing she could do but invite her to lunch at Mogosoëa. George refused to attend and left the house early that morning. Jean Apolzan carried out his duties as usual, but "made disapproving faces behind the lady's back."

All through that autumn Marthe's thoughts were with her friends in England and with her grandson Jean-Nicholas. On her visits to Bucharest she was fatally drawn—much against her will —to the map in the window of the German Information Office that showed the Luftwaffe's onslaught on the British Isles and to pictures of cities in flames. "Will they survive or sink—together with our darling schoolboy?" Marthe asked her diary.

One morning in October, when the trees were all red and gold, George walked into Marthe's bedroom at Mogosoëa, looking ill. He was coughing up blood. "There is something very wrong with the Prince. He must go into the hospital," Jean Apolzan told Marthe. "They give him strange injections in Bucharest that seem to make him worse."

It was an odd, rather sinister situation; Marthe was convinced that Elena Leonte, whose husband and brother were doctors and had links with the Iron Guard, was poisoning George with mysterious injections, which he assured Marthe were only vitamin shots. Knowing his weakness with women, she would not have been surprised if he had let himself be persuaded by his mistress to leave her a large sum of money and possibly the Bucharest house. Did he not sell some land a few years ago to provide a dowry for La Toboso's daughter on her marriage? As George insisted on remaining in the Bucharest house and pretended that he was perfectly all right—"I have a horror of showing that I am ill," he repeated like a child—she dispatched Jean Apolzan to watch over "the master" in town. She herself had to remain at Mogosoëa to obtain the release of her papers, which had been confiscated during a recent lightning raid carried out by a platoon of the Iron Guard. They arrived—as police in totalitarian countries do—at an early hour of the morning, while Marthe was still asleep, swarmed over the house, opening cupboards, throwing contents of drawers on the floor, breaking locks and tapping walls in search of hidden safes. They were not interested in jewelry or money, only documents; it was obvious that the government suspected Marthe of some sort of subversion. All was seized: family photographs, archives, letters, but above all Marthe's manuscripts and her notes for *La Nymphe Europe*. Even a book of Claudel's poems and a manuscript donated by Anatole France were judged suspect and taken away. Marthe was devastated and immediately set about to recoup them. No stone remained unturned; it took time, some precious items were lost, but eventually the bulk of them was returned. It had been a sobering experience.

But the annoyance and the fury caused by the Iron Guard's raid were nothing compared with her mounting anxiety over George's health; he now looked like a shadow of his former self, emaciated and barely able to walk. In December, Jean Apolzan came to say that "the Prince is too weak to get out of bed." Marthe packed her bags and drove into Bucharest to George's house, where she confronted Elena Leonte. "You must leave at once," she told her. "You have done him enough harm as it is. Go!" La Toboso was a short, dark-haired woman with a prominent bosom and lovely legs. She had installed herself in George's house and obviously considered it her domain. Marthe's unexpected appearance threw her off balance; afraid of scandal (one of her daughters was about to get married), she collected her scattered belongings and left, expecting to return the next day. But Marthe would have none of it; that evening George was moved to a private clinic, the Helias Sanatorium, and put under the care of Dr. Danielopolu, a friend of the family and a specialist in treating cancer. Elena Leonte and her "acolytes" were forbidden access to George's room in the clinic. Thus began a long vigil. For three and a half months, until he was moved to Mogosoëa, Marthe and her daughter, Valentine, mounted guard over husband and father. They occupied a tiny room, next to George's, sleeping in two-hour shifts, waking up whenever a commotion was heard in the corridor. Assassination was an ever present danger, as George, whose anti-German opinions were well known, was one of the people on the Iron Guard's blacklist. It was a time of terror and lawlessness in Bucharest; people cowered in their houses, afraid to be arrested in the street on some flimsy pretext and deported to one of the German concentration camps.

George's illness ebbed and rose, as cancers do. He had a beautiful body with the powerful chest of an athlete. During the regular radiology sessions Marthe observed with a sinking heart the "sinister white mushroom" growing between her husband's lungs. George was amazingly patient and good humored. He, who so often had made Marthe cry because of his brusque retorts and short temper, was revered on the hospital floor for his perfect manners and winning smile. The nurses all adored him and special prayers were said every morning in the small whitewashed hospital chapel for the Prince's recovery. He wanted Marthe near him at all times. "Where is she?" he would ask Valentine if she happened to be away on an errand. "I want her here." One day, as he recovered consciousness after a prolonged bout of fevered delirium, he brought her hand to his lips and whispered, "Forgive me for all the suffering I have caused you. You were so beautiful and so young—how could I?" Marthe, tears streaming, buried her face in the blankets.

At the end of April, as the cancer spread to the lower parts of his body and all hope of recovery receded, Marthe brought her husband to Mogosoëa. It was the proper setting for his last days. "We moved him here in an ambulance, accompanied by two nurses and one intern," she wrote to the Abbé Mugnier. "He is delighted to be home and is feeling better already; the lovely spring air, the flowers and the blessed peace after the hell of the Helias Sanatorium, which Valentine and I nicknamed 'Hell Helias,' make him happy. Yesterday he was able to sit up in bed and eat a soft-boiled egg by himself—great progress. . . . It is tragic to see this indomitable spirit laid low, our traveler in the skies, reduced to being fed bouillon by the spoon and given tiny amounts of milk every two hours. As his illness progresses, he does not hear the morning concert of the birds under his windows anymore, the nightingales and the croaking of the frogs in the night. But he can still see the fields of blue irises and smell the aroma of the acacias in flower. . . . He enjoys seeing little George play around and now and then—for a very short time—receives a few visitors."

George died on Wednesday, July 2, 1941, at 2 a.m., holding Marthe's hand. He was buried, according to his wishes, in the little chapel of St. George, next to Mogosoëa's main house. "If you don't mind being in an Orthodox church, I would like you to be buried next to me," he said to Marthe shortly before his death. But, sadly, his wish would be thwarted by coming events.

She had never imagined how much she was going to miss him. Married since the age of fifteen—almost a child—she had been his wife for nearly forty years; their personalities often clashed, they spent more time apart than more conventional couples. He was—in the manner of Balkan husbands—chronically unfaithful to her, and yet there was an indissoluble link between them; whenever one or the other contemplated divorce they always withdrew from the brink. "It is tragic that he should have been taken from me," Marthe confided to the Abbé Mugnier, "at a time when we could have settled down and spent the rest of our lives in agreeable companionship, which has always existed in spite of our intermittent quarrels." In years to come Marthe was to realize that fate had been kind to George to allow him to die when he did, in the dignity of his ancestral home, surrounded by those who loved him. He would never have adapted to the life of a penniless exile.

When in June 1941 Germany attacked Russia, her recent ally, Romania, which in the course of the year had become a German-occupied territory, was immediately drawn into war against the Soviets on the German side. She was also forced to declare war on Britain, the country which had been a steady friend, guaranteed her independence and had only the year before condemned Russian annexation of Bessarabia. All communications with England, except through the Red Cross, were now cut. The staff of the British Legation and the British Council left for Greece; it would be a long time before the family would have news of young Jean-Nicholas. As in a rerun of a film of twenty-five years before, Bucharest was again being bombed; this time by Soviet planes based in Odessa. Marthe sent little George, with his English governess, Miss Leggett, to the safety of Posada in the mountains; she herself remained at Mogosoëa, with Valentine, on guard against marauding soldiers. Communiqués from the front trumpeted the German Army's victorious progress into Russia. "Smolensk . . . the Berezina

. . . Mogilev; shades of Napoleon's campaign. Will it end the same way?" Marthe asked, putting a large question mark in her diary.

Christmas that year, the first since George's death, was subdued. A French Catholic priest, a guest at the Byzantine Institute of Bucharest, celebrated the Midnight Mass in the presence of the family and a handful of French and Swiss guests. Among them was Jacques Truelle, the French Minister in Bucharest, a charming, cultivated man, a friend of Proust's and an admirer of Marthe's writing, whose company gave her much pleasure and delighted Antoine during his periodic visits to Mogosoëa.

"You must start writing again," the Abbé Mugnier advised Marthe in one of his letters. It had been more than a year since she had looked at the pages of *La Nymphe Europe*. Work seemed strangely irrelevant during the time of George's illness; all her strength and mental resources were focused on saving him or at least making him comfortable; she now turned toward it as the only solace against pain.

But first something had to be done to make Mogosoëa livable during one of the fiercest winters on record. The house had been built and arranged as a spring and autumn residence to receive the first and the last rays of the sun. In the past Marthe never spent winters there; because of the delicate condition of her lungs, George insisted that she always leave Romania before Christmas. She usually moved in again in late March, with the arrival of spring, which in the Balkans comes early. With most rooms opening up to the sky and the gardens, winter winds coming all the way from Siberia and "howling like wolves" whistled through the colonnades and ornate chambers, bringing with them sheets of snow. To winterize one of the smaller drawing rooms, an ingenious arrangement of curtains and screens was made. Arcades opening up to the sky were closed with boards, and heavy curtains, black on the outside as camouflage against enemy bombers and oatmeal white on the inside, were suspended from rings in the ceiling. The whole effect was one of a tent, and Marthe called it the tent of Abd-el-Kader. It enclosed a large stone fireplace, heated by logs. In this snug little room Marthe now spent most of her time writing or entertaining visitors; the library next door, also boarded up with planks, served as the family's dining room. "You would laugh if you saw these arrangements," Marthe wrote to Rosita de Castries in Biarritz, "but at least we are surviving the winter. Come March we will resume normal living, if such a thing still exists."

⚜

With Romanian soldiers being forced by their German masters to fight on the Russian front in Odessa, Bucharest hospitals were filling with wounded. At the Office for Air Prisoners, where Marthe worked, she was being besieged by petitions from soldiers' relatives, begging for medicines and anti-infection drugs. Her own medicine chests were depleted; what if one of her family contracted pneumonia? Little George certainly would not survive it. Marthe decided to attempt a short trip to Switzerland.

René de Weck, the Swiss Minister in Bucharest—a good friend—arranged for a Swiss visa and a three-day transit through Italy. Hungary, where she would have to get off the plane, was no problem; the difficulty was to obtain an exit and reentry permit from the authorities in Romania. "They will be quite glad to let you leave," said de Weck; but she needed to be allowed to return. Finally, after many disappointments and false alarms, the necessary permits were granted—a tribute to Marthe's persistence and to her influential contacts.

Marthe could not be blamed for feeling tremendous relief when the plane finally took off from Bucharest. After leading a sad and cloistered existence for the last two years, it was only natural to look forward to a change and to a wider world, beyond the confines of the war. In Budapest, where she stopped for a night, she was greeted by her friend Louise de Vilmorin, now involved in a passionate affair with Count Esterhazy and on the point of leaving Pali Palffy. She too was waiting for an exit visa, but it would take her a year to return to Vichy-occupied France.

In Rome, Marthe returned to the Grand Hotel and to the memories of King Alfonso XIII, who had died the preceding year. The Italian capital glittered in late spring sunshine, but was "strangely silent and deserted," she noted. She hurried on to Geneva and Lausanne. After successfully arranging for a shipment of medicine from the Red Cross and replenishing her own personal pharmacy, Marthe traveled to Berne, where she had a long meeting with the American Minister, Leland Harrison, who knew Bucharest well and had visited Mogosoëa. He received her privately, as Romania was considered an enemy country, using Marthe as a channel to send an unofficial message to the Romanian Foreign Minister advising him to withdraw Romania's troops from the Russian front "as rapidly as possible" and to keep them "strictly within their own frontiers." Only then could Romania expect favorable treatment from the Allies and special protection from the United States at the postwar peace conference.

Marthe's last day in Switzerland was spent at the grave of her sister Marguerite and her mother in Clarens. The two cypresses she had planted had grown; she was relieved to see that the grave had been well looked after. Marguerite, her favorite sister, had now been dead for twenty-four years; she still missed her. How long, she wondered, will it take me to reconcile myself to George's going? "The rest of my life," she concluded as she slowly walked back to the car and drove to Geneva Airport. She hurried back to Mogosoëa for the first anniversary of her husband's death; a memorial service was to be held in the Orthodox chapel next to the main house, where his body lay in the family vault.

Mogosoëa looked wonderfully green after the recent rains, suffused with the delicate scent of lime trees in full bloom. Marthe spent the anniversary alone with her thoughts and her grief. More than ever she missed the Abbé Mugnier's conversation, his gentle wit and wise guidance. "Never, in the course of my entire life, did I need you more than I do now," she wrote to him on December 10, 1942. "It is two years since I have last seen you, but I should not complain, I have your letters, so we are not out of touch." The Abbé was now over ninety and quite frail; she dreaded to hear of his death. One day Jacques Truelle, the French Minister, who was also a friend of the Abbé, arrived at Mogosoëa and announced that he was the bearer of sad news. Marthe looked stricken; she was certain that the Abbé Mugnier had died. But it was Charles-Louis de Beauvau-Craon, her old love, who had died at the Château Haroué in Alsace. "Strange and ungrateful as it may seem,"

Marthe confessed to her diary, "I breathed a sigh of relief. Charles-Louis was dear to me, but I need the Abbé far more." "Yet, I cried like a fountain that evening," she noted, "when the memories of Charles-Louis came flooding back. He was my first real love and the man on whom my life centered for at least five to six years."

As 1942 drew to a close, faint rays of hope began to pierce the all-enveloping gloom at Mogosoëa. The Germans did not take Moscow after all, nor did they take Stalingrad. In November the British won the battle of El Alamein, defeating Rommel in Egypt. Was the tide turning?

In the spring of 1943 came the North African landings; *"Alger —La France Libre vous parle,"* Marthe heard the magical words one early morning on her radio. They echoed throughout the house, bringing joy and hope that there might be an end to this war. At night the family repaired to the "catacombs," the underground suite of vaulted chambers, dating back to the days of Byzantium, where they could listen to the BBC news undisturbed.

Marthe continued to work in the Office for Air Prisoners, but she found Bucharest depressing. The town was overrun by German soldiers, who filled the streets and commandeered restaurants and hotels. The country was gradually being stripped of food; the outdoor markets, an integral feature of Bucharest, had disappeared; the gypsies, threatened with extinction, had repaired to the mountains; no more music was heard at street corners; Cismigliu Park, where generations of young Romanians used to court and promenade in the evenings to the strains of gypsy orchestras, was now silent; flower beds looked neglected, and weeds grew over the once well-maintained paths. Shopping for food was becoming a nightmare for town dwellers, but even in the country it was not much better. Antoine, the fastidious gourmet, on his visits to Bucharest from his house near Turnu-Severin, where he was marooned by the war, regularly repaired to the Jockey Club, where, he said, there was still half-decent food. He was not a popular member; in prewar days, as a rich and distinguished diplomat with a reputation as a snob, he was known for his devastatingly funny jokes at the expense of his fellow members. They now took their revenge by snubbing him. "What's your name, by the way?" asked a crusty old boy, reclining in a deep leather armchair in the library; Antoine was outraged. "I've forgotten," he said, and stormed out.

"*Alger—La France Libre vous parle.*" Twice a day the Mogosoëa household, which now included various nieces and children, gathered to hear the war bulletins. In April, Jacques Truelle, whom Marthe nicknamed "Frère Jacques" because of his cheerful disposition, secretly left for Constantinople to rejoin the Free French in Algiers. It was becoming clear that the balance was swinging in the Allies' favor.

Did Romania back the wrong horse? Its new Foreign Minister, Mihai Antonescu—no relation to Ion Antonescu the dictator—was convinced that the time was ripe to start negotiating the terms of Romania's surrender with the Allies. Mussolini's downfall and Italy's capitulation that summer made it desperately urgent. He dispatched Alexander Cretzianu, a conservative politician and friend of Prince Stirbey's, to Cairo to "test the waters." But Cretzianu's tentative démarche, though sympathetically considered by Britain and the United States, failed because of Stalin's determination to punish Romania for siding with the Germans and sending its troops to fight in the Crimea. Disappointed, the Foreign Minister decided to try unofficial contacts: this would involve sending someone to Constantinople. Turkey, which had remained neutral in the conflict, was where representatives of the belligerents met, talked, dined and spied on each other. Both Ankara and Constantinople teemed with spies and agents of every description. There is no official confirmation either in her diaries or in the Romanian State Archives that Marthe was asked to try where her predecessor had failed, but we do know from letters of Archibald Gibson, the *Times* correspondent in Ankara and a most reliable witness, that she spent about six months in Constantinople "acting as an emissary of Foreign Minister Mihai Antonescu in his efforts to open negotiations with the Allies." "To my joy, among the recently arrived visitors was Marthe Bibesco, a prominent figure of aristocratic background in Bucharest society," Gibson recalled. "She contacted me and I wished her the best of luck in her mission."

This time there were no difficulties about an exit or return visa, but the Orient Express, which she boarded on September 25, 1943, took a long time to arrive at its destination. Marthe occupied herself by updating her diary. She got off the train in Sofia, which was bedecked with black flags for the death of King Boris, who had suffered a heart attack after his interview with Hitler in Berchtesgaden. When she finally arrived at her destination she was met by the Romanian Minister to Turkey and the Spanish Ambassador Casa-Rojas. She settled into a large room, rented from a Turkish acquaintance, Madame Ratib Bey, with a superb view of the Bosphorus. For the first time since George's death she felt that life could be pleasant.

Though Marthe's "mission" was doomed to failure from the start—the timing was wrong and well-wishers among the Allies were shackled by the doctrine of "unconditional surrender"—the stay in Constantinople revived her. Dabbling in international affairs, meeting powerful people who were "in the know," was what she had always enjoyed and was used to. She was surrounded by an international elite: diplomats, particularly the Casa-Rojases, whom she saw almost daily, Brazilians, Swiss and Swedish journalists, resident British and French officials, and politicians and visiting writers, like Steven Runciman, the Byzantine expert and biographer of the Crusades. "I feel young again," she wrote in her diary. Being able to devote time to *La Nymphe Europe*, in the place which formed the background for her first volume, was also a source of immense satisfaction. On January 28, 1944, while she quietly celebrated her fifty-eighth birthday by reading and resting in bed, she received—much to her surprise—a huge bouquet of fresh cyclamens from Félix Guépin, the director of Dutch Shell in Ankara, a handsome and cultivated man of great charm. He had met Marthe at a dinner party two weeks before and was impressed. Looking her up in the French Who's Who, he noticed that her birthday was that very week and sent flowers. Marthe found this token of a younger man's admiration particularly thrilling. "It makes up for being one year older," she confessed to a friend. "Today I feel as if I could be any age."

Early in March, Prince Stirbey, on his way back from another unsuccessful round of negotiations in Cairo, suggested that it was time for Marthe to return home. Further peace initiatives were hopeless, as long as the Russians insisted on retaining Bukovina and the whole of Bessarabia and—worse—putting Romanian armed forces under the Red Army's command. By now Marthe was quite ready to return to Romania. She had had only intermittent news of her family and she worried about the state of affairs at Mogosoëa, for since George's death it was she who had to make all the decisions.

Marthe knew that the future for her country looked bleak; the victorious Russian counteroffensive, sweeping the German armies before it, would soon be within striking distance of Bucharest. The German occupation was bad, but life under the Soviets was bound to be even worse. In future years she was to remember the Constantinople interlude as the last, almost carefree episode in her life.

Marthe returned to Bucharest on April 2 after a terrifying train journey during which she and her maid, Blanche Caniot, nearly perished under a U.S. air bombardment. Many people were surprised to see her back. "They said I left because I was afraid and I came back because I am stupid," she laughed. "Our Bucharest gossips never change." Shortly after her return she moved the family to Posada, safer from marauding soldiers and farther away from the bombs than Mogosoëa. She remained there with Valentine, her husband and little George, living in a forester's cottage covered with firs, while wave after wave of Allied bombers flew over their heads. "At least 300 U.S. planes passed over our little retreat in the woods," she noted in her diary. "Little George is as good as gold, he only worries about his puppy and his two favorite sheep coming to grief. So far we have escaped—Isvor is still untouched. . . . Survival is like a lottery, a deadly game of roulette."

She was still in Posada when news came of the Abbé Mugnier's death. Marthe had been steeling herself for this news for some time; the Abbé was ninety-two years old, yet his death affected her deeply. In him she lost not only a devoted friend and confessor but a brilliant literary adviser, whose shrewd judgment had guided her through the years. Years later she paid tribute to their thirty-four-year friendship by compiling three volumes of their correspondence, which not only give a picture of the period but also reveal the inner Marthe, even more than her diaries.

Marthe had not seen much of King Michael since he ascended the throne. The King was not under house arrest; people saw him walking around Bucharest or visiting troops, but his duties were a constitutional charade. He had no power and his every move was watched. Antonescu had filled the palace with spies, and Marthe realized it was better to keep away so as "not to embarrass the royals." Yet the young King was courageous; he insisted on visiting a prisoner-of-war camp, where U.S. airmen shot down over Romanian territory were being held, and inquired about their welfare. He also intervened several times on behalf of Romanian Jews, who were threatened with deportation to Auschwitz. By the summer of 1944, with the Russian troops at the frontiers of Romania, the King told Marshal Antonescu that he *must* make peace with the Allies and take Romania out of the war—no matter what the conditions. But the Marshal would do nothing without consulting Hitler. It was then that the King decided to act.

On August 23, 1944, having secretly assured himself of the support of the Army commanders, he summoned Marshal Antonescu to a meeting at the royal palace and gave him an ultimatum: sign an armistice immediately or resign. When the Marshal refused, the King signaled to two of his trusted palace guards, who arrested Antonescu at gunpoint. He was marched upstairs and locked in a walk-in safe. In the next few hours, while messages were being sent to loyal Army units to secure bridges and access roads and while the German garrison, sensing danger, was put on alert, the country's future hung in the balance. Manfred von Killinger, the German Minister in Bucharest, a brutal Nazi, demanded an immediate audience with the King. "Where is General Antonescu?" he asked. The King told him that he was "in a safe place." At ten o'clock that evening Marthe and her family, alerted by the gardener from Mogosoëa that "something unusual was happening," heard the King announce to the country that Romania was no longer an ally of Germany.

In Bucharest cheering crowds gathered in front of the palace, while fierce fighting began on the outskirts, but the key bridges and roads were successfully defended by loyal Romanian troops. During the next few days, the Luftwaffe systematically aimed their bombs at the royal palace, forcing King Michael to take refuge in the country. But by then the German armies were in full retreat throughout Romania, abandoning their vital sources of oil, chrome and aluminum, pursued by the Red Army and Romanian troops. King Michael's coup hastened the end of the war by many months.

After the final defeat of Germany, Romania expected Britain and the United States to honor the pledges of democracy and free elections made at Yalta. They did not know of the 1944 bargain struck between Stalin and Churchill in Moscow which gave the Soviet Union "a 90 percent predominance" over Romania. King Michael called it "a death sentence," and he was right: it resulted in the country's disappearance behind the Iron Curtain for the next forty-six years.

The most immediate result of King Michael's coup, however, was the signing of an armistice agreement between the government of Romania and the Allied High Command. Soon after, representatives of the Allied Control Commission, a body created to administer former enemy territories, arrived in Bucharest. The head of the mission was a Soviet general; his staff included U.S. and British officials. British and American officers were a welcome sight in Bucharest's streets, but there was little they could do in the face of the terror unleashed by the Russian armies. Marthe, returning to Mogosoëa from Posada, watched them requisition everything: cars, agricultural implements, bicycles, even telegraph poles. They were like an army of locusts. In the city people cowered behind locked doors. "Here comes the comrade"—the cry of terror rang out all over Bucharest.

The Romanian Communist Party, outlawed for a number of years, now emerged from underground and gradually assumed local power. Marthe knew that it spelled doom for Mogosoëa and Posada; in the new order of things she and her family would become "enemies of the people." Yet there was still a little time left to fight. With the help of a few "old-time" officials in the new government of Petru Groza, she succeeded for the time being in having Mogosoëa classed as a "historical monument." Her tractors and farm implements were confiscated, but she was allowed to keep a few gardening tools, with which her two gardeners, who now doubled as armed guards, had to manage.

For a brief period Mogosoëa reverted to its former role—an oasis of peace amidst general turmoil. "It was an amazing experience," Nigel Davies, then a member of the Allied Control Commission in Bucharest, told me, "after the tense, war-torn city to find oneself in these magical surroundings, greeted at the door by a butler in white gloves and ushered upstairs in the presence of the Princess Bibesco, presiding over a multilingual assembly of diplomats and assorted military, including a Soviet general." Thanks to her vegetable garden and generous contributions of food and drink from the Allied commissary, supplied by visiting diplomats, Marthe could still entertain in the old way. But time was running out and she knew it. The lunch party she gave for her birthday on January 28, 1945, was her swan song. In the large dining room, cleverly protected from the cold, warmed by a huge fireplace with scented logs, she entertained an extraordinary mixture of guests: members of the Romanian government, officials of the Control Commission, diplomats from neutral countries and the Soviet military. It took all her finely honed skills as a hostess and her sense of humor to make the party a success. To the Soviet Ambassador, who harangued her on the advantages Romania would derive from its association with Soviet Russia, she replied tartly, "Don't forget, Ambassador, that you are in the house of a prince who, together with his four sons, was beheaded by the Turks for pursuing policies friendly to Russia. That's where it got him."

In the spring, as war in Europe was ending, Marthe was questioned by the Securidad, the Romanian police, now headed by a dedicated Communist. They let her go, but it was an unnerving experience. On V-E Day, as she was leaving church after the Thanksgiving service in the Bucharest Cathedral, a member of the French Legation led her aside and told her, "It is time for you to go—now." She still had her government passport, issued when she traveled to Turkey, and there would be no difficulties about a French visa. By an extraordinary stroke of luck she managed to obtain the vital Soviet exit stamp, essential for leaving the country. Yet she still hesitated; the beauty of Mogosoëa tore at her heart, and uppermost in her mind was the question of when the rest of the family would join her. "My mother looked me square in the face," Valentine later recalled, "and asked, 'What should I do?' " Both Valentine and her husband wanted to stay behind "for a bit," hoping that things might improve. There was still much misguided faith at the time that the Romanian government—under pressure from the Allies—would abide by their promises of free and democratic elections. Valentine assured her mother she could cope with Mogosoëa; Dimitri would administer Posada, or whatever was left of it. They hoped to join her in Paris in a year's time.

Air Vice-Marshal Donald Stevenson, chief of the British Military Mission in Bucharest, acted as Marthe's "angel protector." Convinced that she was in real danger from Romanian and Soviet authorities, he arranged passage on one of the RAF cargo planes to Italy and then to Paris. On September 7, at five o'clock in the morning, Marthe presented herself at the airport, carrying one small suitcase and her fur coat. She was never to see Romania again.

❦

16

The
Last Challenge

*I*n the early morning of September 10, 1945, Max, the old porter at the Paris Ritz, who had worked there since he was a fifteen-year-old bellboy, was standing in front of the Place Vendôme entrance, contemplating the array of military vehicles in the square. Since the Liberation of Paris the previous August, the Ritz had been home to high-ranking Army personnel, assorted war correspondents and harassed Allied government officials; it was all very dull. When will the smart people start coming back? he wondered.

Suddenly, driving from the direction of the rue de Rivoli, came a blue RAF station wagon and from it disembarked a familiar figure whom Max had not seen in six years. It was the Princess Bibesco, wrapped in furs against the morning cold, distinguished and elegant as ever. To Max's astonishment, she arrived with only one suitcase. Where were the mountains of luggage and the Hermès-designed crocodile-skin *nécessaire de voyage* with silver mountings he remembered so well? But at least here was a civilian and a great lady at that; she had even brought her own maid. He rushed forth and greeted her warmly.

It had never occurred to Marthe that the Ritz might be full or that, its being Army VIP territory, she might lack the necessary authorization to stay there. She flew to it like a homing pigeon, and of course the management found her a room. It was small, far from the luxury suites she used to inhabit in the old days, but it had a lovely view of the garden, the crisp linen sheets she remembered, and it promised to be heated in the winter. Blanche Caniot was found a tiny maid's room under the eaves.

Her first move was to unpack her address book and attempt to discover who was in town. Telephones in post-Liberation Paris barely functioned, but word of mouth and the grapevine were as active as ever. She knew that many of her friends had remained in the capital through the war; others had returned since the Liberation. Over the next few days she walked back and forth across the city, looking, remembering and seeing friends from the past. It did not take her long to be back "in the swim," dining with Philippe de Rothschild, Gaston Palewski, now chief of de Gaulle's cabinet, Paul Claudel, Christian Bérard, the stage designer, and above all her dearest friend Rosita de Castries, who was with the Abbé Mugnier during the last weeks of his life. Post-Liberation Paris—almost totally devoid of traffic—was beautiful, cold and abnormally clean, but it struck Marthe as hollow, "like a mask." The majority of apartments were unheated; people huddled in their rooms wearing overcoats and fur-lined boots; there were frequent electricity cuts; food shortages were acute and the black market was thriving. At the Ritz hot water was rationed—the old boiler needed to be replaced—but at least it was warm. She was struck by the general shabbiness of the place. "Whiting on the menu and paper napkins on the table," she moaned.

All of it was nothing, however, compared with the changes that had taken place among the people. Far more than in post-1914 Paris, Marthe's friends were divided among themselves, even within families. Those who had stayed behind were intent on establishing their good behavior, and one way to do that was to blacken the reputation of a neighbor. Paris was a welter of accusations and counteraccusations. Anyone who had given a meal to a German, treated him medically or sold him clothes vociferously proclaimed that he could not have done anything else, and anyway his colleagues across the road had done much worse. Only the Gaullists, who had spent the years after France's collapse abroad, and members of the Resistance, were exempt from the taint of collaboration. The term *épuration* (purging), which at first Marthe did not quite understand, was on everyone's lips. She soon noticed that there was "a terrible discretion" among her friends; certain subjects were scrupulously avoided unless you knew somebody very well and were alone. Even the sales staff in smart shops, who had happily served Germans and their ladies in the past four years, now hypocritically refused to serve the wife of a suspected collaborator.

Marthe's friend Louise de Vilmorin, Countess Palffy, who these days spent most of her time at the British Embassy's Residence in a happy triangular relationship as mistress of Duff Cooper, the Ambassador, and best friend of his wife, Lady Diana, was hauled in front of the *comité d'épuration* and ordered to answer charges, as her name had been inscribed on the blacklist. She answered that in 1937 she had married Paul Palffy, lived in Slovakia and Hungary during the war and *had* to mix with Austrians and Germans. She was exonerated, particularly when it became evident that a mysterious Mr. Stasi, with whom she had been living in Budapest in 1943, turned out to be the pro-Allied Count Esterhazy and not a member of the Gestapo as her accusers had claimed. Moral judgments at the time were capricious.

Prominent artists and writers did not escape their share of criticism. In their excellent book *Paris After the Liberation*, Anthony and Artemis Beavor tell how Sacha Guitry, the famous actor, who as a dramatist and an actor was often compared to Noël Coward, was arrested early one morning. "He was hustled in wearing yellow-flowered pyjamas, jade green crocodile pumps and a panama hat and taken to the mairie of the 7th Arrondissement. When asked by the examining magistrate why he had agreed to meet Göring, Guitry replied 'par curiosité'; he said that he would have been just as interested to meet Stalin, which was probably true."

Two famous women, the actress Arletty (of *Les Enfants du Paradis* fame) and Coco Chanel, were declared collaborators. They both had taken German lovers and lived with them at the Ritz. It was rumored that after her arrest Arletty had had her head shaved; Coco Chanel, in spite of distributing hundreds of flacons of Chanel No. 5 to GIs, was also arrested, but later was released; she stayed out of France for the next eight years.

Marthe, who disliked Colette since the days of Henry de Jouvenel, did not feel particularly sympathetic when she heard that the famous writer was put on the blacklist for contributing to the collaborationist paper *Le Petit Parisien*. (On the other hand, she hid her Jewish husband, Maurice Goudeket.) Another of Marthe's close acquaintances, and Colette's neighbor in the Palais Royal, Jean Cocteau, whose behavior during the occupation had been at least equivocal, was let off easy; the Gaullists felt contempt for him rather than hatred. "He is only a dancing girl" was the answer when someone contemplated prosecution. For a long time afterward Cocteau went on boring people explaining at enormous lengths how "he had owed it to his art *not* to join the Resistance."

In spite of all the disturbing crosscurrents which marred the harmony of many a social gathering, Marthe, who had been deprived of Paris life for so long, plunged back into it with satisfaction. Her first priority, however, was to see her grandson John at school in England (he now preferred the English form of his name). She was upset to discover, when she visited the British Embassy, that her British visa, which she had always been taking for granted, was no longer valid. Because of postwar restrictions, it took two and a half months and the intervention of highly placed friends to obtain a new one.

While waiting to visit England, Marthe took stock of her situation. Money was her most important problem, as from now on she would have to be the family's breadwinner. It was a formidable responsibility for a woman, almost sixty, in delicate health, who had been used to a life of luxury and a large steady income.

Before leaving Romania, Marthe arranged, with the help of René de Weck, the Swiss Minister, to let Mogosoëa to the Swiss Legation for a year; the rent, payable in Swiss francs, would take care of her immediate expenses. She decided, for the time being, to remain at the Ritz, where as a valued prewar customer she was given particularly favorable terms. The "impossible to heat" Quay Bourbon apartment was let to Guy Millard, who, as a member of the British Embassy staff, enjoyed special allocations of heating oil. "I remember Marthe Bibesco in those days," Sir Guy Millard told me. "She was a formidable personality, awe-inspiring to a young attaché like myself. Still good-looking, she seemed to know everybody. In a Paris almost totally devoid of taxis, she could be quite demanding when it came to driving her to some reception. But she was scintillating company, so one did not really mind."

The immediate present was secured, but what about the long-term future? School fees for John had to be paid; his younger brother, George, was expected in Paris the following year and later possibly Valentine and her husband. Cut off from her Romanian revenues, she would have to earn the money through her writing. Could she cope? She had no illusions and no doubt. "I have never lacked courage," she told Rosita de Castries, "and this is not the time to start feeling anxious."

Marcel Bourdel, the editor-in-chief of Plon, who had published Marthe's books in the past, offered her a generous contract for the projected three-volume correspondence with the Abbé Mugnier, a chronicle of social and literary life in Paris covering a period of thirty-four years. He even supplied a secretary to help classify the letters. Marthe also signed a second contract, under which Plon agreed to pay her a modest life annuity in exchange for world rights to *Isvor, Croisade pour l'Anémone, Images d'Epinal* and *Feuilles du Calendrier*, which they planned to reissue in new editions. By all contemporary criteria the publishers did her proud; it was now up to Marthe to deliver, which she did—though often late—for the obstacles in her path multiplied every year.

Marthe spent a happy Christmas in England that year, reunited with her seventeen-year-old grandson, John. It was the first time since the war that young Ghika was with a member of his family and not "parked" for the holidays with the parents of a friend. They went to Midnight Mass at London's Farm Street, praying for his parents and brother back in Romania. After Christmas, Marthe gave a cocktail party. The Lloyds, the Asquiths, the

Palairets, Ishbel and Malcolm MacDonald, Enid Bagnold—they all came; it was as if she had never left London. She rejoiced in her English friends. Though postwar austerity was more severe than in France ("Who won the war?" she wondered), there was none of the mutual suspicion she had found so troubling in Paris.

In the third week of January she returned to a Paris made uneasy by de Gaulle's resignation. The general atmosphere of instability contributed to her own depression. News from Romania was bad; the Communists were gaining more and more power, the free press was being suppressed, protesters were beaten up, show trials were beginning to be held and thousands of people were being deported as slave laborers. King Michael was again stripped of his powers and yet, when he appealed to the British and American governments to honor their pledges, he was told he must cooperate with the Russians. In November 1947 he flew to England to attend the wedding of his cousin Prince Philip to Princess Elizabeth. He returned the following month—much to the annoyance of the Communists—and announced his engagement to Princess Anne of Bourbon-Parme, whom he had met during the wedding festivities. Determined not to allow the continuation of the dynasty, the Communist government of Petru Groza forced him to abdicate. Like Marthe, King Michael departed into exile with only a few personal belongings. Romania ceased to be a monarchy and became a People's Republic.

Marthe's recurring nightmare was that Valentine and her husband were going to stay in Romania too long and not be able to leave. There was still—she was told—a window of opportunity to make an exit before the barriers came down.

In the spring of 1946, Antoine Bibesco appeared fresh from Bucharest—outwardly unchanged, laughing, sarcastic, "the golden prince with emeralds in his pockets," as Enid Bagnold called him. But something in him had gone; he was poor and he had so loathed poverty! He had never dreamed it could happen to him. His wife, Elizabeth, had died in Bucharest during the war; his estates had been confiscated by the Communists; there remained only his Quay Bourbon apartment, a few scattered investments and his sense of humor. Like Marthe, he was determined to survive.

At about the same time a telegram from Valentine came from

Romania: "George and Miss Leggett arriving London May 4," just as Marthe had arranged before her departure. Glad that the plan had worked out, she rushed to London to meet them. "Little George" was now nearly ten years old; an attractive, but difficult boy, badly in need of continuity and the discipline of a boarding school. On Michael Palairet's suggestion he was sent to one at St. Leonard's on Sea while waiting to go to Ampleforth, like his older brother. For Marthe it meant two school fees plus clothing and boarding expenses. "I will cope," she told Sheila MacDonald, as they were sitting together at the theater during the gala performance of Enid Bagnold's *National Velvet*.

Back in Paris, Marthe plunged into work, but it was becoming obvious that the advances from Plon would not be enough to support her and the boys. The *Revue des Deux Mondes* commissioned a series of articles on current topics; the House of Guerlain, about to launch a new scent, decided to call it Isvor and pay Marthe for the use of the name; and the filmmaker Robert Bresson offered a modest advance for a script entitled *Au Hazard—Balthazar*, which, unfortunately, never materialized into a film. All this took Marthe away from her writing, and when Marcel Bourdel arrived expecting the first volume of her correspondence with the Abbé Mugnier, he was told by Marthe in no uncertain terms that he would have to wait until her other engagements were completed. She explained that in order to write—and write well—it was essential for her to be free of nagging financial worries. She needed more money than her editors were prepared to offer, a request that spawned a long series of negotiations, which became progressively bitter and ended only with Marthe's death.

On March 13, 1949, as Marthe was returning home from the theater with Paul Claudel and his wife, she was handed a letter just arrived from Romania. It contained dreadful news: *"Maman chérie,"* Valentine wrote from Bucharest, "we are to be deported to Curtea de Arges, which will be our place of exile. I understand we are leaving tomorrow. Two days ago, as we were fast asleep at Mogosoëa, we were awakened at 2:30 a.m. by loud banging and shouts at the front door. Two members of the local militia burst into our bedroom, ordering us to hurry up and dress; they remained in the room while we dressed. They allowed us to pack one pair of sheets, two blankets, two pillowcases, one change of clothes, some underwear, a pair of shoes each, also two spoons, two knives, two plates, two cooking pans and one glass each. Marioare [the cook] managed to slip in some provisions; I had to calm her down, as she was hysterical with indignation, threatening the men with all sorts of curses—you know her. . . . We were not allowed to take a single book or a piece of jewelry, but they allowed us a little money, not very much. We were then loaded onto a horse-drawn cart, where we sat on top of our belongings, like our peasants, and taken to Bucharest in pelting rain. Once in town we were hauled in front of the Revolutionary Committee, who announced that a new decree nationalizing the land and everything connected with it has just been passed. According to our interrogators, we have become 'enemies of the people.' We are not allowed to remain in our home and are being deported to Curtea de Arges tomorrow. Posada too has been nationalized; we haven't been able to go there for some time now. . . . Goodbye, darling Mother, pray for us; I hope that we will not be exiled for too long. Vally."

Marthe was devastated. From then on, rescuing her daughter and son-in-law became the single motivating force in her life, all other activities being subordinated to this one aim. "The thought of Valentine in a village jail dwelled with me through the night, replacing sleep," she wrote in her diary. "Every morning I reviewed what could be done to help them: whom to see, whom to write to—I became a slave to their cause."

Her agony was to last for seven and a half years. She lost count of the number of letters addressed to military and civilian authorities, of the "important people" in various countries contacted, of endless journeys undertaken with "the children" in mind. Getting them out of prison was for her a moral obligation—a goal, superseding in importance any agreements concluded with her publishers. In the meantime, as money was urgently needed for school fees, the boys' holidays and other expenses, which the advance from Plon could not cover, Marthe undertook a crushing burden of assignments—magazine articles, lecture tours, short "potboiler" books for mass circulation. She even attempted to write lyrics for a Marquis de Cuevas ballet. Anything that would bring instant cash. Not surprisingly, all this activity played havoc with her deadlines for Plon. "You must understand my situation and be patient," Marthe wrote to her editor in response to an inquiry about the fate of the first volume of *La Vie d'une Amitié*, her correspondence with the Abbé Mugnier, contracted some six years before. "I must have money to live and to support my family—it will not help you at Plon if I die." Finally the first volume was ready and published in the early fifties, but even though *La Vie d'une Amitié* was well received by the critics, by then it was no longer so timely, as interest in the prewar era had temporarily vanished in France.

But Marthe still had a formidable literary reputation in France, and *Isvor*, *Le Perroquet Vert*, *Images d'Epinal* and her other books had made her publishers vast sums of money in the past. They felt morally obligated to help. A contract was drawn up for *La Nymphe Europe*, the gigantic epic in twenty-seven volumes. Again Marthe was to receive a monthly payment and an advance for each consecutive volume as they appeared.

The immediate problem was providing for her grandsons. John was a source of pleasure and pride. After successfully graduating from Ampleforth, he passed the exams for Oxford with flying colors, entered a military training academy and received a commission in the Irish Guards. He and Marthe had a close, affectionate relationship. John's younger brother, George, was a rebel—undisciplined and hard to manage. His early childhood, overshadowed by the war, left him with a deep sense of insecurity; it was aggravated by the fact that Marthe could not provide the boys with a home in England. She came over regularly for their school holidays, but had to borrow places from friends or take them to often depressing small boardinghouses. "Why do I always have to pack?" young George would explode in a rage. It distressed Marthe, for this boy was to her the son she never had (his name had been legally changed to Bibesco) and the heir to the great tradition of the Hospodars of Wallachia. But he disappointed and deeply hurt her; at sixteen he ran away from school, joined the merchant navy in Australia and changed his name to Moore.

In spite of the daily struggle for existence and the ever present worry about Valentine, Marthe still had occasional moments of happiness. One autumn, while staying with the Londonderrys at Mount Stewart in Ireland, she met a clever, charming and unusual man named Assis Chateaubriand. A descendant of French-Portuguese parents who emigrated to Brazil at the end of the century and made a fortune in São Paulo, he founded the São Paulo Museum of Modern Art. He invited Marthe to give a series of conferences in Brazil under his auspices, paid all fees and bought first-class tickets on a luxury steamer for her and her grandson. It was a wonderful solution to the problem of young George's summer holidays and a way to earn some money. They embarked on the SS *Andes* on August 9, 1952, arriving at Rio de Janeiro twelve days later. Marthe was enchanted with the trip and the warm hospitality with which she was received in Brazil. As it happened, the wife of Brazil's current Foreign Minister was a Romanian, a Gafencu, a relative of the "gourmet Gafencu" Marthe and George used to dine with in Bucharest. Delighted with Marthe's arrival, she took her firmly under her wing, escorting her on a tour of the interior and the virgin forests of the Amazon. In São Paulo, Assis Chateaubriand was her host. In September they returned to Paris and Marthe described her impressions of Brazil in two long articles for the Paris review *Hommes et Mondes*. As a memento of the trip she brought back with her a green parrot, called Pereire, who became her inseparable companion, much to the annoyance of Blanche Caniot, whose voice the bird managed to imitate with uncanny precision.

In the autumn of 1954, Marthe became the recipient of a prize from the French Academy of Literature, awarded "for the entire body of her work." But an even more distinguished honor came the next year when the Royal Academy of French Language and Literature in Belgium elected her as a life member to succeed the distinguished Canadian writer Edouard Montpetit. At first it was rumored that she was to succeed Colette, who had died shortly before; that particular honor, however, went to Cocteau. Marthe was relieved that the customary eulogy for the predecessor did not fall to her. "A speech extolling the virtues of the French language and of Edouard Montpetit will be far easier to deliver than one eulogizing Colette," she told her friend the Baroness Vaxelaire, sister of the president of the Belgian Aeronautical Federation, who used to be a close friend of Marthe's husband. Marthe's speech, delivered in "jewel-like French," was universally admired. She much enjoyed the series of official dinners and receptions, at which she appeared "as if she had no care in the world." But later, during a long, intimate lunch with the widowed Queen Elizabeth at the royal palace in Brussels, she at last let her tears flow when talking about her "imprisoned children." For some time now the Queen had been trying to help Marthe through the International Red Cross, of which she was then president, but her mediation was rejected by the Communist authorities of Romania.

More honors followed. The Toulouse Academy of Jeux Floraux, dating back to the days of the Troubadours, awarded her a prize for *Isvor*, while a year later *La Vie d'une Amitié* brought the much coveted Prix Sévigné. She was warmly congratulated by her publishers, who expressed the hope that the first volume of *La Nymphe Europe* might now be delivered without delay.

News from Romania was scarce and depressing. The only communication with Valentine and her husband, imprisoned in the depths of the countryside, was by way of Red Cross postcards, which told nothing. Mogosoëa was being turned into a museum; Marthe was wryly amused to hear that her Hermès *nécessaire de voyage* with silver fittings was now in the possession of the Chief of Staff of the Army—a Communist—who enjoyed traveling with it.

Jean Apolzan, the faithful butler, who spent his life in the service of the Bibesco family and loved them all, died in 1950; in his room in the small village hut where he now lived, he had kept a picture of Marthe and her husband on their wedding day. It was preserved by the old retainers at Mogosoëa.

In 1951, two witnesses of Marthe's youth died: the Kronprinz, who had been eking out a sad, embittered existence in the provinces, and Antoine Bibesco, the cousin she had loved as a brother. "This immensely civilized man," wrote the *Figaro*, "was one of Proust's closest friends; his life was intimately interwoven with the social and intellectual life of Paris from early in this century." And

Enid Bagnold, Antoine's friend for over forty years, in a moving tribute to him in *The Times*, praised his eccentricity, humor and gift for friendship. "Unique, advisory, mocking, affectionate and impatient, swept by sudden depressions and as sudden laughter (against life or himself), he would sit in these last years, quite unchanged in his wisdom, in the tarnished silver quiet of his house by the Seine, with the river reflected in mirrors through his rooms, just as he had done when he lived beside another river with his brother Emmanuel in London."

When Stalin died in March 1953, Marthe hoped that the Iron Curtain might be lifted. She redoubled her efforts, but the Romanian government remained obdurate. Finally, in the spring of 1956, the long-awaited miracle happened. Air Vice-Marshal Donald Stevenson, Marthe's rescuer from Bucharest, sent on a government mission to Moscow, had an interview with Bulganin and in the course of a long conversation obtained from him the promise to put pressure on Romanian authorities to release the Ghikas. Marthe was in London when, on July 12, Evelyn Bark of the Red Cross telephoned: "The Ghikas have been released and are being granted exit visas. They will fly to London on August 2."

Marthe was ecstatically happy. To Michael Palairet, who called to congratulate her, she said, "At last I shall be able to die—I have laid down my mandate." On Thursday, August 2, 1956, a few minutes after midnight, the Bucharest plane landed at Heathrow. Valentine, thin, pale and leaning heavily on a cane, fell into her mother's arms. "Thank you for getting us out of hell," she told her. They were not in good physical shape; Valentine had damaged her knee while in detention; it had been carelessly operated on and she was left with a limp for the rest of her life. Her husband, though nervously drained, was much better. After a short stay at the London Clinic and a thorough medical checkup, they rejoined Marthe and their son John at a cottage in Ascot, lent by Yvonne de Rothschild. It was a time of great happiness. "Like Persephone, my Valentine finally emerged from hell," Marthe wrote in her diary. "Only her journey took eleven years." Having won her children's release, she now had to find the means to support them.

Finding a place to live for Valentine and Dimitri was the first priority. An important consideration was the climate, and Marthe, remembering her stay with her friends the Abdys near Truro, decided to look in Cornwall. She had always loved that part of England for its benign climate and ideal gardening conditions, which she knew Valentine would enjoy. Tullimaar was the answer to their dreams. A white late Georgian house, on a plateau overlooking a tidal river, it was surrounded by a park full of mature trees and was approached through a winding drive. It was in good condition, and the price, because of its isolated location—it was one of the houses General Eisenhower had used as a retreat before D-Day—was reasonable. Above all, it offered peace and security. They bought it from the proceeds of the sale of two apartments in Paris that had once belonged to Dimitri's parents.

Marthe enthusiastically launched into furnishing Tullimaar. She had always loved being in England, and the prospect of owning property and spending more time in that country, where she felt so much at home, filled her with joy. While touring the local antique shops for bargains, she recalled the words of Lord Thomson, some forty-odd years before, when after the destruction of Posada he said to her, "One day I will give you another country."

By early spring the house was ready for occupancy. It was high time, for even the most generous friends could not be expected to provide hospitality for the Ghika couple for too long. In time Marthe turned Tullimaar into what the neighbors teasingly called "a Napoleonic museum." "It was a happy house," John Ghika, Valentine's son, recalled. "My grandmother had great taste and she furnished it very well on odds and ends. She also assembled in it most of the Napoleonic mementos we owned, with the lovely painting of Emily Pellapra in pride of place in the drawing room." A portrait of Napoleon as First Consul, lent by the National Trust, dominated the winding staircase. The garden, with its profusion of shrubs and wildly rampaging plants, was a delight.

But Marthe could not spend all her time at Tullimaar. She had to return to her work in Paris, as her commitments were heavy.

Tullimaar was an expensive house to run. In order to defray some of the costs, the Ghikas tried to grow rare camellias and flowers for the London market. Though quite successful, they were up against strong competition. Unforeseen disasters, like the explosion of a boiler or the need to replace a window after a storm, assumed catastrophic proportions. It may be said that it was reckless of Marthe to have chosen such a large property for her children, instead of a small, unpretentious little cottage, where they would probably have been just as happy. But Marthe was Marthe—she liked grandeur and her standards had always been high. She was not going to capitulate at this late stage in her life. She also felt very strongly that, after all her years of agony, Valentine "deserved" nice surroundings and she was determined to earn what was needed.

While *La Nymphe Europe* languished, well behind schedule, Marthe embarked on a new series of books and articles, which promised more immediate financial rewards. Early in 1957, shortly after her seventy-first birthday, Albin Michel published Marthe's *Churchill et le Courage*, a short, enthusiastic biography of Winston Churchill, which was widely translated and brought her a considerable sum of money. Clementine Churchill, to whom Marthe sent a copy in French, thanked her with a delightful letter; they had known each other since the twenties and Mrs. Churchill appreciated Marthe's contribution to the numerous biographies which had been flooding the bookshelves since Winston's eightieth birthday. Eleanor Roosevelt's reply to Marthe's book was the dispatch of a charming photograph of President Roosevelt meeting Churchill in Washington in 1942.

The moment *Churchill* was finished, Marthe—on the advice of her editor at Albin Michel—launched into another "mass audience book": a biography of the newly enthroned young Queen Elizabeth II; destined for the Japanese market, it too brought immediate financial rewards. Then came another slender volume on Proust, *The Veiled Wanderer*, a collection of letters and reminiscences, followed by a historical romance, *Theodora of Byzantium*, and a series of sketches of women who played minor colorful parts in French history, such as Laura de Sade, the Duchess de Berry, the Duchess de Baune and others. Added to all this was a veritable avalanche of articles Marthe wrote for French, Belgian and U.S. publications. Looking at them today, one is struck by the volume of her output and the range of her subjects: from a piece celebrating violets—Marthe's favorite flower—to personal reminiscences of Claudel, Jean Cocteau and Saint-Exupéry; from a profile of Dior to reflections on fashion, marriage and modern love. This enormous activity helped to pay the bills at Tullimaar, but left Marthe little time for getting on with what she called "real writing." Not surprisingly, the first volume of *La Nymphe Europe* turned out to be disappointing. Overly long, even turgid, it is a long way from the crisp, elegant prose of *Isvor*, *Le Perroquet Vert* or *Catherine Paris*, from "the language that flows like a river, peopled with landscapes and shadows," as the literary critic of *Le Monde* once wrote of Marthe's books. Lost in a forest of genealogies from Byzantium to Greece and ancient Dacia, the story of Marthe's ancestors fails to engage interest; it is boring. Hoping that Marthe's reputation would sell it, Plon published it nevertheless, but much of it languished unsold on booksellers' shelves. Somehow Marthe seemed to have lost her magical way of writing. Was it because she was cut off from her native roots? Or because she was physically exhausted and harassed by money worries? Or because, as she often complained, "writing for popular consumption has silted my inspiration"? Or was it simply because she had chosen too complex a subject? It is hard to know, but the result was depressing both for Marthe and for her publishers, who understandably refused to finance the next volumes, which meant that she would lose her monthly retainer. But nothing would ever affect her determination to "keep the flag flying." She continued to produce articles and book reviews and to give conferences and radio talks. At the age of seventy-eight, suffering from a painful attack of shingles, she embarked on a well-paid lecture tour through North Africa. But still the bills kept coming; Marthe was swamped.

Already some years before, she had started selling things from her Paris flat: "Today sold to a M. Goldenet for 250,000 francs Vuillard's 'Violets,' a present from Emmanuel," reads an entry in her diary. A year later a cherished family jewel found its way to

Christie's in Paris. "It hurt" was Marthe's only comment. As years passed, a number of pictures, including her portrait by Vuillard, were disposed of; so was the famous bracelet once owned by Marie Walewska, which had been presented to her by Philip Sassoon. She mourned it like the loss of a very close friend. And in the early sixties the famous emeralds were acquired by a London jeweler.

As her possessions dwindled, so did her circle of old friends. Paul Claudel's death in particular affected her deeply. They had known each other for many years and had a friendship based on mutual admiration and amused understanding of each other's foibles. The great houses of the *Belle Epoque* also were disappearing; the last one, the Murat mansion in the rue de Monceau, witness to many of Marthe's social triumphs, closed with the death of its owner, "the great Aunt Cécile Murat."

Whenever she could, Marthe spent time with her family at Tullimaar, where she also could entertain her English friends. She felt the English appreciated her and shared her love for animals and flowers. It is generally difficult for a woman in her sixties and seventies to make new friends, but Marthe still managed to gather a circle of admirers around her in Cornwall. "She was a great woman—such courage," the historian A. L. Rowse, a neighbor, told me when I asked how he remembered Marthe. "She never complained and never spoke of the riches and grandeur she lost; she adored life and was determined to maintain standards at all costs. I thought she was simply magnificent."

Enid Bagnold described her as being "beautiful, but . . . much more—she is tremendous. She has veils and a white stick, like the blind, and Napoleonic jewels. . . . She is a whale to meet and a whale for anyone I ask." Enid Bagnold's description of Marthe in the last phase of her life is accurate. Age did not diminish her impact on people. "As she entered a room, one knew immediately that here was someone quite special," recalls Sir John Plumb, the historian. "She had great charm, was wonderfully articulate and could recite stories, like Scheherazade . . . perfect to entertain guests during a rainy weekend in the country."

At some point in her sixties Marthe gave up conventional

clothes and adopted a somewhat theatrical, ageless costume: long, shapeless, kaftanlike tunics of wonderful materials, made for her (at a special price) by her friend Madame Bricard at Dior, turbans fastened with a diamond aigrette and masses of necklaces to replace the real jewels she had sold. This was the way her granddaughter-in-law, Judy Ghika, remembers her from her first meeting before her engagement to John, Marthe's beloved grandson.

"I had a great joy this morning," Marthe wrote in her diary of August 7, 1968. "John has just announced his engagement to Judy Davidson-Smith, an English girl of a good family. At last he is getting married!" John was forty, a lieutenant colonel in the Irish Guards, with a brilliant military future. He had done everything right in his life and was now bringing a charming, attractive girl to Tullimaar to meet his formidable grandmother. As Judy recalls: "She lay extended on a chaise longue, the folds of her voluminous robe around her, hair swathed in a turban with a diamond aigrette, a green parrot perched on a nearby table. She opened her arms to me. I liked her. She was warm and perceptive, with a great sense of humor, though quite imperious at times."

Another great joy—one for which Marthe had been waiting over thirty years—was the award of the Légion d'Honneur, France's most prestigious decoration, at a formal ceremony in Paris, presided over by her old friend General Catroux. What made it even more special was that the cross and insignia were the ones previously worn by the Abbé Mugnier. Congratulations came from all over Europe. If ever Marthe had doubts about being a well-known and well-loved figure in England, France, Central Europe and the Balkans, here was the proof. She rejoiced and answered every single letter.

Marthe now entered on the last stage of her life's journey: her health, always fragile, was giving way; she suffered from recurrent attacks of shingles, which made her utterly miserable and prevented her from traveling. She spent most of the time in her Paris "lantern" overlooking the river, within earshot of the bells of Notre Dame, cared for by the faithful Blanche Caniot, surrounded by her "parterres" of flowers—single blossoms in small vases on windowsills, tables, writing desk, wherever space could be found. Flowers were Marthe's lifelong passion and kind friends ensured an unending supply. In spite of almost constant pain and discomfort her daily routine remained unchanged. Every morning, assisted by her excellent secretary, Madame de Charnacé, she handled a vast amount of never diminishing correspondence, answering letters from friends and admirers and planning forthcoming articles. At the age of eighty-six—a year before her death— she had written five articles for assorted French magazines and was making plans for two books. In the afternoon she rested, but she was always home at teatime. Friends came and went and they found her wonderful company. "Marthe had a kind of magic, which could turn a routine event into something special and festive," the Duchess d'Harcourt, one of her Paris friends, told me. "One day she telephoned asking us to a Venetian fete. We assumed she was giving a party and got all dressed up for the occasion. We arrived to find her place full of people in evening clothes—the cream of Parisian society—drinking lemonade and cheap white wine, to which they certainly weren't accustomed, gazing at the brightly lit *bateaux mouches*, the tourist boats, passing under the windows. Where was the comparison with Venice? But no matter, somehow Marthe contrived to create a wonderful ambiance and turn the evening into a festive occasion. The party went on till all hours."

It was the same mixture of fantasy and courage that helped her to disregard her financial difficulties, which toward the end of her life became acute. In spite of the help of a number of friends— Elie de Rothschild and Sonia Cahen d'Anvers, among others— daily living was becoming a problem. There were times when Blanche Caniot had to dip into her own savings to help with her mistress's grocery bill. But then another article would be written and the emergency would temporarily recede. Unexpected help came from a London librarian, who arranged the sale of some of her manuscripts and letters from prominent correspondents to the University of Texas in Austin, where they form a much prized Marthe Bibesco Collection.

During those last years a great friendship illuminated her existence: Charles de Gaulle entered her life after she sent him an inscribed copy of *La Nymphe Europe*. Unlike others, he understood the significance of the book and thanked her in his beautiful prose and in the most flattering terms. Regular correspondence ensued; Marthe became a fervent admirer of the General—"almost a groupie," her friends teased her. But woe to those who dared criticize her idol in her presence. At the General's invitation she again attended functions at the Elysée, as in years past. "I have been a witness to history," she noted after a reception de Gaulle gave for Chancellor Adenauer, during which she saw the two statesmen confer on what she imagined was the subject of German-French rapprochement. When in 1968 General de Gaulle visited Romania, he took a copy of *Isvor* with him, sent by Marthe. "Through it," he wrote to her afterward, "I saw many things that might have otherwise passed unnoticed during the short time I spent in your country."

It was General de Gaulle who best understood and defined Marthe's importance in the context of her time. In friendship he paid tribute to a woman from a Balkan country who encapsulated so many aspects of Europe—old and new—an entire range of relationships and traditions, which all her life she strove to fuse into one. When in early 1970 she sent him a copy of an article entitled "Napoleon and the European Idea," which she had just published in the *Revue de Paris*, the General answered in terms that filled her with justifiable pride: "Napoleon's idea for Europe comes close to yours—you do personify Europe to me." *"Dominus non sum dignus!"* Marthe exclaimed. "This letter fills me with such joy that I would like to die now—holding it." But it was General de Gaulle who preceded her by almost exactly three years. His death on November 10, 1970, was a terrible blow. "I had to fight hard to continue with the rest of my engagements that day," she recalls in her diary. "It hurts—this gigantic shadow under which I so loved to shelter is no more." He was the last love of her life.

Wednesday, November 28, 1973, dawned bright and sunny. The river sparkled and, as usual, Marthe spent the morning working on her correspondence. Death came to her quietly that evening—unannounced and unexpected, while, comfortable in her armchair, facing the lights of the river, she toyed with a draft of a letter to Madame de Gaulle on the third anniversary of the General's death.

She died as she had always wished—of heart failure.

Rosita de Castries arrived and put the crucifix of the Abbé Mugnier on Marthe's chest.

She was buried in the presence of her family at Ménars, the ancient seat of the Chimays, home to George's mother, Valentine. On her tomb they put the epitaph:

MARTHE BIBESCO
Ecrivain Français

To which should have been added: "Daughter of Europe."

Epilogue

One day in the summer of 1995, John Ghika, a brigadier in the British Army and Marthe's grandson, was surprised to receive a letter from Bucharest with the intriguing heading "Fundatia Culturalae Marthà Bibesco." It invited him and his family to visit Romania to acquaint themselves with the work of the recently formed foundation, dedicated to "the person and writings of Marthe Bibesco" with the object of using her work and ideas to help with the "speedy integration of Romania into the European community of nations." It was a startling announcement, for Marthe's writings had lay covered with dust in Romania's libraries and archives for the preceding fifty years.

Fifty-six years had passed since that autumn morning in Posada when John Ghika, then a schoolboy, was hustled onto a plane to Athens and then London to enable him to return to his school in England. Since then he could only dream of his homeland. Throughout the long, dark years of Communist rule his family's name had remained on the regime's blacklist. Since the fall of

Ceausescu he occasionally wondered what it would be like to go back on a visit. But he was a busy man, living in the English countryside with his wife and two children, with a job and many duties to perform. The unexpected letter made up his mind.

Matters have certainly gone full circle since the Communist days. When John Ghika and his wife, Judy, landed in Bucharest, they were received with enthusiasm not only by representatives of the Bibesco Foundation but also by the press and the public. The airport was brought to a standstill, with TV cameras, photographers and the press jostling to get a closer view of the couple. Their pictures appeared on the front page of every Bucharest newspaper.

After a day of reminiscing about Marthe and discussing the plans for translating her works into Romanian (she wrote in French) to give them a nationwide circulation, they were at last allowed to drive to Mogosoëa. "It still lives," John Ghika later told me. The beautiful setting is unchanged except for the addition of a few unattractive cottages at the edge of the park. The house is now a museum and a center for the restoration of manuscripts and old vestments. It is run by a knowledgeable and pleasant woman curator. As a special favor John was allowed to see his old room; it was barren, but the huge marble bath he had so enjoyed as a boy was still there (the only one left in the house). There were not many traces of the woman who had spent seventeen years of her life restoring Mogosoëa. The palace was now government property, but the memories of the Bibescos lived on among the few remaining retainers. Marioare, a former cook, now nearly eighty, who had known John as a child, wept with joy; others came bringing the traditional welcome of bread and salt. There was much talk of old times and many tears were shed for the Principul and the Princessa. They were told how during the darkest days of the Communist rule the villagers of Mogosoëa were ordered to erase the paintings of the Bibesco family from the walls of the chapel where Prince George lay buried. They instead plastered over them—"put them to sleep for a better day," as one of the villagers told John. A short time before the Ghikas' arrival the paintings were uncovered. Here again was the old Prince, George's father, George himself and Marthe as a little girl, shining through the diffused light of the old Byzantine chapel.

A solemn service of Thanksgiving—a welcome for the family —was sung in the local Orthodox church. John and Judy Ghika promised to return to Mogosoëa with their two children to open the Princess Marthe Bibesco Summer University, planned for Comarnic, near Posada.

In the meantime the work of the foundation goes on. Romania, a small country at the edge of the Western world, wants to rejoin the European community and hopes that Marthe's spirit will guide her.

Bibliography

The main sources for this book are the sixty-five volumes of Marthe Bibesco's diaries from 1908 to 1973, the year she died, the Ghika family archives, the Fonds Bibesco at the Bibliothèque Nationale in Paris and the Central National Archives in Bucharest, Romania. I have also consulted the following:

Almedingen, E. M. *The Emperor Alexander II*. London: Bodley Head, 1962.

Anet, Claude. *Les Roses d'Ispahan*. Paris: Juven, 1907.

Asquith, Margot (Lady Oxford). *Autobiography*. London: Methuen, 1985.

Bagnold, Enid. *Autobiography*. London: Heinemann, 1969.

Bonsal, Stephen. *The Little Nations at Versailles*. New York: Prentice-Hall, 1946.

Cahen d'Anvers, Sonia. *Baboushka Remembers*. London: Private printing, 1972.

Callimachi, Anne-Marie. *Yesterday Was Mine*. London: Falcon Press, 1952.

Channon, Sir Henry. *Diaries of Sir Henry Channon*. New York: Penguin Books, 1984.

Clary, Prince. *A European Past*. London: Weidenfeld & Nicolson, 1978.

Curtiss, Mina. *Other People's Letters*. London: Houghton Mifflin, 1978.

Deletant, Dennis. *Studies in Romanian History*. Bucharest: Editura Enciclopedica, 1990.

Diesbach, Ghislain de. *La Princesse Bibesco: La Dernière Orchidée*. Paris: Perrin, 1986.

———. *Proust*. Paris: Perrin, 1991.

Ghika, Matila. *Heureux Qui Comme Ulysse* . . . Paris: La Colombe, 1953.

Gunther, John. *Inside Europe*. New York: Hamish Hamilton, 1936.

Household, Geoffrey. *Against the Wind*. London: Michael Joseph, 1958.

Jenkins, Roy. *Henry Asquith: A Biography*. London: Collins, 1964.

Jouvenel, Renaud de. "Histoire d'une Amitié," *Revue des Deux Mondes*, March 1981.

Mackintosh, Mary. *Romania*. London: Robert Hale, 1963.

Marquand, David. *Ramsay MacDonald*. London: Jonathan Cape, 1977.

Masefield, Sir Peter. *To Ride the Storm*. London: William Kimber, 1982.

Mee, Charles. *The End of Order: Versailles, 1919*. London: Secker and Warburg, 1980.

Nicolson, Harold. *Peacemaking*. London: Constable, 1933.

———. *Diaries and Letters, 1930–39*. London: Collins, 1966.

Painter, George. *Marcel Proust*. London: Chatto & Windus, 1961.

Pakula, Hannah. *The Last Romantic: Biography of Marie Queen of Romania*. London: Weidenfeld & Nicolson, 1984.

Rose, Kenneth. *George V*. London: Weidenfeld & Nicolson, 1983.

Rowse, A. L. *Memories of Men and Women*. London: Eyre & Methuen, 1980.

Seton-Watson, R. W. *A History of the Romanians*. Cambridge: Cambridge University Press, 1962.

Sitwell, Sacheverell. *Roumanian Journey*. Oxford: Oxford University Press, 1992.

Teodorescu, Magda. "Princess Bibesco in Texas," *Romania Literata*, 1994.

Trefusis, Violet. *Prelude to Misadventure*. London: 1942.

Acknowledgments

I wish to thank, first of all, Marthe Bibesco's grandson Brigadier Prince John Ghika and his wife, Judy, for their unfailing support and encouragement during the writing of this book. Not only did they grant me access to all their family papers and answer innumerable queries; they also extended the hospitality of their country home on the days when research lasted into the night. Without them there would have been no book.

My friends Laurence and Linda Kelly were kind enough to introduce me to Princess Odette Bibesco in Paris; her personal recollections of her cousin Marthe and those of her nephews Constantine and Michael Brancovan were enormously helpful. I also wish to thank Antoine Bibesco's daughter Priscilla Bibesco-Hodgson for allowing me to see Marthe's Quay Bourbon apartment, where she now lives, and the Princess de Beauvau-Craon for lending me the photographs of her grandfather Charles-Louis de Beauvau-Craon.

My thanks go to Sherban Cantacuzino, who introduced me to

John Ghika, to Baroness Elie de Rothschild for sharing with me her memories of Marthe, to Sir John Plumb at Trinity College, Cambridge, to Jane Lady Abdy, Hugo Vickers, John Saumarez Smith, Mary Young, Julia Brown, Mrs. Adrian Berry and Baron Vaes and to Peter Schoenburg von Hartenstein for allowing me to use his mother, Princess Schoenburg's memoirs and descriptions of pre-1914 Bucharest.

During my trips to Bucharest I was extremely fortunate to be the guest of John R. Davis, U.S. Ambassador to Romania, and his charming wife, Helen. Their interest in the project opened many doors.

I have derived inspiration from the enthralling biography of Queen Marie of Romania by Hannah Pakula (although I differ with her in her interpretation of Marthe); also from Ghislain de Diesbach's *La Princesse Bibesco: La Dernière Orchidée.* Sir Peter Masefield's biography of Lord Thomson of Cardington has also been helpful, for it provided information on the R.101 episode.

Finally I want to thank my editor, Jonathan Galassi, for his help and encouragement.

C.S.

Index